GW01606776

CHILDREN OF AFRICA

GARY MOORE

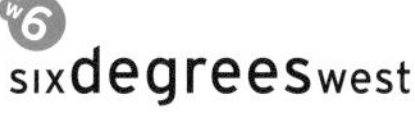

© 2001 – Published on behalf of Aidlink and GOAL by

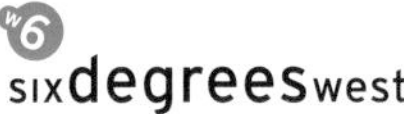

Six Degrees West Limited, 9 Herbert Place, Dublin 2, Ireland
Telephone: +353 (1) 676 0298, Facsimile: +353 (1) 676 3865,
Email: info@sixdegreeswest.com, Web: www.sixdegreeswest.com

Publisher: Gary Moore

Designer: Siobhan McNabb

Photographic Printer: Adrian Ensor

Digital Image Preparation: Xat Houatchanthara & Stephen Quinn

Printers: Brookfield Printing Company Limited

Reproduction: Lithographic Plate Plan Limited

Binding: Library Bindings Limited

ISBN 0-9540508-0-0

The publishing of this book was very much a collaborative effort. In addition to the hundreds of children that we photographed along the route, an army of people in Africa and Ireland were involved in the production of this project and my thanks go out to everyone listed below. In particular I would like to pay a special tribute to Louise Leakey in Kenya and to Simon Burch and Siobhan McNabb in Ireland for their professionalism, hard work and support.

Ireland: Michael Holland, John Hick, Tony Bennett, Stephen Quinn, Xat Houatchanthara, Paul Holmes, Alan Holmes, Colin Newman, John Newman, Dave Walsh, Tony Bell, Jennifer Caldwell, Owen Binchy, Aonghus Geraghty, Richard Kendrick, Pauline McNamara, Tracy O'Connor Marion McLornan, Brian O'Malley, Jessica Felton, Colm O'Brien, Stephen O'Connell, Lisa Mitchell, Sue Patterson, Nicky Gogan, Denis O'Reilly, Vincent DeVeau, Lennie Moore, Adele Moore, Simon Durham, Paul Gingel, Jackie Byrne, Colin Farrell, Anne Cleary, Zelie McGrath, Mick Dunne, Tom Owens, Nora Hayes, Martin Black, Joe Collins, Alan Warnock, David O'Mahony, Conor Kenny, Annemarie Bird, Nev Roddie, Paula Mullooly, Pauline McGowan, Gay Needham, Zita Lloyd, Jasmine Guinness, Gerry Hoban, Danielle Considine, Simon Flanagan, Leszek Wolnik, Maureen Kearney-Wolnik, Mark Restan, Hannah Moore, Aoife Reilly.

England: Adrian Ensor

South Africa: Dr Kader Asmal, Nurunessa Patel, Nomani Pikie, Margot Winer, Simon Winer, Christa Pieper, Sipho, Liz Armstrong, Nick Davis, Diane De Kock, Francis and Natalie Mandy, Craig Morgan, Debbie, Peter and Kari Green

Namibia: Marcella Munangua

Zimbabwe: Violet Moyo, Margaret Ncube, Jade, Nick and Vee Shaxson, Flip and Harry Millbank, Amanda and Rob Millbank, Torben and Erica Hanson, Paul and Caryl Kuhn

Zambia: Monica Banda

Malawi: Gladys Saka, Mr Nyiranda, Liz Fry

Tanzania: Leleshwa Alekaria, Sinyangwai Simel, Njokut

Kenya: Samira Leakey, Mwangi Njagi, Farouk Mohammed, George Muodi, Julius Olepose

Uganda: Gerald Wamereye, Tawemo Samuel

Rwanda: Eric Kabera

Ethiopia: Bekele Debalke, Fantu Shawaz, Asefash Haile Selassaie, Bekele, Rachel, Haimanot, Roland Sims

THE PROCEEDS

All of the proceeds from this book will go to fund educational projects in sub-Saharan Africa. Through Aidlink, the proceeds will go directly to educational projects funded or operated by Aidlink and GOAL in-partnership with local organisations. Projects already earmarked for funding include education programmes for street children in Addis Ababa and Nairobi; the building and funding of a new school in Ileret, Kenya; the funding of an Aids education programme on the Malawian/Mozambiquan border and the funding of an educational programme for Aids orphans in Zimbabwe. A lot of the children that you see on these pages will benefit from its sale.

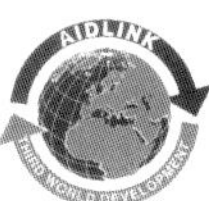

Aidlink is a Third World Development Organisation. It aims to relieve poverty in the Third World by funding long term sustainable development projects and by ensuring the full participation of local communities. Founded in 1982, Aidlink is a non-denominational non-governmental organisation focusing on the support of small to medium sized long-term community development projects in Africa, Asia and Latin America. These projects are in the areas of Health, Education and Training including Adult Literacy, Care of Street Children, Rural Development/Agriculture, Construction and Water Provision among others. Many of these projects are facilitated in the field by missionaries and/or local organisations. Community participation in all stages of the project cycle is encouraged to give a strong sense of ownership and to guarantee sustainability of the project. Over the last year Aidlink has been involved in the support of 40 projects in 18 different countries in Africa, Asia and Latin America. These include: The Abebech Gobena Orphanage and School, Ethiopia; The Nutritional Nursery Programme, Turkana, Kenya; Youth Centre, Otukpo, Nigeria; Chisomo HIV/AIDS Centre, Malawi; Afya-Maendeleo Health and Training Programme, Kibera Slum, Nairobi, Kenya; Songea Vocational Education Training Programme, Tanzania, Ggaba Kindergarten, Women's and Youth Vocational and Literacy Centre, Uganda. Aidlink – Tel: +353 (1) 496 6956, Fax: +353 (1) 496 3320, Email: aidlink@indigo.ie

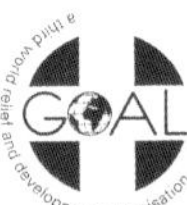

GOAL is an International Relief and Development Agency dedicated to alleviating the suffering of the poorest of the poor in the Third World. Founded in 1977 by John O'Shea and four friends, GOAL is non-denominational, non-political and believes that every human being has a right to food, water, shelter, literacy and medical attention. At present GOAL is operational in thirteen countries, and provides financial support to a whole range of indigenous groups and missionaries who share our philosophy. Since inception GOAL has sent more than 700 volunteers to work in Third World regions and spent 90 million pounds reaching those in greatest need. GOAL keeps its administration costs to a minimum – 5% over the last 23 years. GOALs runs programmes for street children in Sierra Leone, Angola, Honduras, Ethiopia, Mozambique, Kenya, Uganda and India.

DONATIONS

If you would like to make a personal or corporate donation to the Children of Africa appeal, you can do so by contacting Aidlink or Six Degrees West at the numbers above or you can make a deposit or transfer to either of the following bank accounts.

Aidlink/Children of Africa Appeal:

Bank of Ireland, Blackrock, Co Dublin, Ireland.
Deposit Account – 122 692 26. Sort Code – 90 10 28

Allied Irish Bank, Stillorgan, Co. Dublin, Ireland:
Deposit Account – 108 580 35. Sort Code – 93 35 70

KADER ASMAL

SOUTH AFRICAN MINISTER OF EDUCATION

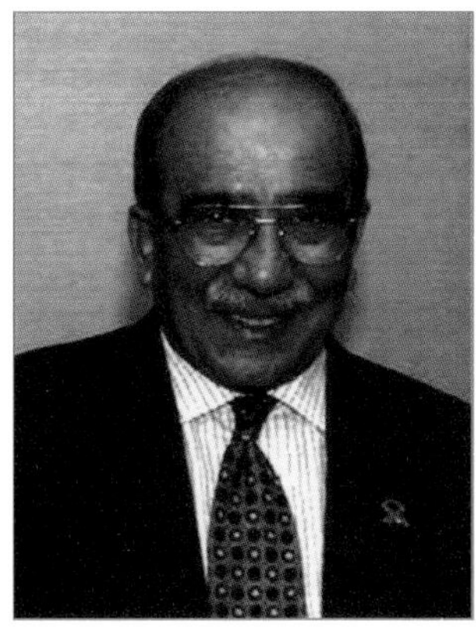

As Minister of Education for South Africa I am often asked why education is so important. Take a look through this book, see the faces charged full of hope and innocence, read the children's stories and I defy you to not immediately see for yourself why education is so important to the Children Of Africa.

If not immediately obvious I will try to explain further. A nation without education is a nation without a future. Each and every one of the children featured in this book will one day inherit their respective country's economic, social and political future. However, it is a future they should look forward to inheriting. Not fear. With education such fear can disappear. With basic education, such as literacy skills, comes knowledge. With knowledge comes self-sufficiency. With self-sufficiency comes pride and with pride comes a nation that can at last make its way in the world.

We have been given 21 per cent of our country's budget to spend on education and we have already devised a dynamic new curriculum, within a completely new policy framework, which I believe, will be the key to unleashing the massive potential currently existing within our young people.

In Ireland in recent years you will have seen how education can unlock such potential and in doing so lead to a new generation of educated students. These people attract industry and as a result, valuable employment opportunities for all.

In order to do likewise in South Africa we too have changed our educational focus in recent years. We are moving from a syllabus, which in the past based itself on division, 'civil service' subjects and sectarianism, to a syllabus including a strong focus on basic literacy, science, and functional technology.

However, South Africa is only one country out of many on our vast continent. Many more are not as fortunate. Yet the desire to learn remains – no matter what the fortunes or adversity of the individual country.

Let me offer you an example. Even amidst the battles fought on a daily basis against hunger and poverty, the number of children attending Primary School in Sub Saharan Africa has quadrupled since 1961. The suspicion in which education was once held dwindles with each new opportunity presented to our young people. There now exists a very real enthusiasm for education.

The resources from the purchase of this beautiful book will help harness this enthusiasm and the thirst for knowledge in some of the Continent's children. Combine these elements with a good basic education and we shall see a powerful catalyst for change in Africa.

In the past this catalyst for change was easily misplaced. The lucky few who received an education had to move to cities or even abroad to utilise their newly found skills, leaving their own communities even more depleted as a result.

With the money from this book, teachers will be trained and in conjunction with the elders, parents and children of each community, a programme will be decided upon to work with local resources. They will also be taught how to make their resources sustainable and thus break the vicious circle that has enslaved our children for so long.

Put simply, education is the engine for change in Africa. It is a vast continent with many different problems on national and local levels. But it will take time.

Through this book and the projects that it funds, your contribution will help provide the educational opportunities that help create the empowerment of children the world over.

Their parents and siblings will learn from them. As will their friends and their siblings' friends. I think you see a pattern forming. I hope you will soon hear and see the rewards of this powerful pattern when it unites with our young and aspiring Children of Africa.

Kader Asmal

Professor Kader Asmal, MP
Minister of Education in South Africa

INTRODUCTION

GARY MOORE

When you look through the photographs in this book what is it you see? Do you see a child or do you see something distant and far removed? Sometimes it is easy to forget that every one of the children you will see over the next one hundred pages or so is an individual with a story to tell. A personal story – sometimes happy, sometimes sad. If you would like to read more about some of the children featured, a selection of their stories can be found at the back of this book.

From the townships of South Africa to the lush farmlands of Zimbabwe, Malawi and Uganda. From the deserts of Namibia, Ethiopia and Kenya to the streets of Nairobi, Kigali and Addis Ababa, all the subjects in this book share one thing in common – they are children. No different to our own young brothers and sisters or sons and daughters. Above all else they are children.

For the most part, the images in this book stand as a visual monument to the spirit, the vitality and the dignity of children no matter how deprived their own personal circumstances are. By and large, as children, they are not the architects of their own fate. They are swept along by forces beyond their control, often falling victim to the avarice, stupidity and wilful neglect of others. Unlike many adults, they are innocent of their own situations.

When I set out to photograph this book I wanted to capture the children along my drive from Capetown to Dublin in a positive light. We have all seen the emaciated and listless images of third world children suffering from the fallout of famine, natural disaster, war and poverty. They are harrowing images, important ones, but they tell a different tale to the one I chose to portray.

Part of the children's remarkable strength lies in the acceptance of their own predicament and their desire to improve on their situation if given the opportunity. To see hardened street children or victims of poverty, laughing and playing as if they have no care in the world is to have hope. Their ability to accept their problems is phenomenal and universal. It is this spirit and vitality I wish to pay tribute to in this book.

They seek what we seek in life, compassion, a sense of belonging, the opportunity to provide for themselves and others and the dignity and self-respect this manifests. Aside from love and support, education is the key to the empowerment of these wonderful kids.

Fifty percent of children in sub-Saharan Africa do not have access to education. Due to economic, social or cultural reasons, some of the children looking at you from the pages of this book are outside the educational loop. They have not been offered any chance of a place on the rungs of the educational ladder. And yet when given the opportunity, the vast majority of them embrace education whole heartedly. Would you see children in the first world walk twenty five kilometres a day so they could attend school? By capturing this hunger to learn, through balanced educational projects carried out in consultation with their respective communities, the full potential of these children can be unlocked.

Access to education, at last perceived to be a fundamental human right, plays a major part in the fortunes of developing countries. Addressing a gender imbalance, whereby two thirds of girls, compared to one third of boys, are without access to education is of vital importance. Case studies from a number of third world nations highlight that the education of girls leads to increased economic productivity, lowers infant and maternal mortality, reduces birth rates and improves environmental management. The Indian State of Kerala, where almost 100% of the girls and boys are literate, rates highly in all of these areas when compared to countries at a similar stage of development. Fact: Education works.

All of the proceeds from this book will go to fund educational projects in sub-Saharan Africa. Through Aidlink, the proceeds will go directly to educational projects funded or operated by Aidlink and GOAL in-partnership with local organisations. Projects already earmarked for funding include education programmes for street children in Addis Ababa and Nairobi; the building and funding of a new school in Ileret, Kenya; the funding of an Aids education programme on the Malawian/Mozambiquan border and the funding of an educational programme for Aids orphans in Zimbabwe. A lot of the children you see on these pages will benefit from its sale.

The years ahead will bring greater pressures to bear on the children of Africa. A dramatic increase in the number of Aids orphans, massive population increases and the spectre of continuing decline in the social and economic conditions for most countries in Africa, mean that the most innocent of all, the children, will continue to suffer unless there are major changes to the political landscapes of the continent's countries. The full affects of the Aids explosion have yet to be understood on the ground and abroad – in the next ten years Aids will kill more Africans than the total number of people who died in every war during the twentieth century! Nine out of every ten people on the continent carrying the virus are unaware they are infected. And yet with these staggering statistics there remains room for hope. Thanks to successful literacy and Aids education programmes, Uganda's infection rate has dropped from 14% to 8%, at a time when the rate in one of it's once comparable fellow states, Botswana has climbed as high as 35%. Fact: Education works.

Coming back to this side of the world I would ask you all to consider one thing. What do you think your biggest achievement will be this year? A new business deal, a new car, an award in sports or in the arts? Look closely at the faces on the pages of this book and then compare that achievement to the achievement of providing opportunity for these children and hundreds of others like them. Your support for this book will help change the lives of these children for the better. They have been let down by circumstance and it is within our gift to provide them with a second chance. If you feel that you can help further, there are contact details on page two.

Their day is between two and three hours ahead of us here in Ireland. I often wonder what they are up to – collecting water, tending livestock or trying to get by on the streets by day. Sleeping and dreaming like all of us by night. As you leaf through the pages try to consider each photograph as an opening scene to their own story.

For all of the children who took part in this project – this book is dedicated to you.

Gary Moore

Dublin, Ireland

May 2001

SPONSORS

Six Degrees West Limited

Brookfield Print Limited

Lithographic Plate Plan Limited

Red Rage Films Limited

McNaughton Paper Ireland Limited

South African Paper Industries

Library Bindings Limited

Atomic Advertising

Windmill Lane Limited

Sink Digital Media

CardBase Technologies Limited

Binchy's Solicitors

Kodak Limited

Michael Holland

Grants Advanced Photo Lab

Posterplan Limited

Kennedy PR

Primary Colour Limited

Photo Logic Limited

Space Limited

Photographics

Adrian Ensor

Easons Limited

O'Mahony's Bookshop

Kennys Bookshop

Hodges Figgis

Waterstones

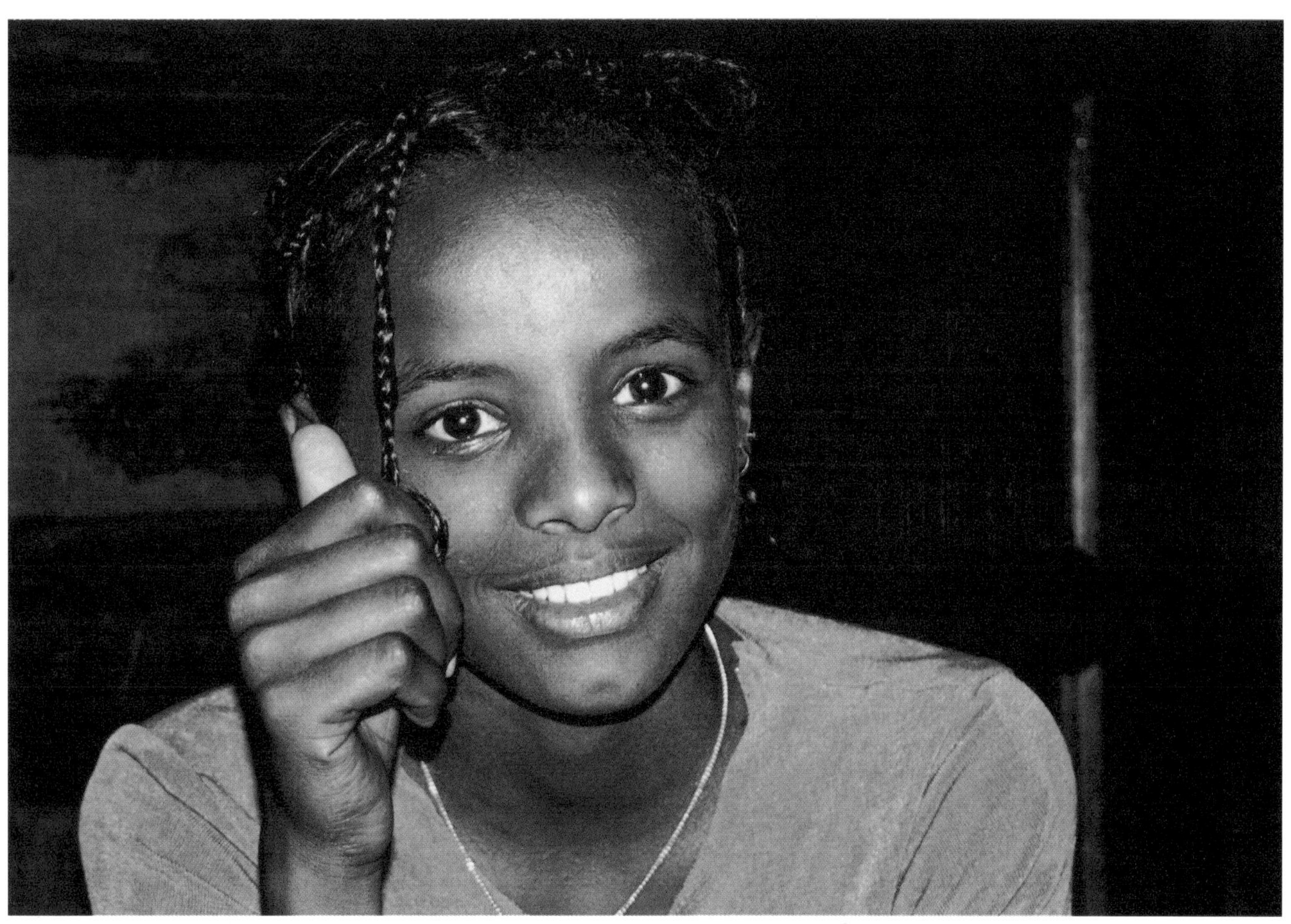

7 **HANA ASEFA CHERENET**

GOAL STREET CHILDRENS PROJECT, WOREDA 21, KEBELE 13, ADDIS ABABA,

ETHIOPIA

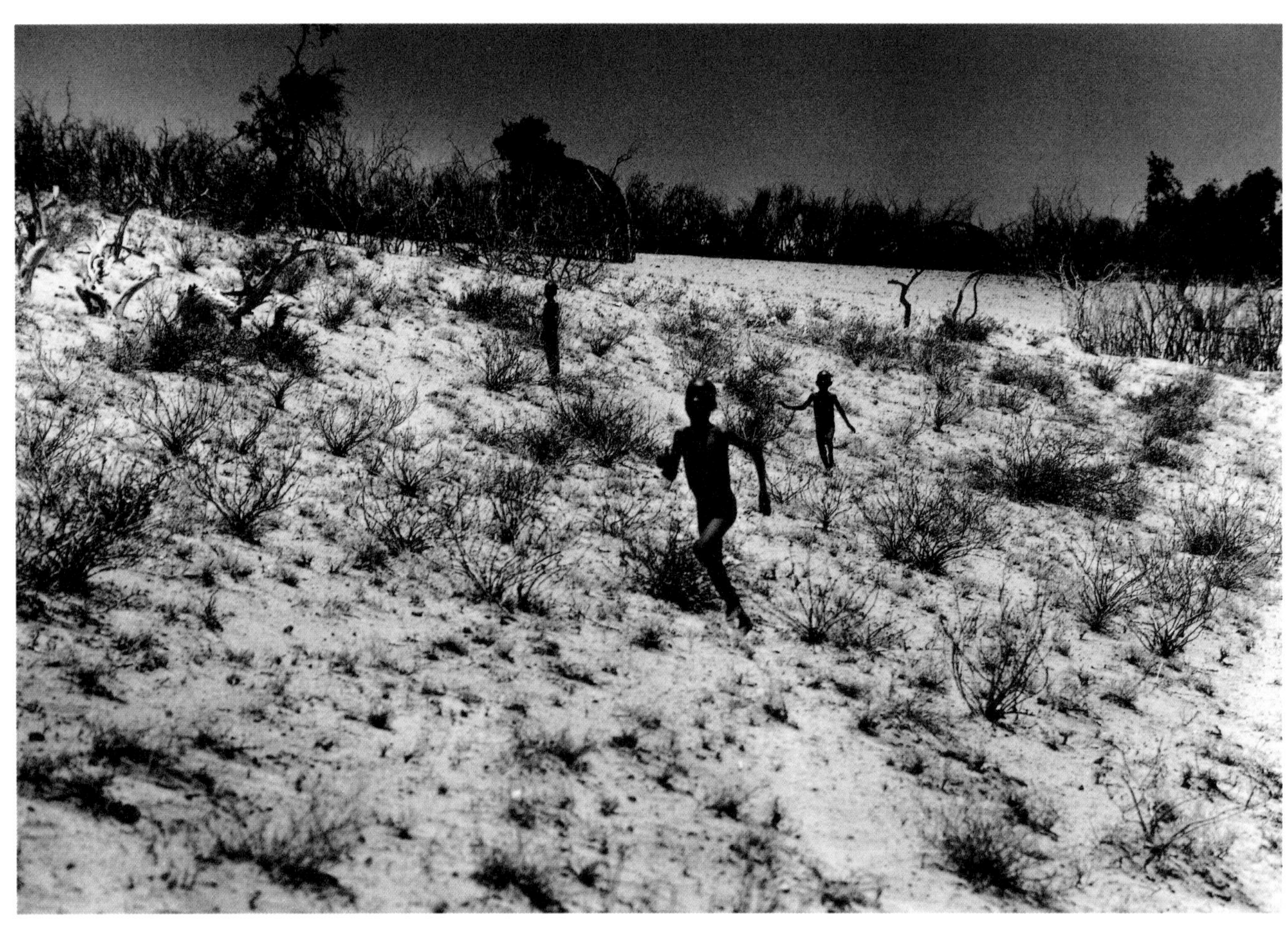

8 **DAASANACH CHILDREN**

DAASANACH TRIBE, GAMO – GOFA,

ETHIOPIA

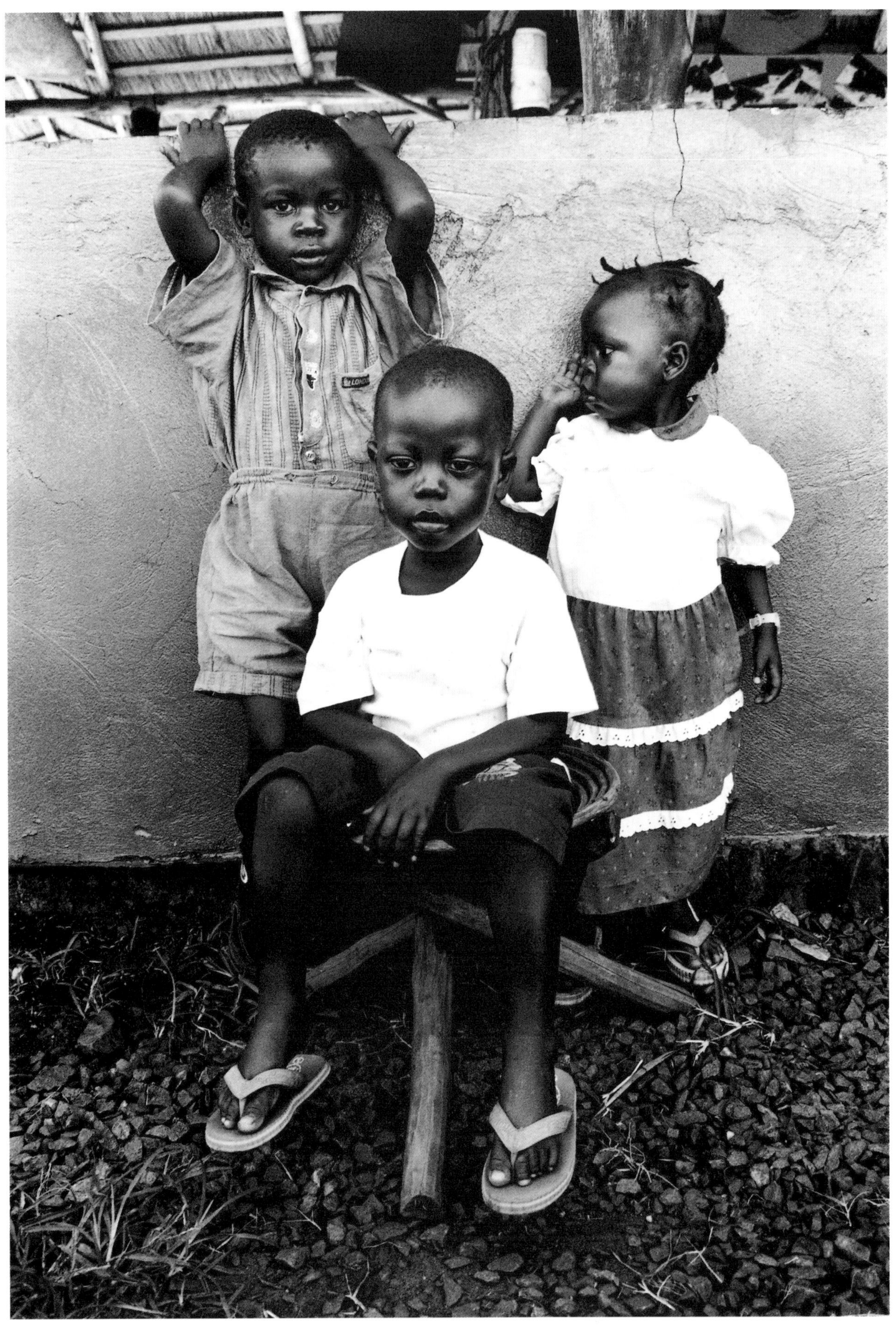

9 HAMUZA KINTU, ALEX BISO & SHARIYA BISO

BUJUGALI FALLS, NILE RIVER, JINJA,

UGANDA

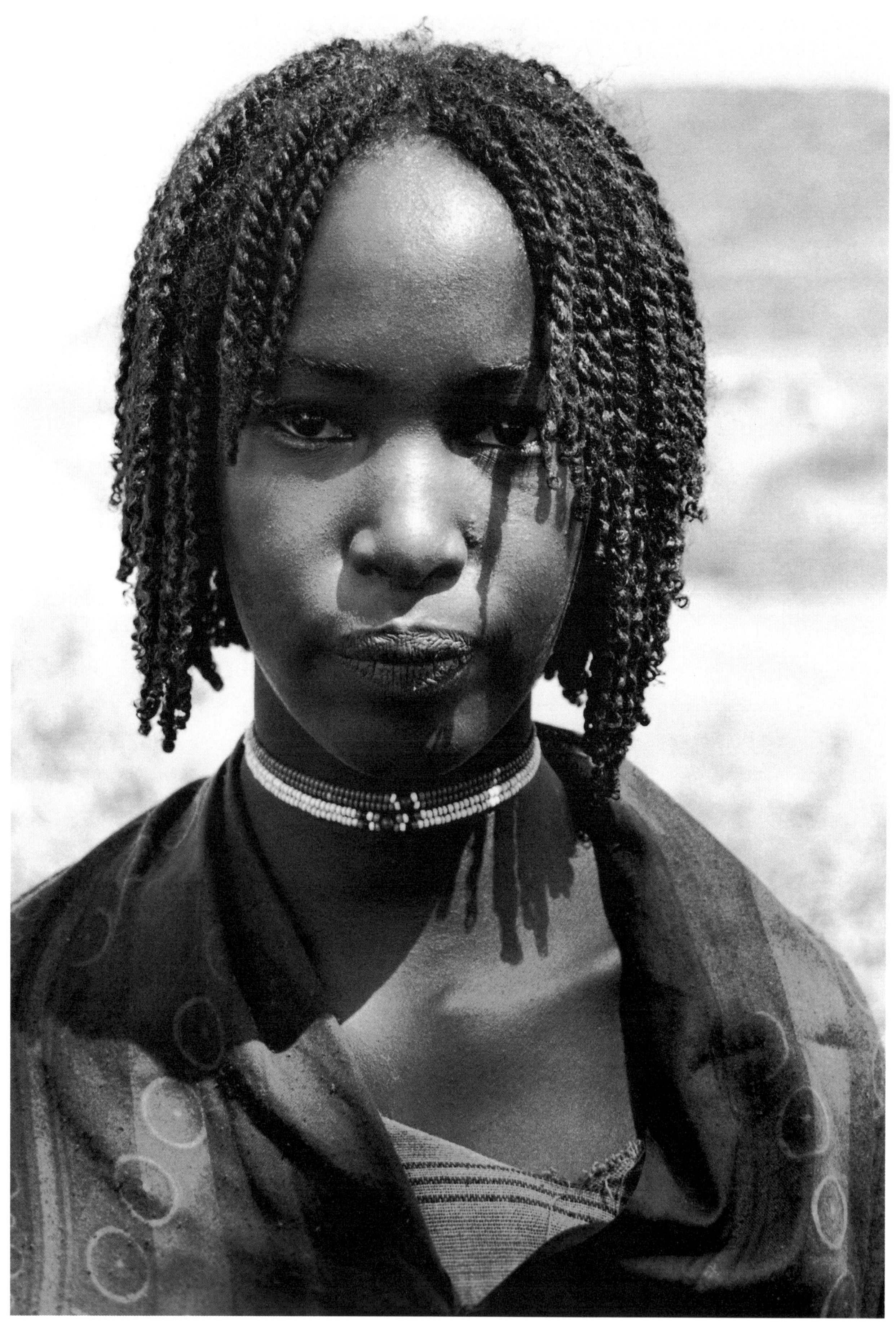

10 **GELLE BOSSET**

KEREYOU TRIBE, DHEBITY, METAHARA, EAST-SHOWA,

ETHIOPIA

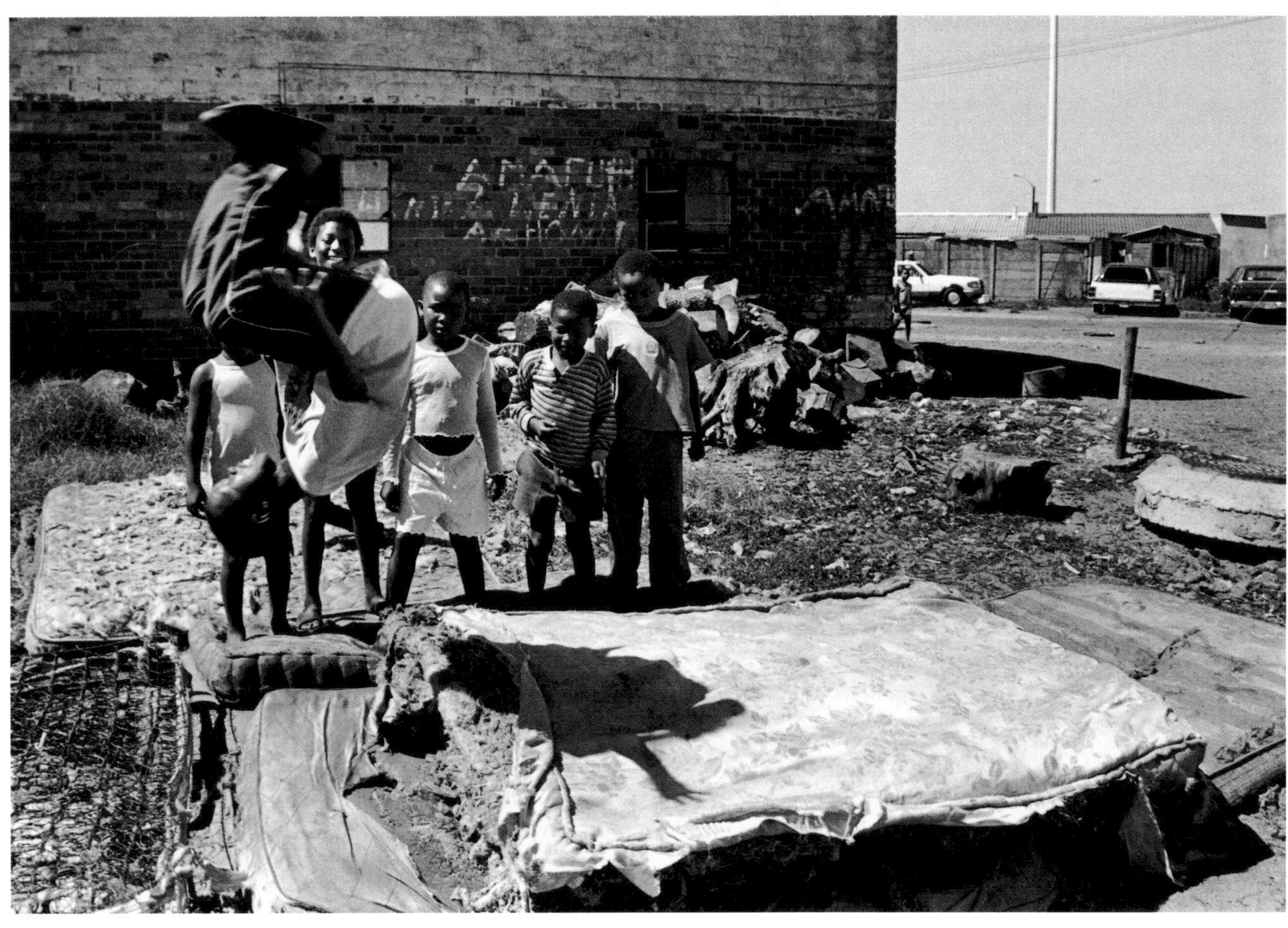

11 **ZUKO, MALIBONGWE, ATTIE, LOZO & DAKI**

LANGA TOWNSHIP, CAPE FLATS, WESTERN CAPE PROVINCE,

SOUTH AFRICA

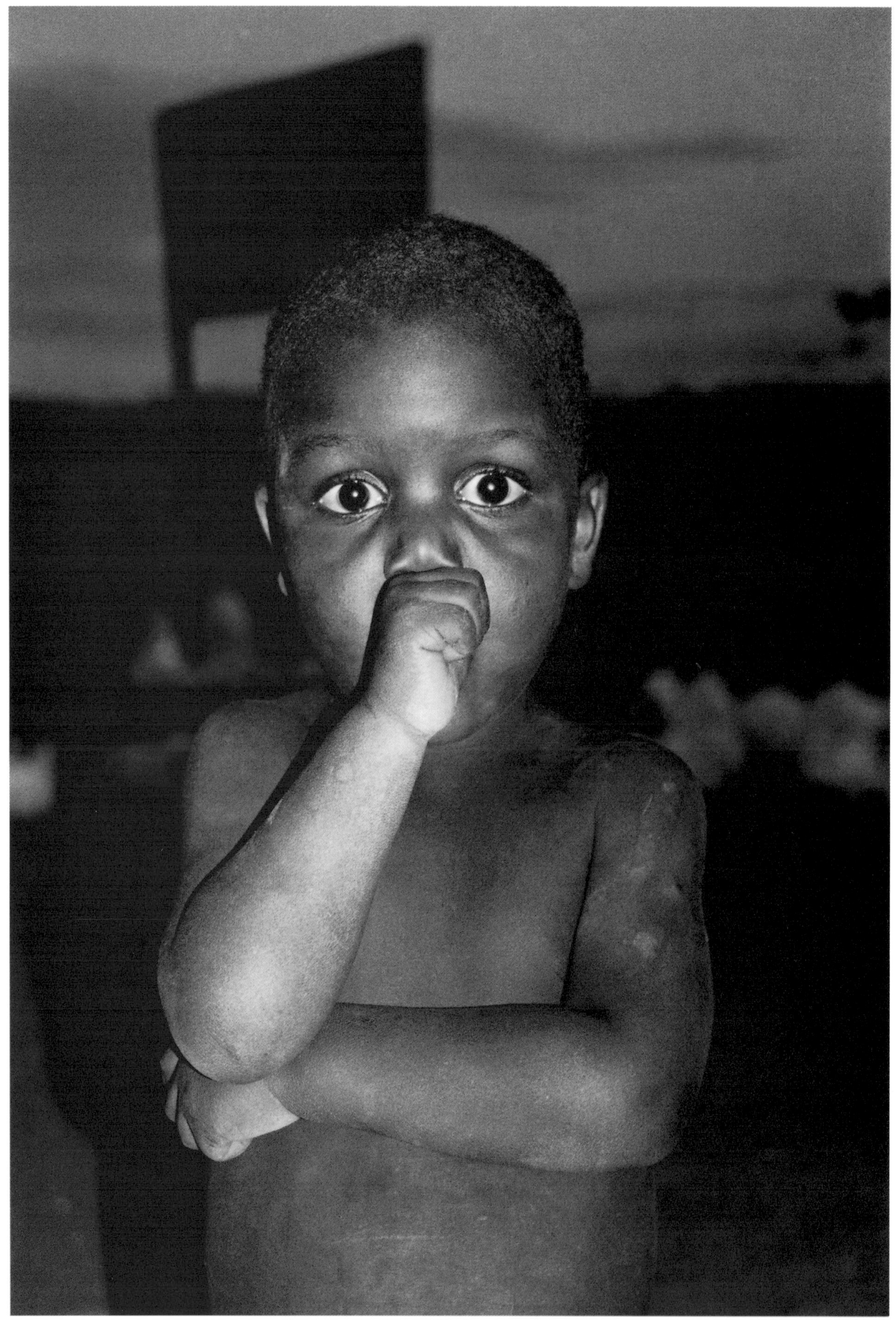

12 **BENET KUTAMUNDU**

MIDDLE OF THE DESERT, DAMARALAND,

NAMIBIA

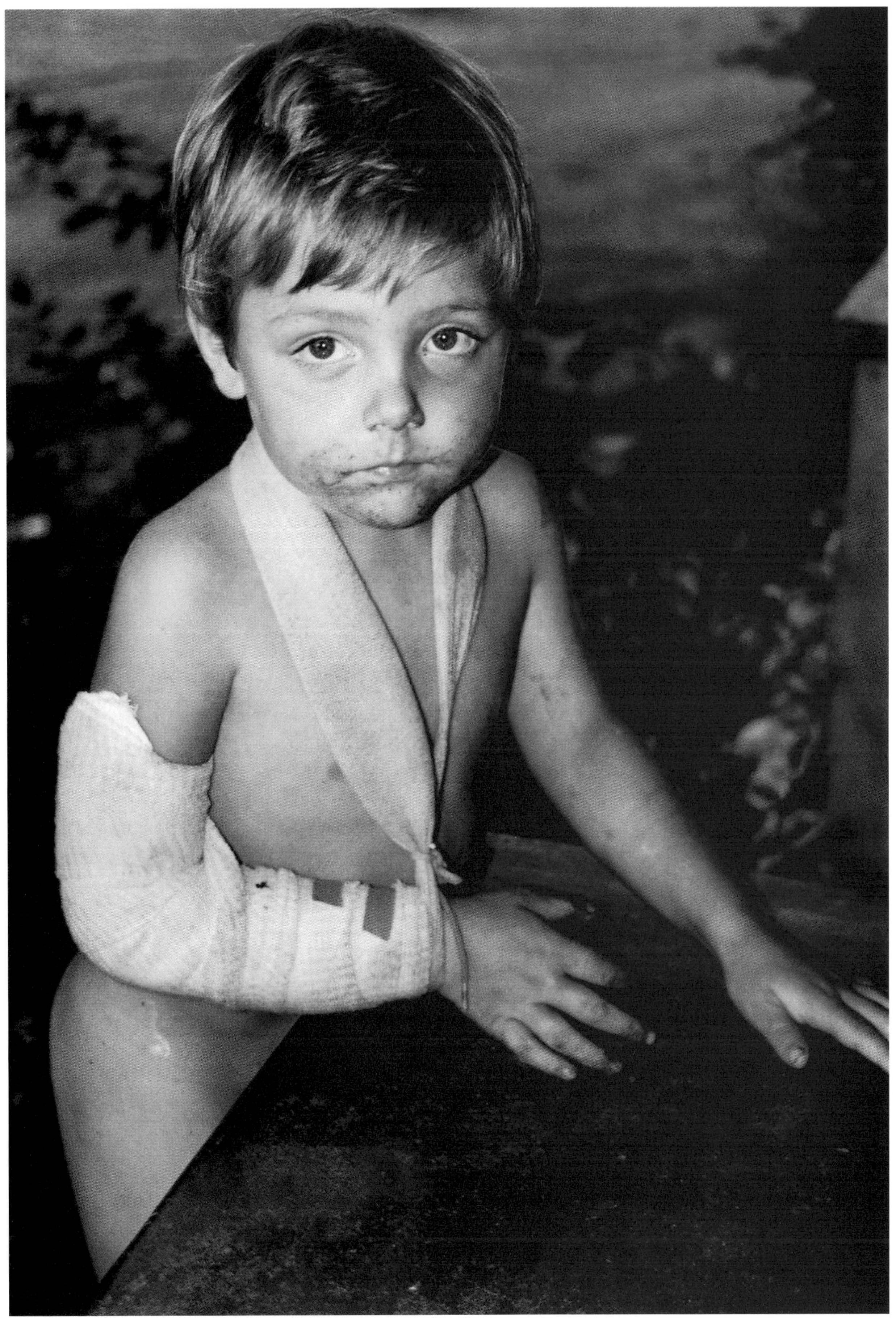

13 **TRISTAN SHAXSON**

MOUNT SELINDA, MANICALAND,

ZIMBABWE

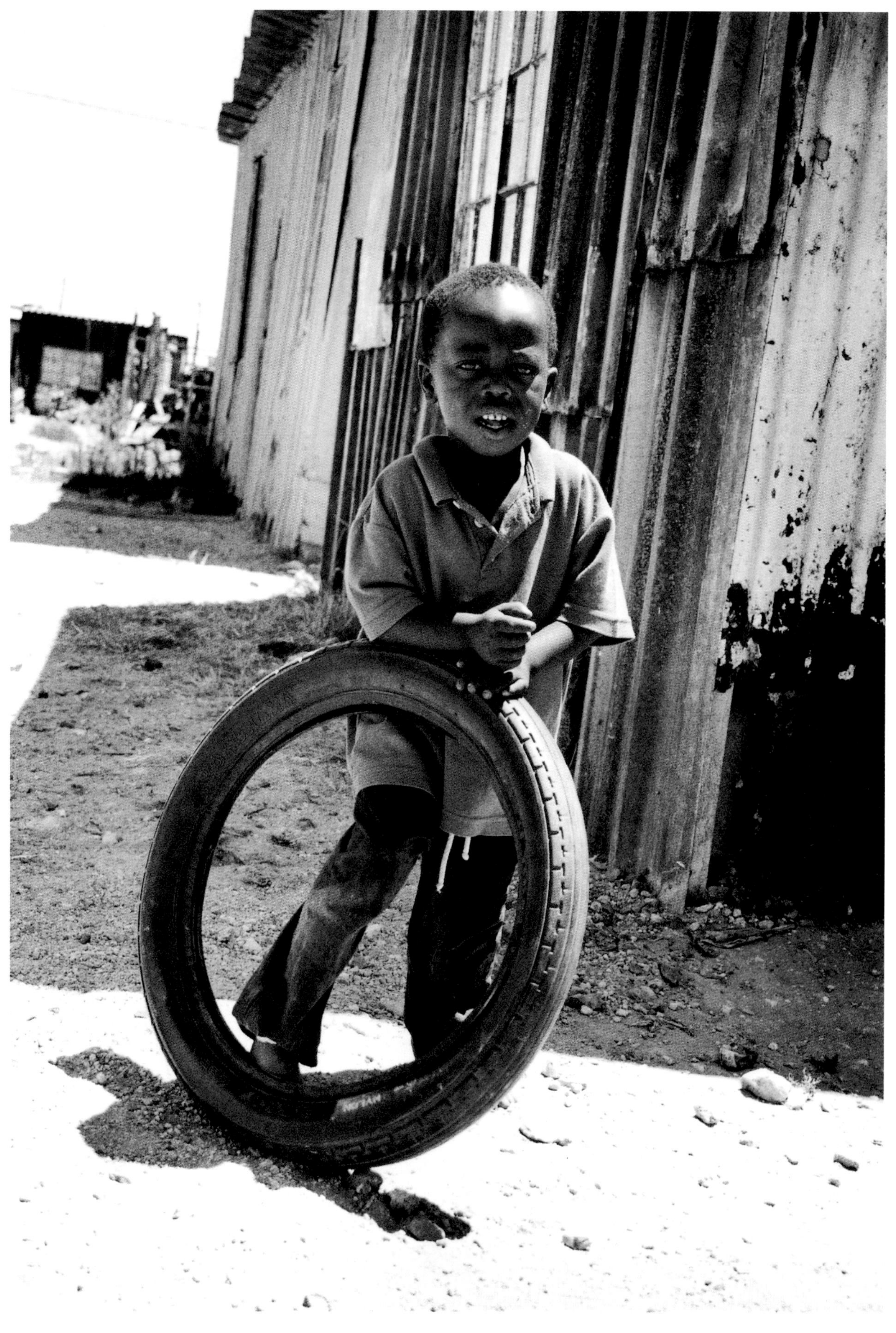

14 **INKWENKWANA**

KHAYELITSHA TOWNSHIP, CAPE FLATS, WESTERN CAPE PROVINCE,

SOUTH AFRICA

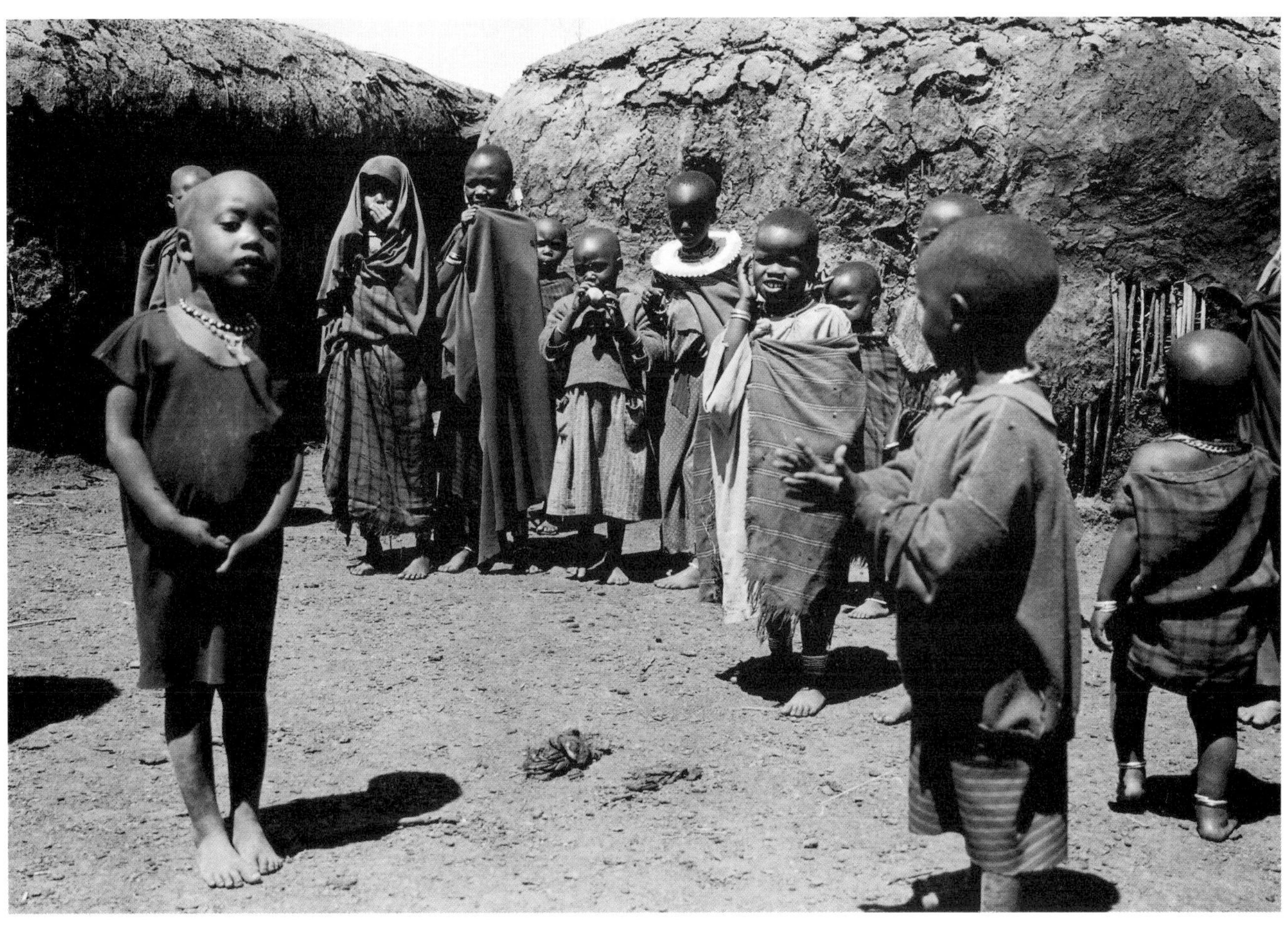

15 **MAASAI INKERA**

KANJIRO SENETO MAASAI BOMA, NGORONGORO,

TANZANIA

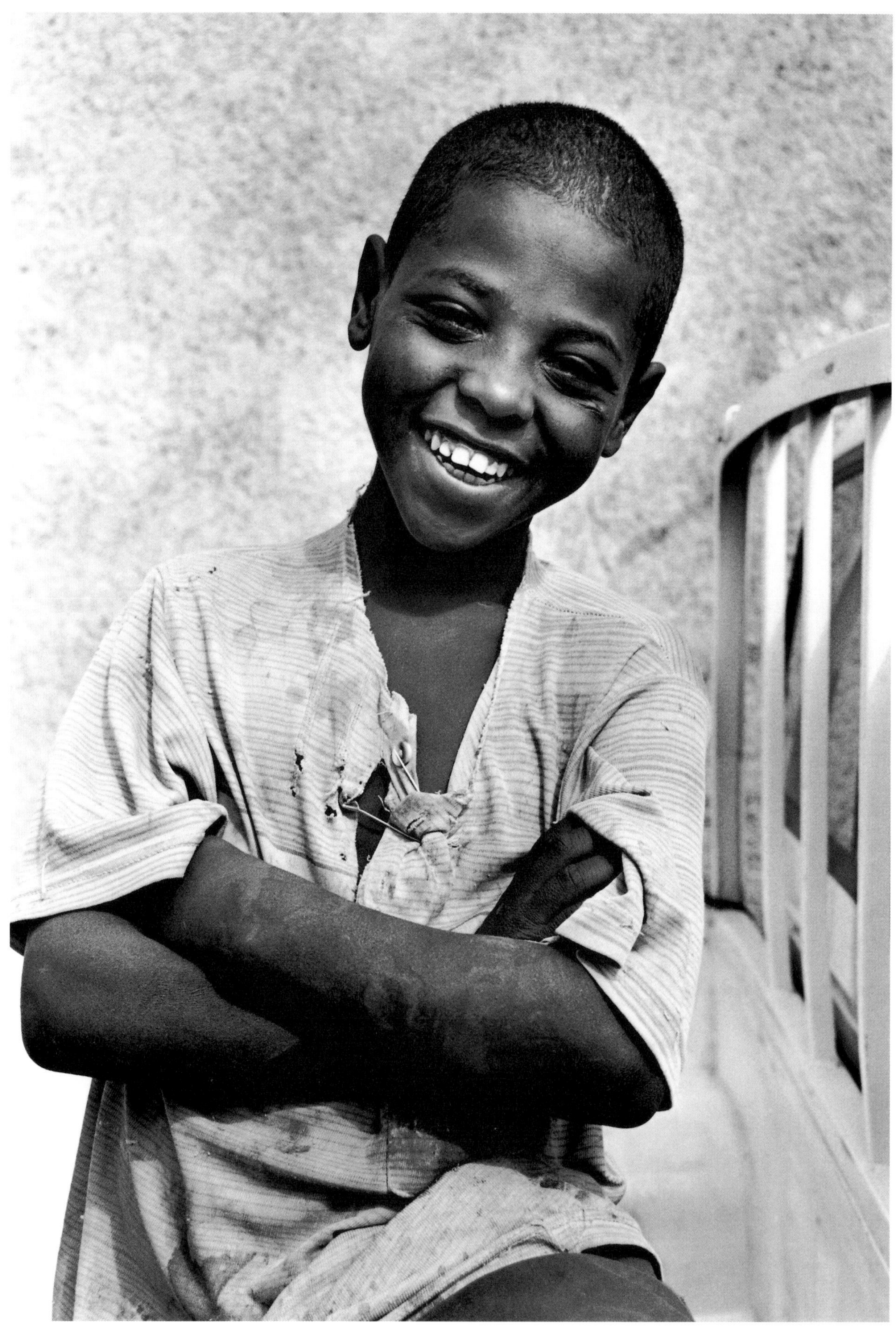

16 **ZERIHUN MENGESTE**

GOAL STREET CHILDRENS PROJECT, WOREDA 21, KEBELE 13, ADDIS ABABA, ETHIOPIA

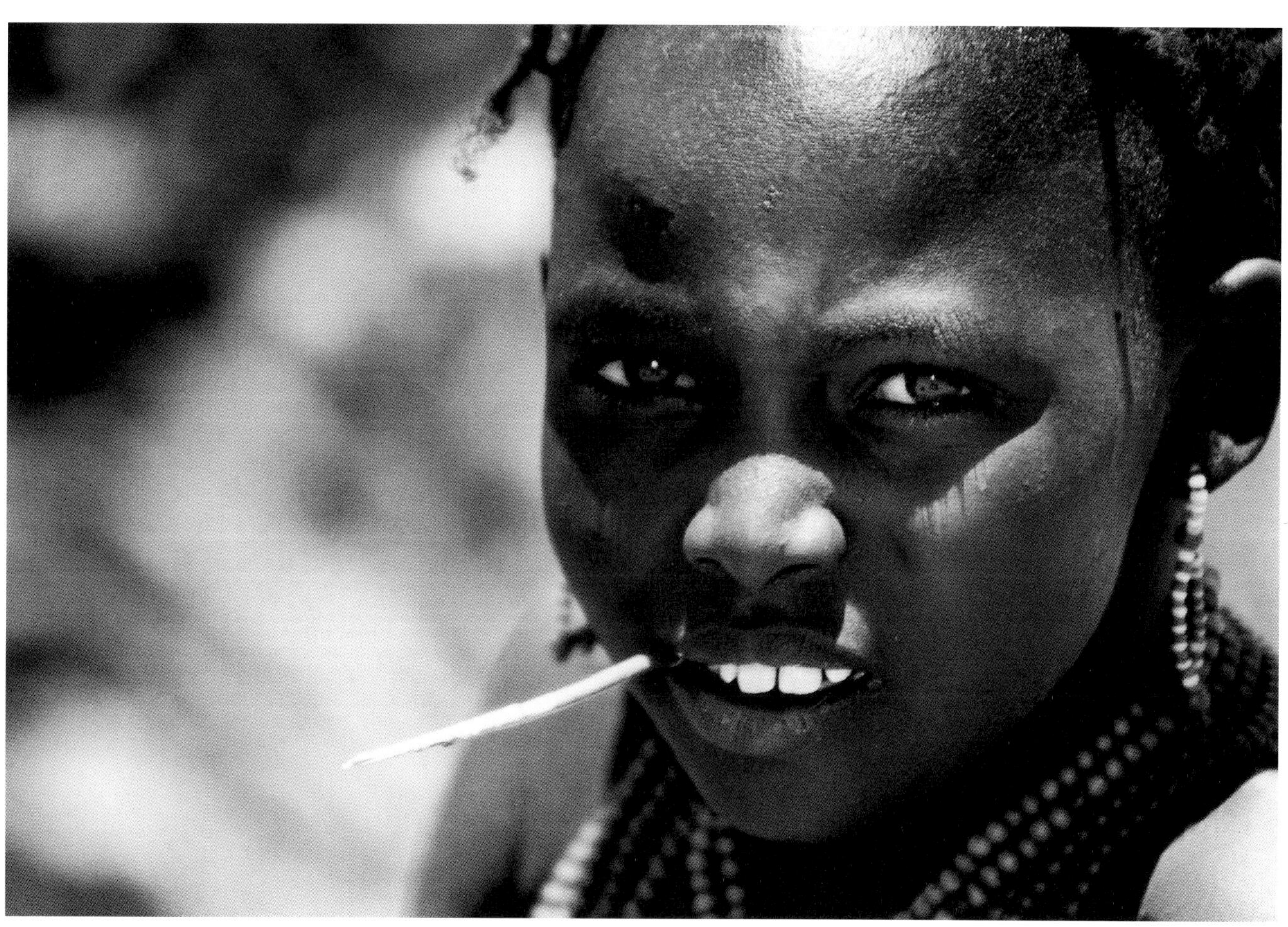

17 **KANNO**

DAASANACH TRIBE, GAMO – GOFA,

ETHIOPIA

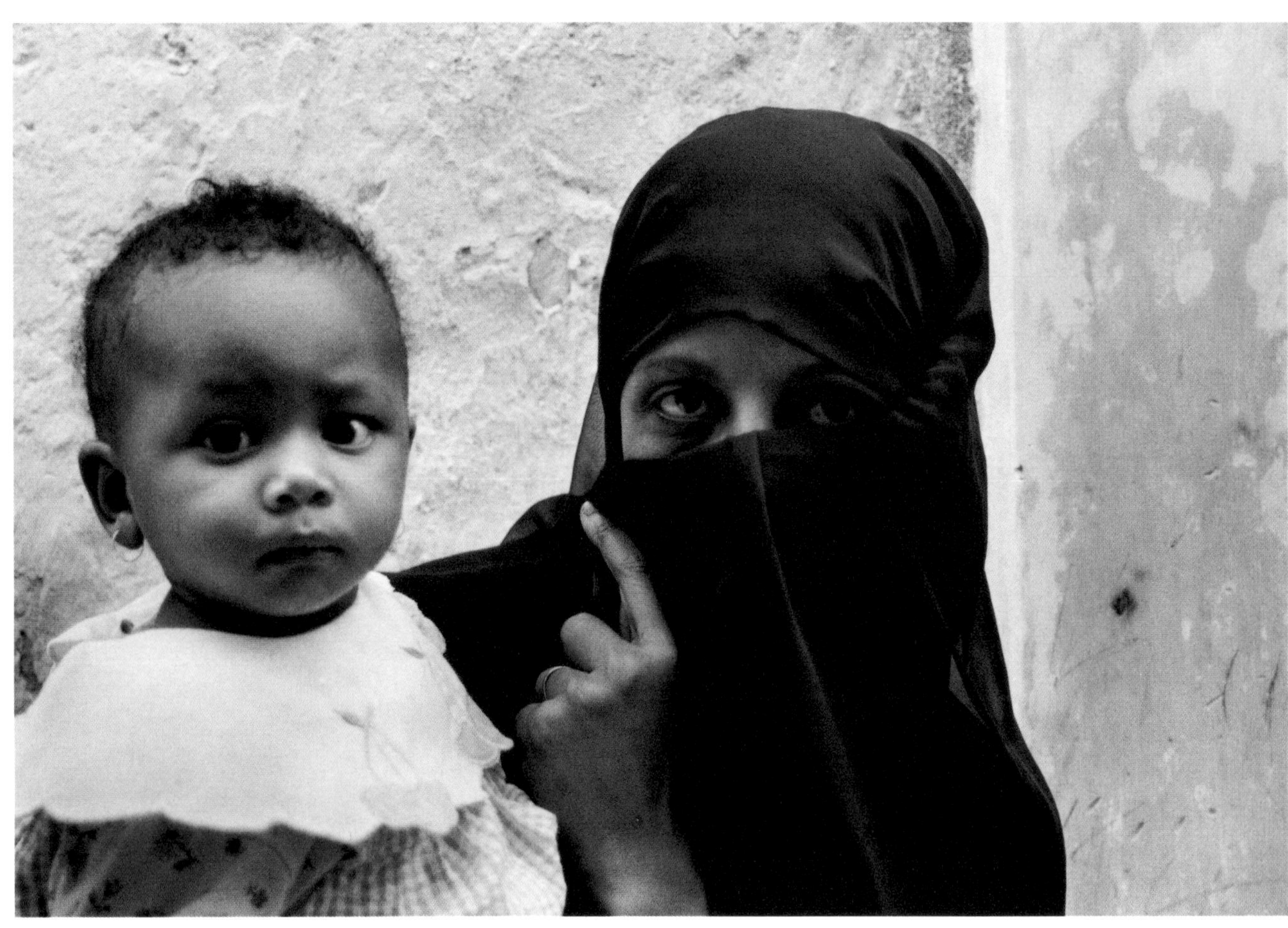

18 **HUSNA & TAUHIDA**

LAMU TOWN, LAMU ISLAND,

KENYA

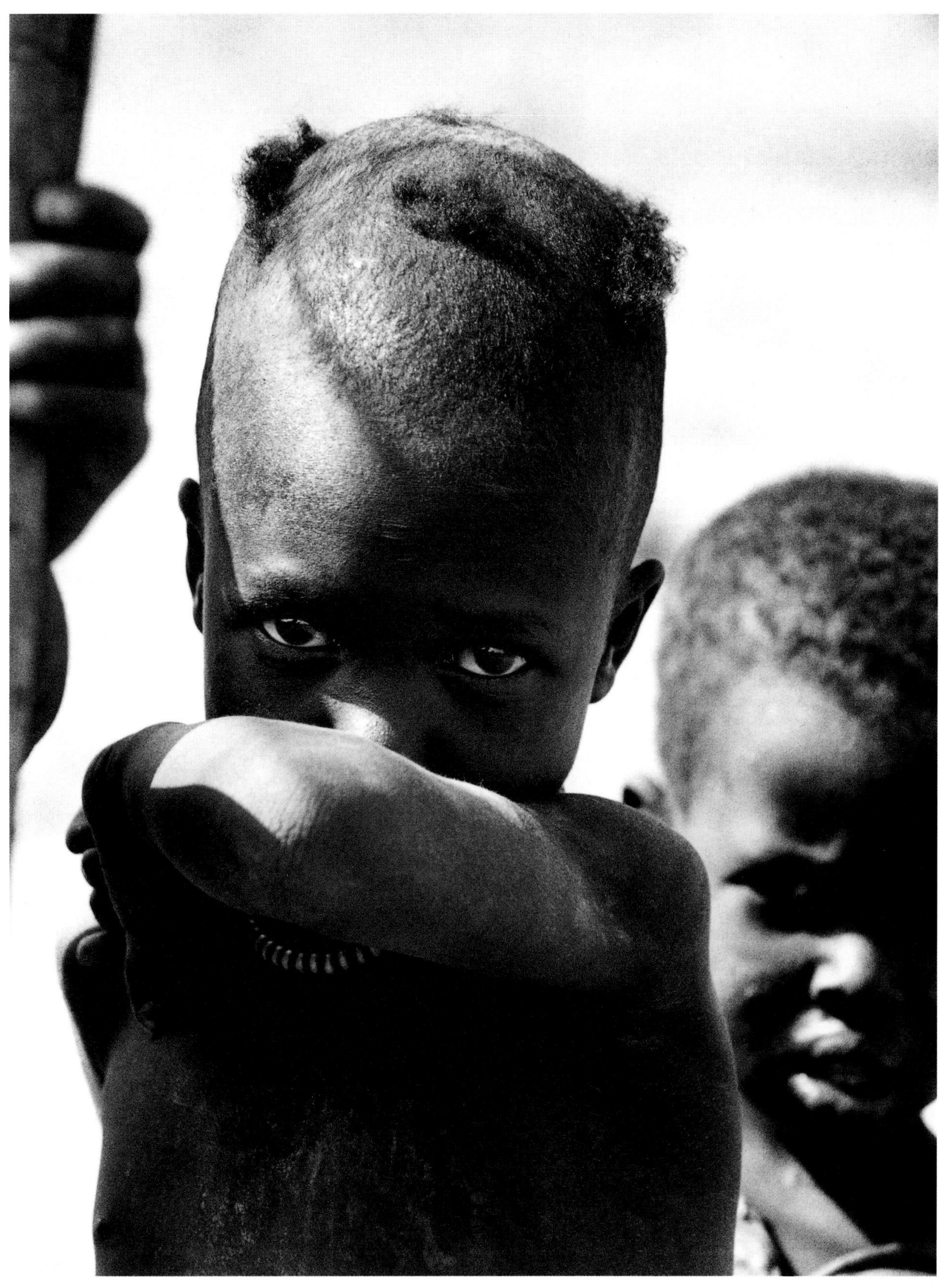

19 **EDAPAL EKWAKOL**

TURKANA TRIBE, LOKALALEI, WEST TURKANA, RIFT VALLEY PROVINCE, KENYA

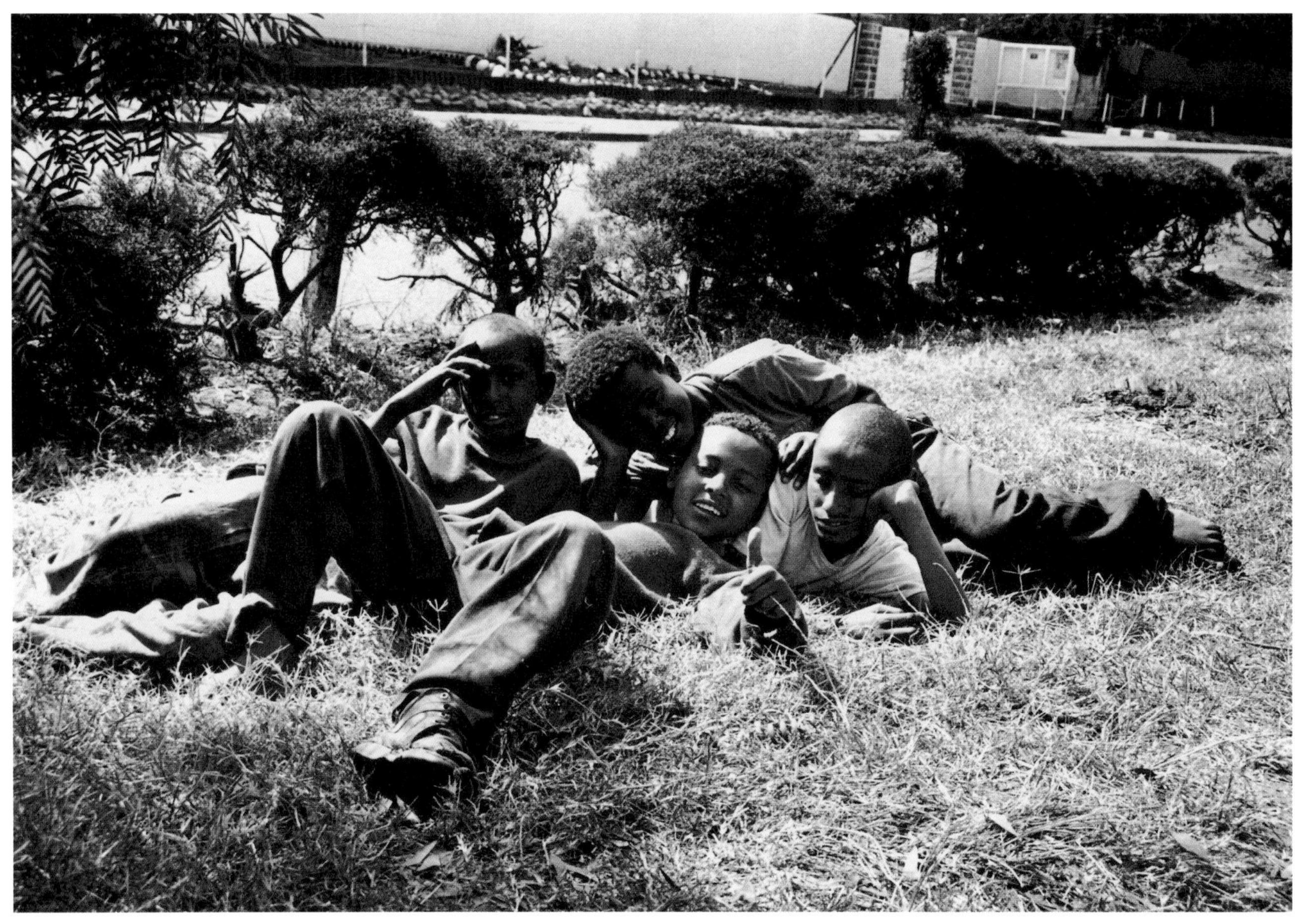

20 **BEHAILU GEBESA, YETAYU LEYEKUN, BELELEGNE ABESA & HUSEN JEMALE**

STREET KIDS, BOLE ROAD, ADDIS ABABA,

ETHIOPIA

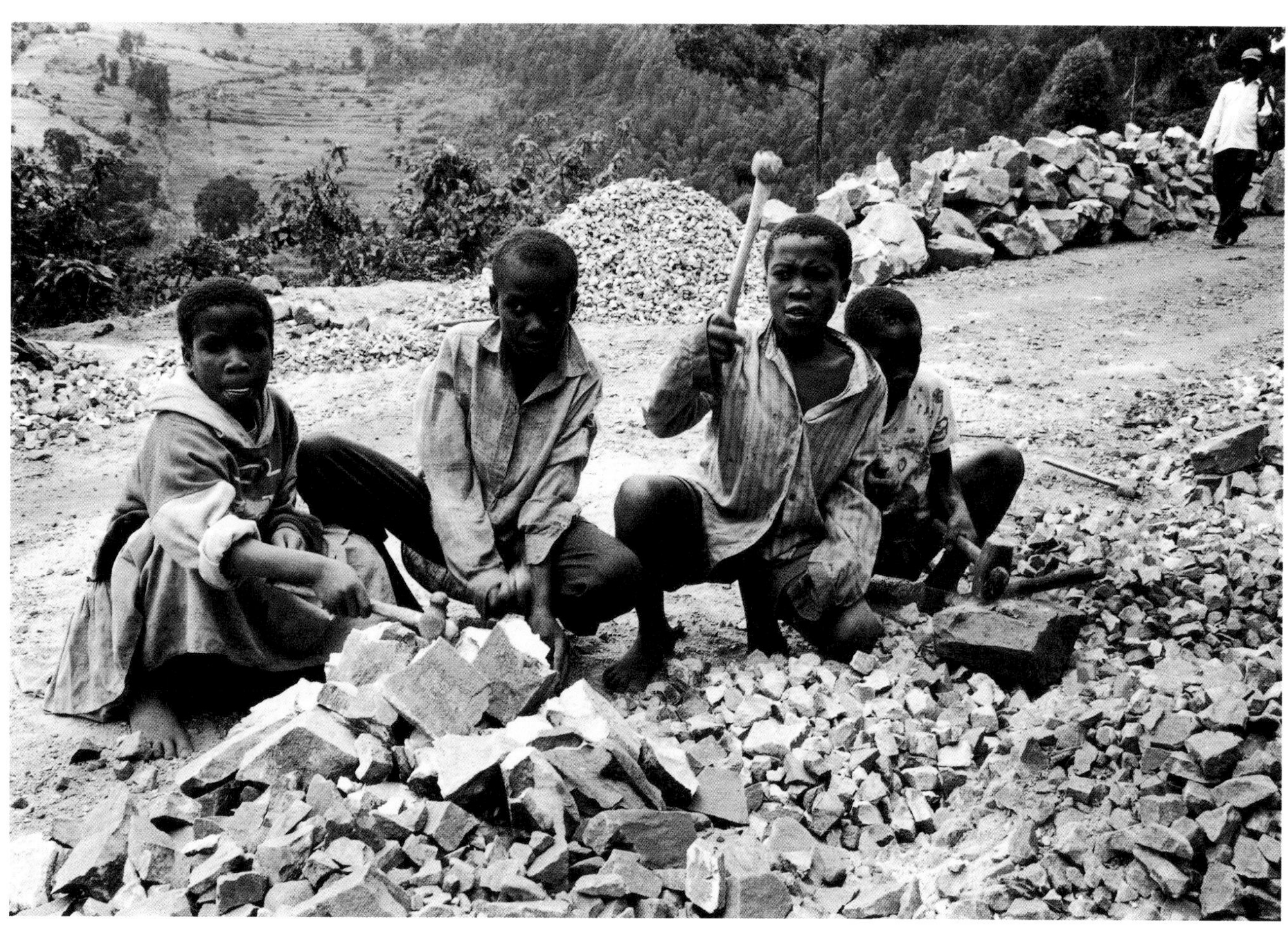

21 **PATIENCE, ORBIN, DIOS & ISAAC**

LAKE BUNYONYI ROAD, KABALE,

UGANDA

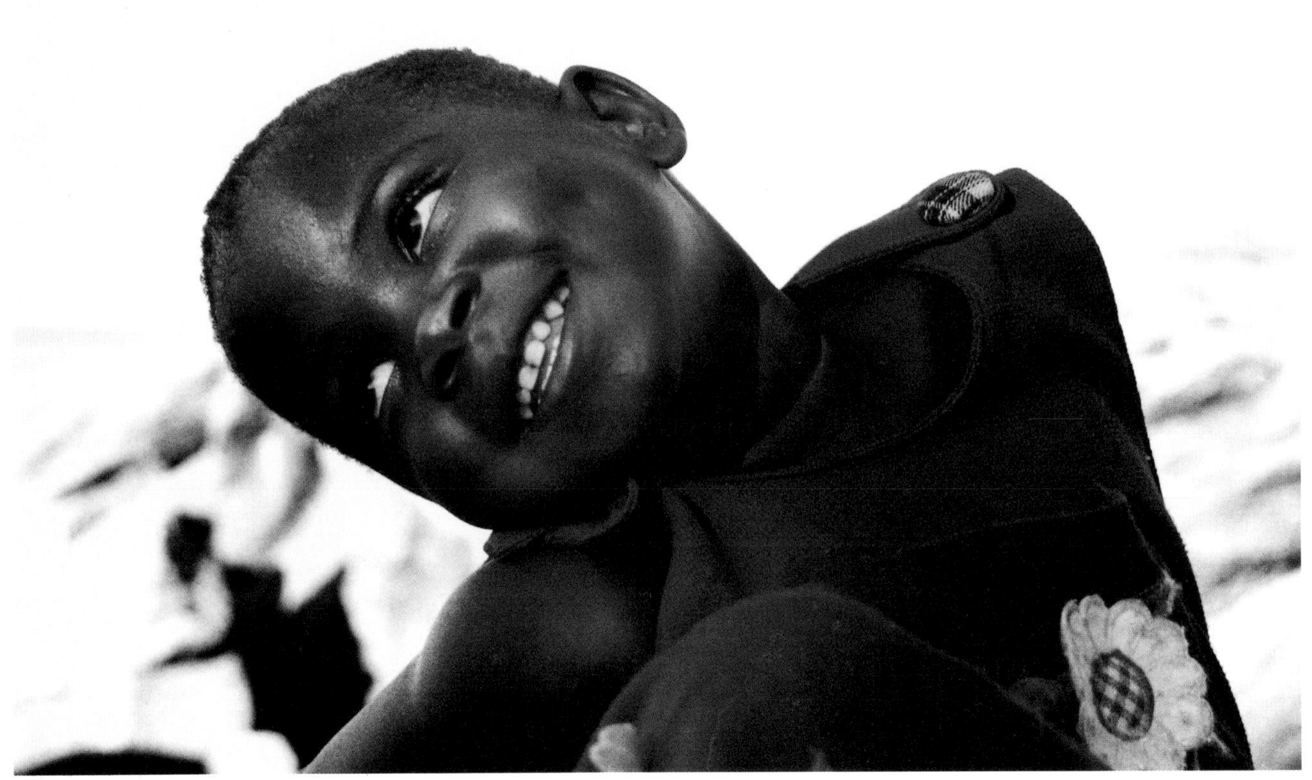

22 **FLORA SAKA**

NKATHA BAY, NORTHERN PROVINCE,

MALAWI

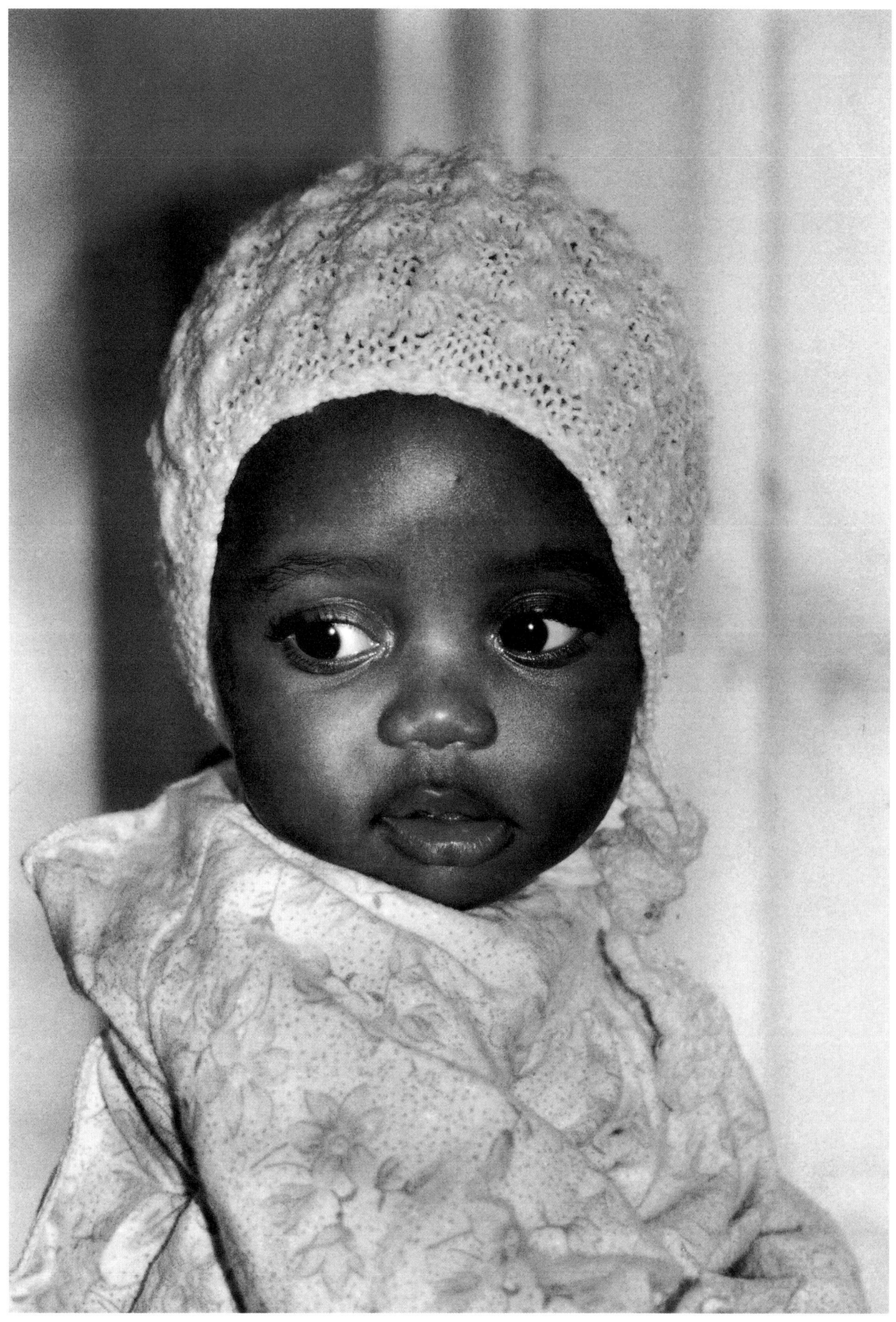

23 **FAITH**

CHINOTIMBA TOWNSHIP, MATABELELAND NORTH,

ZIMBABWE

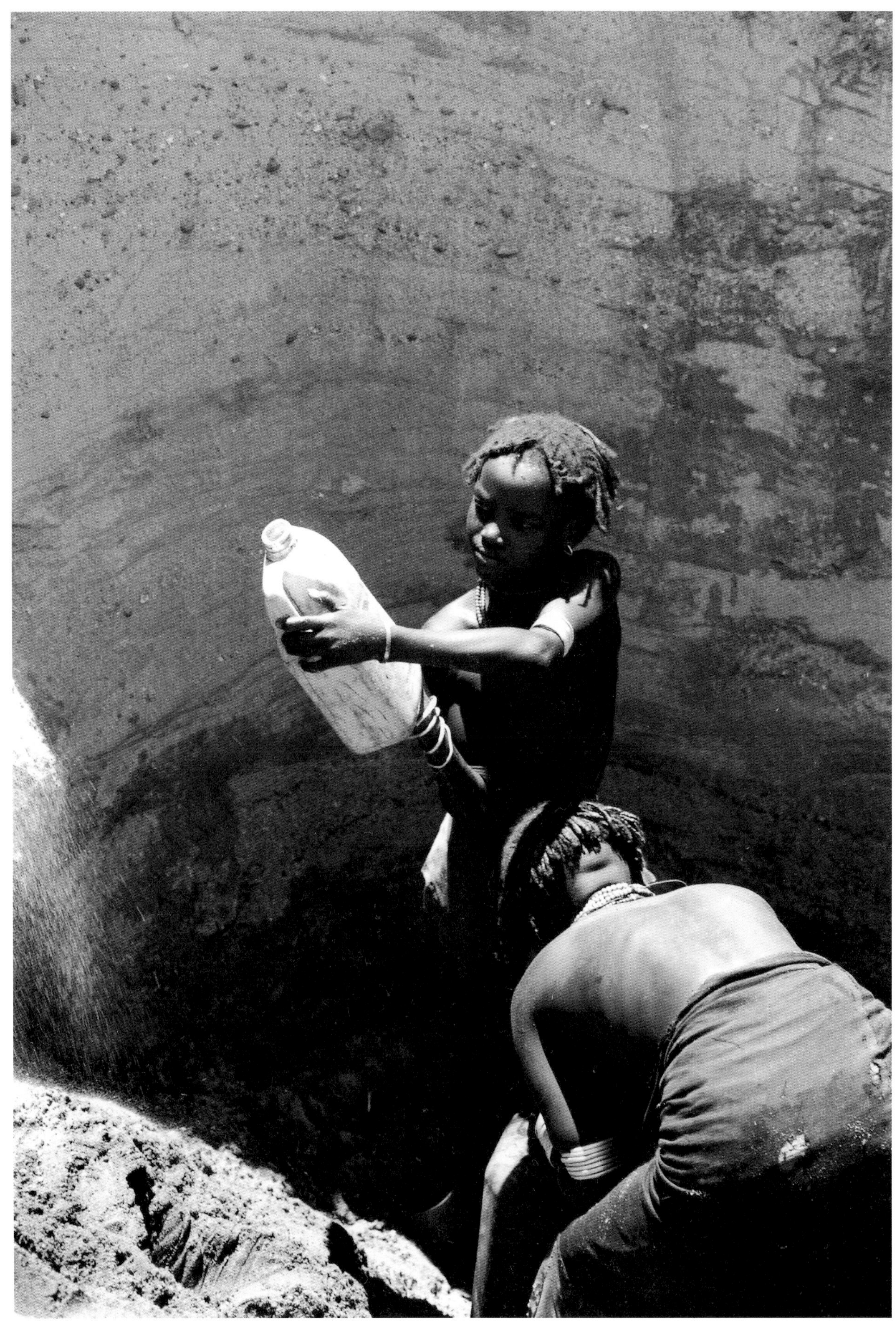

24 **NAKWAR & FRIEND**

DAASANACH TRIBE, GAMO – GOFA,

ETHIOPIA

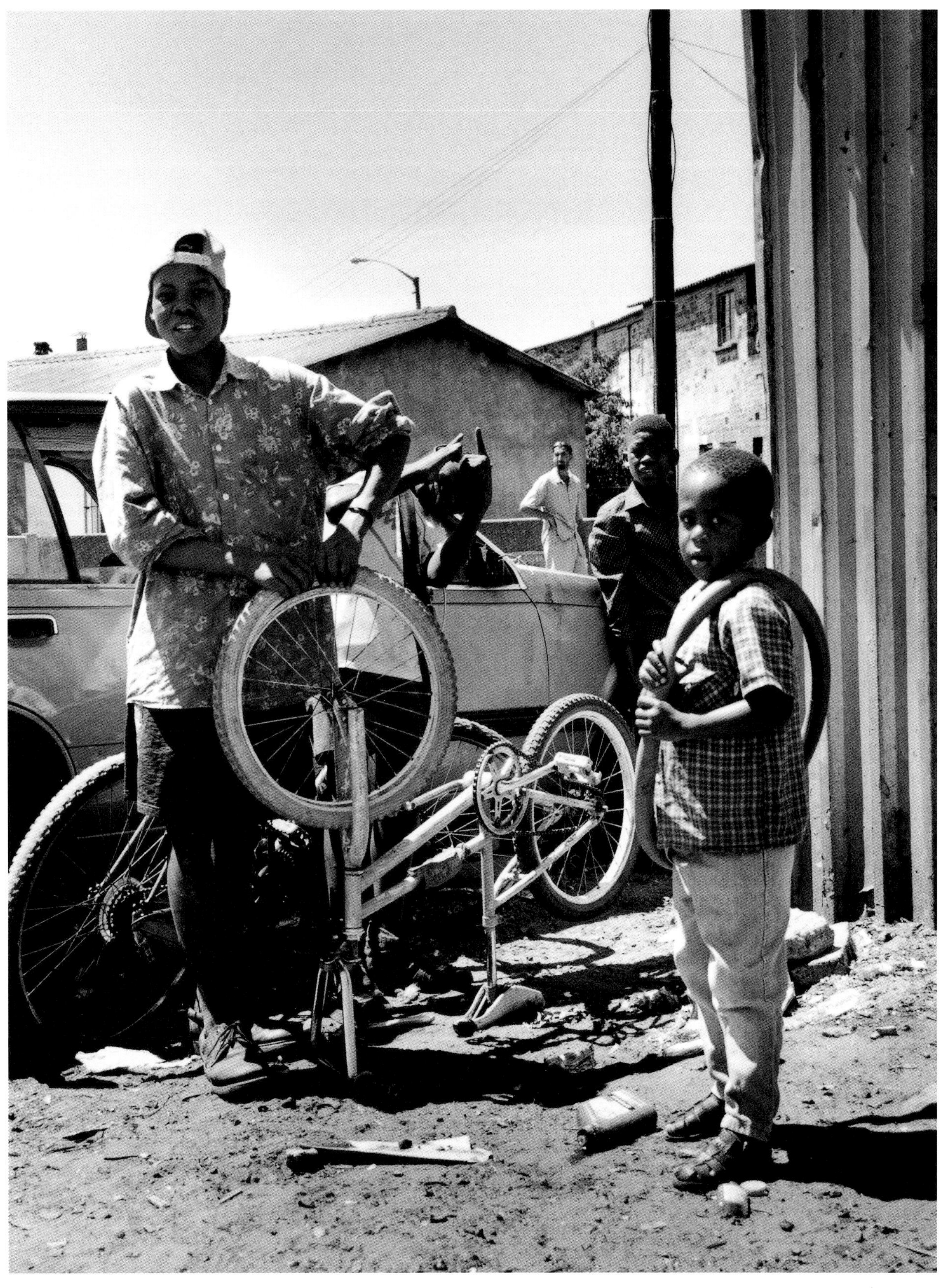

25 **LUNGISA IBHAYISIKILI**

KHAYELITSHA TOWNSHIP, CAPE FLATS, WESTERN CAPE PROVINCE,

SOUTH AFRICA

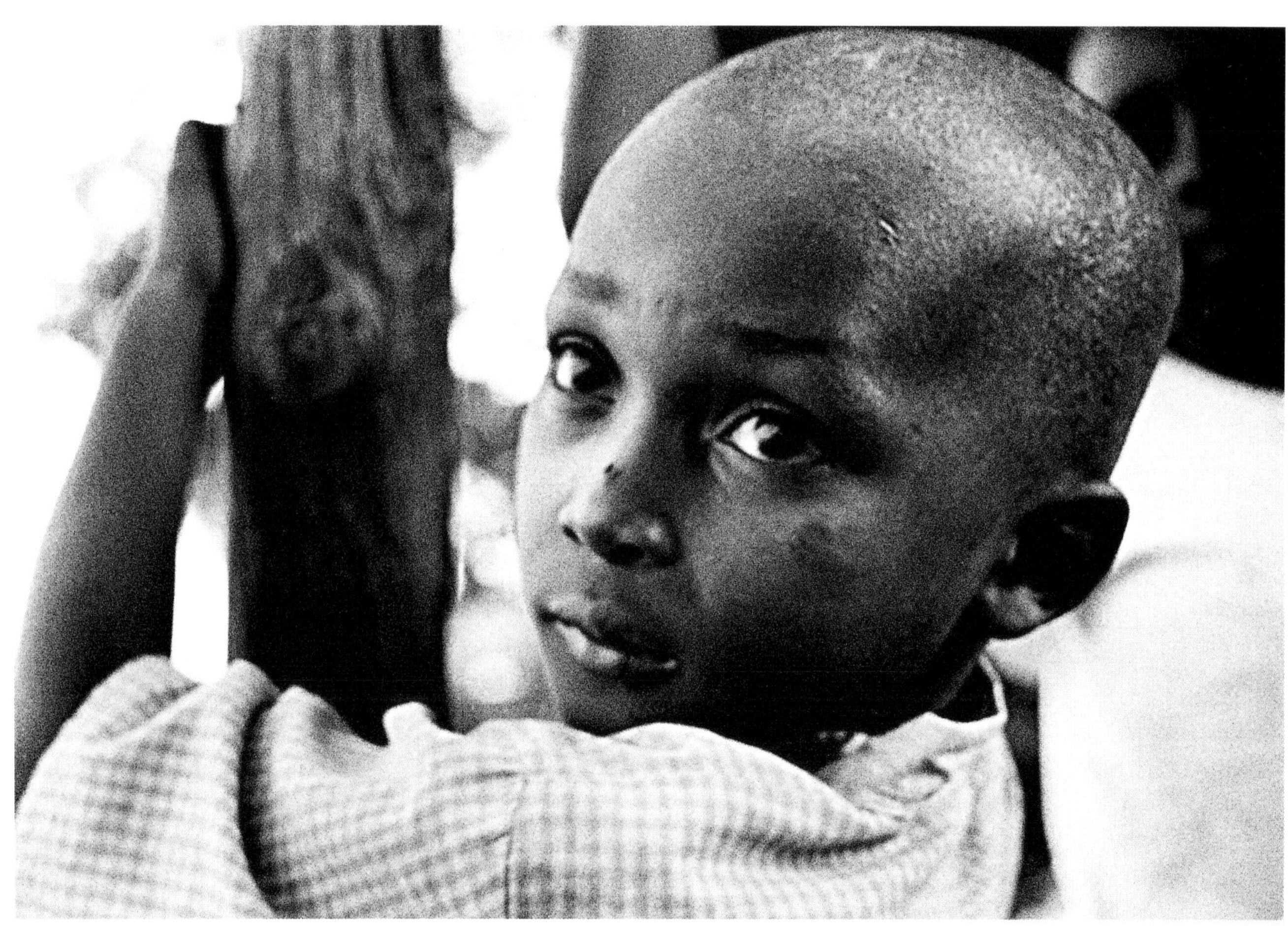

26 **ATHMAN**

LAMU TOWN, LAMU ISLAND,

KENYA

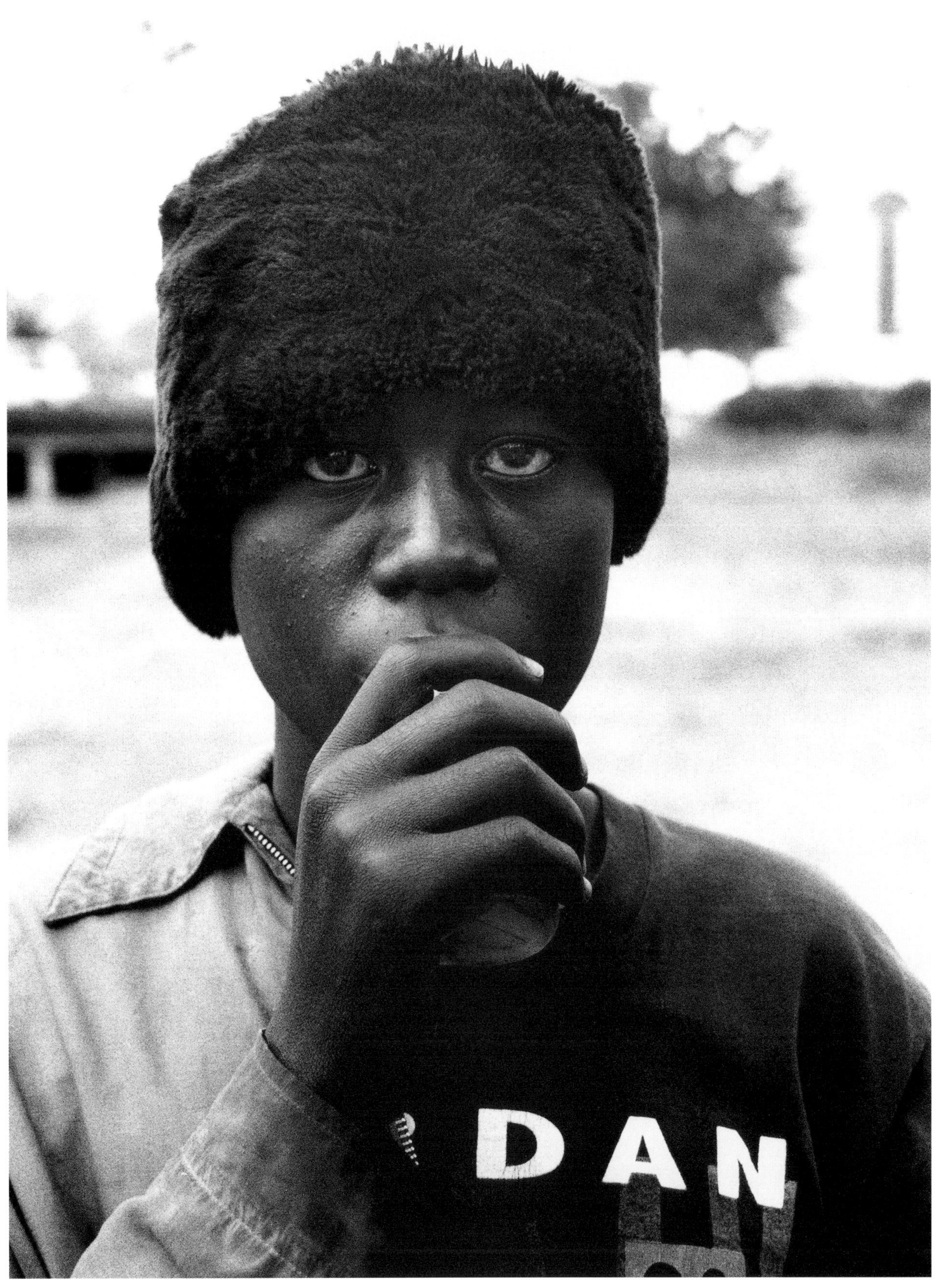

27 **ROBERT ZEWIS**

GLUE SNIFFING STREET KID, NAIROBI, KENYA

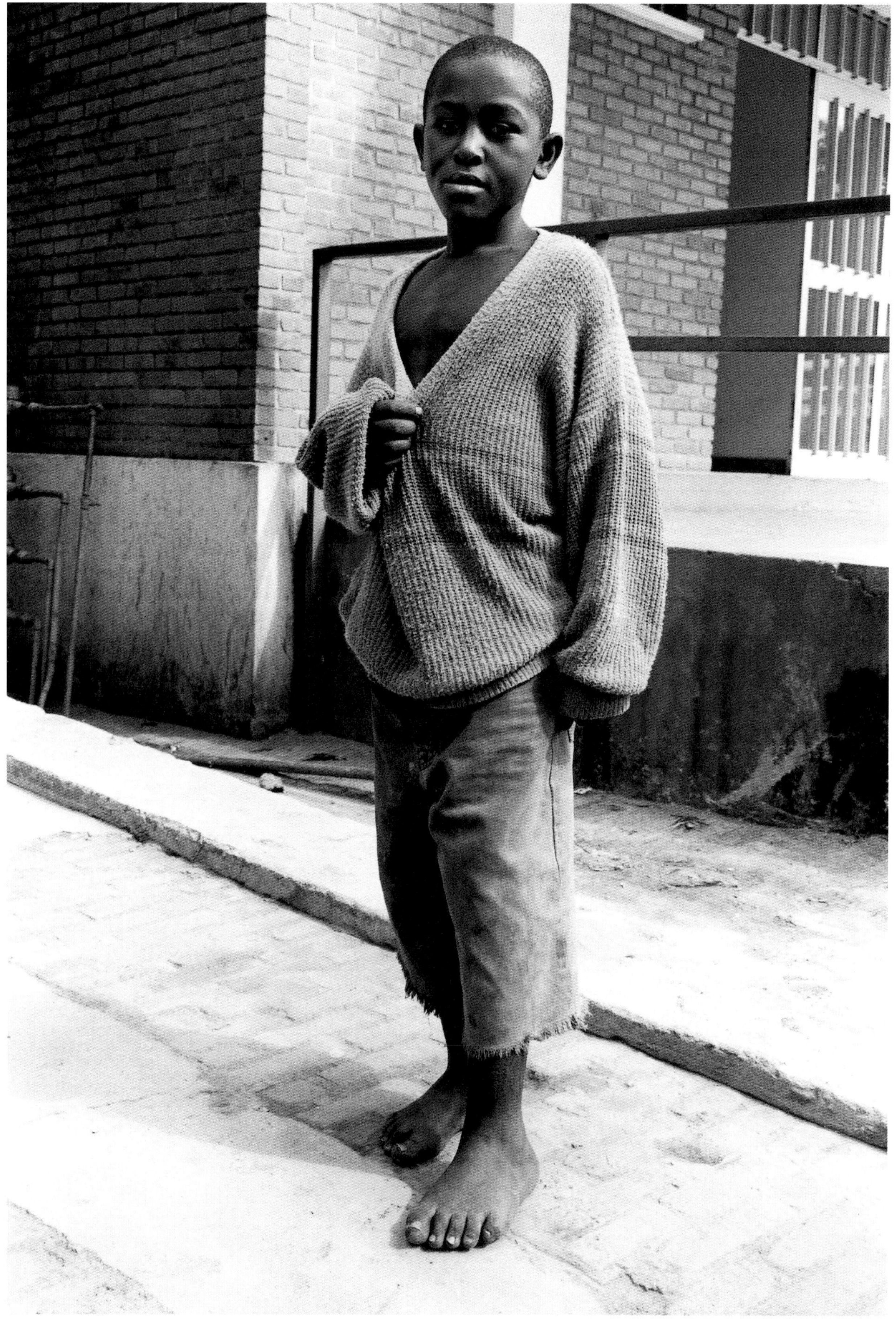

28 GENOCIDE ORPHAN

KIGALI,

RWANDA

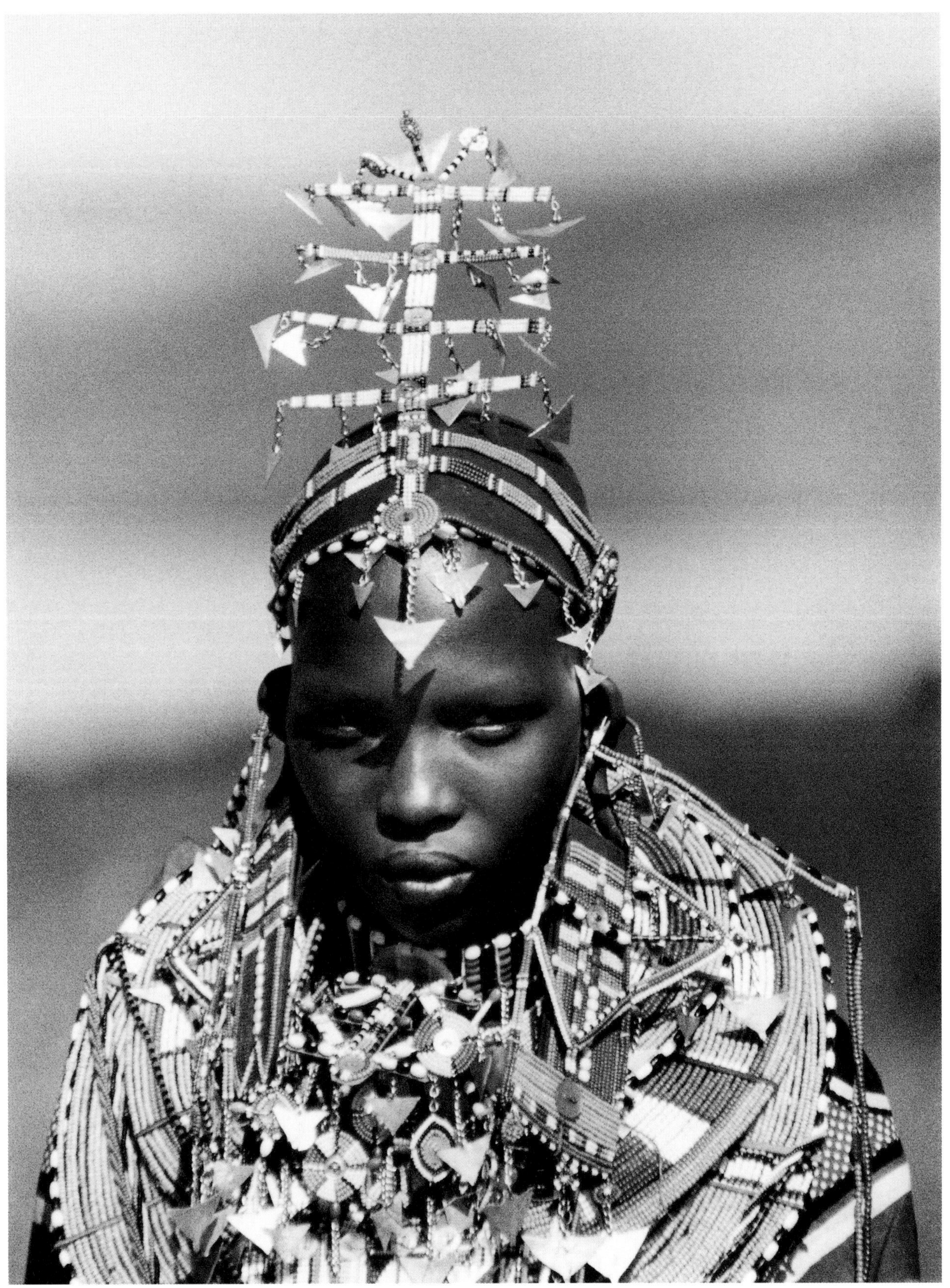

29 **NELOITA**

MAASAI WEDDING, LOITA HILLS, MORIJO,

KENYA

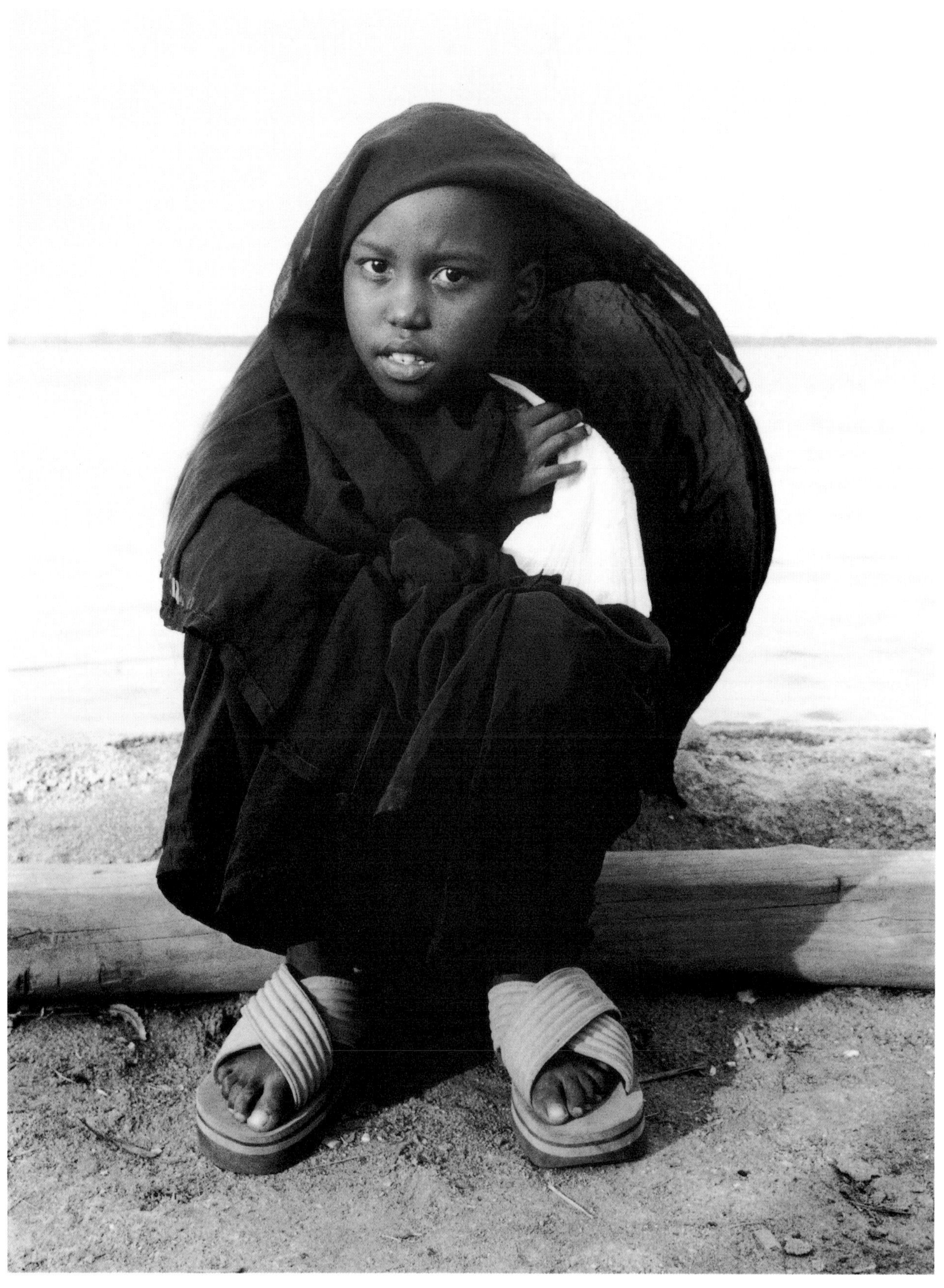

30 **FATIMA**

LAMU TOWN, LAMU ISLAND,

KENYA

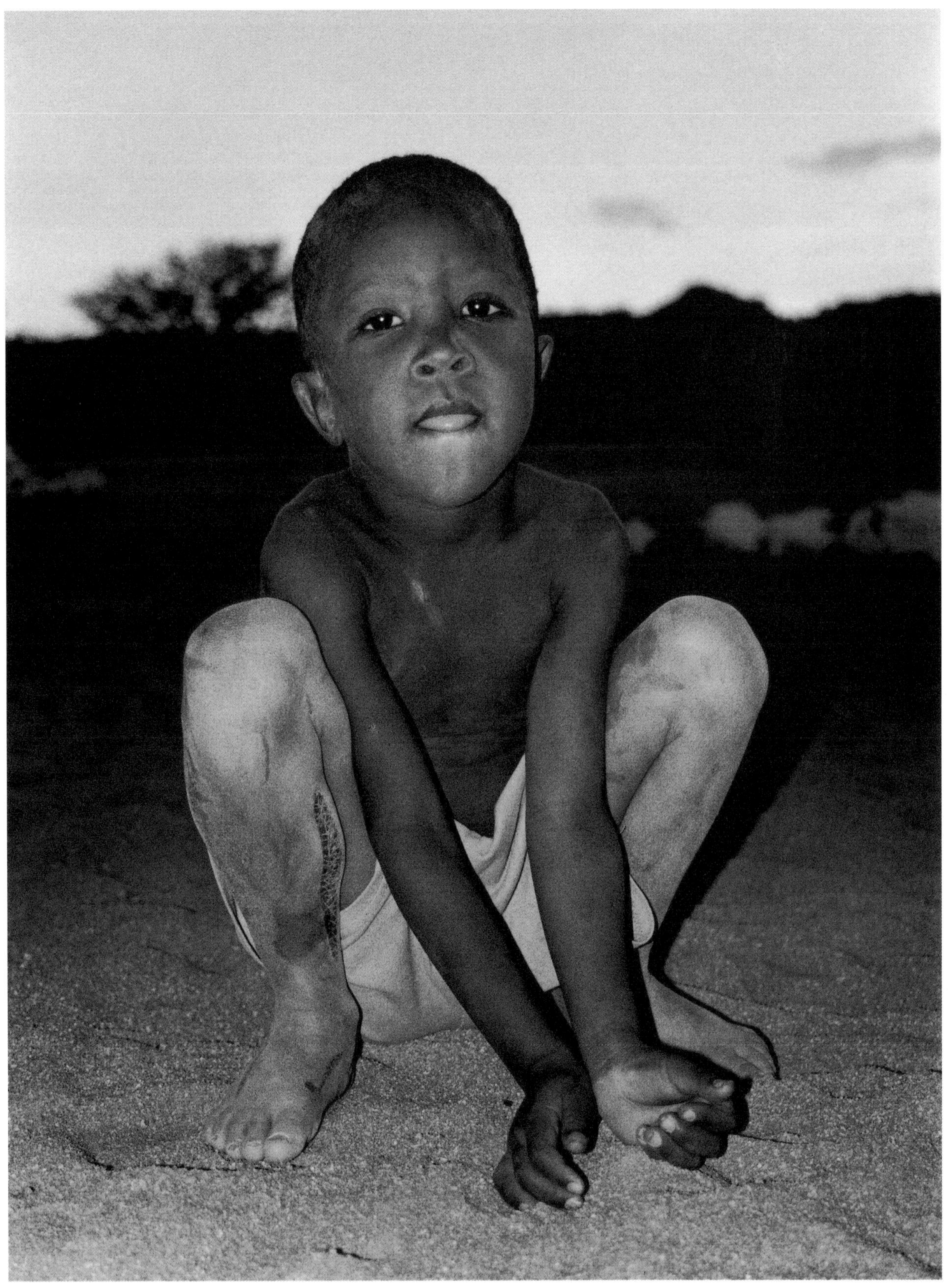

31 **STEVEN KARIKO**

MIDDLE OF THE DESERT, DAMARALAND,

NAMIBIA

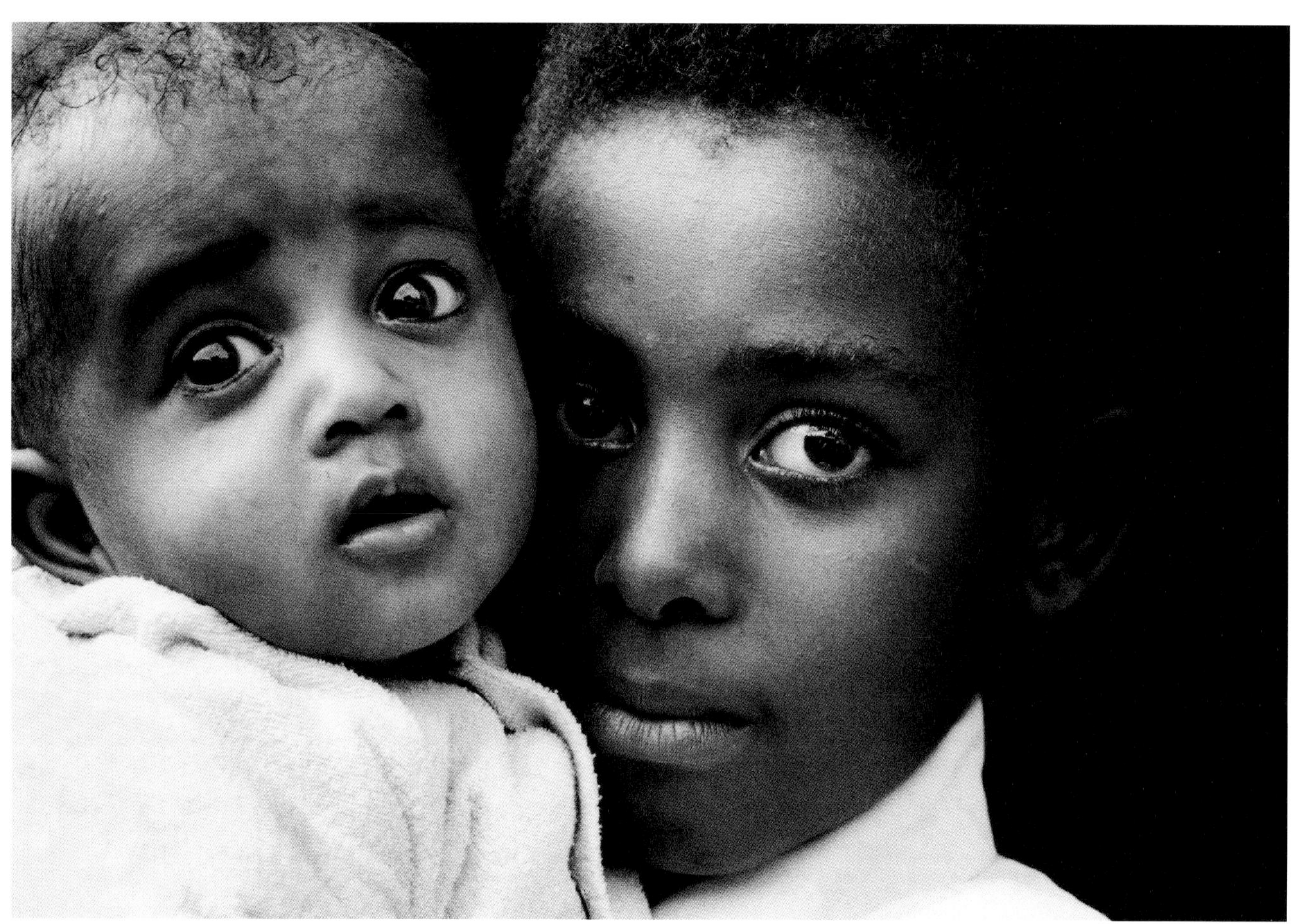

32 **MAMA NA MTOTO**

LAMU TOWN, LAMU ISLAND,

KENYA

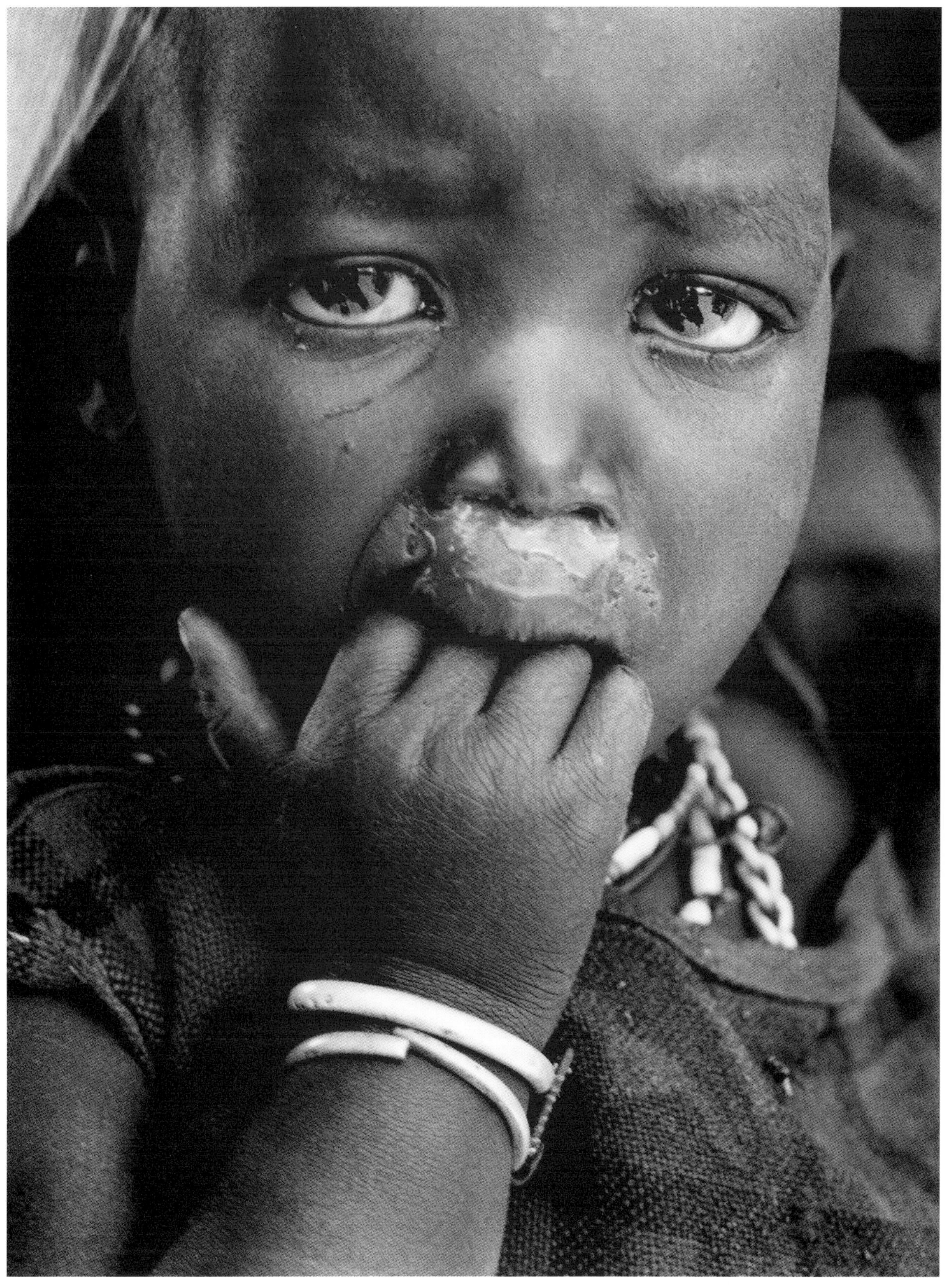

33 **LONGUTT**

KANJIRO SENETO MAASAI BOMA, NGORONGORO,

TANZANIA

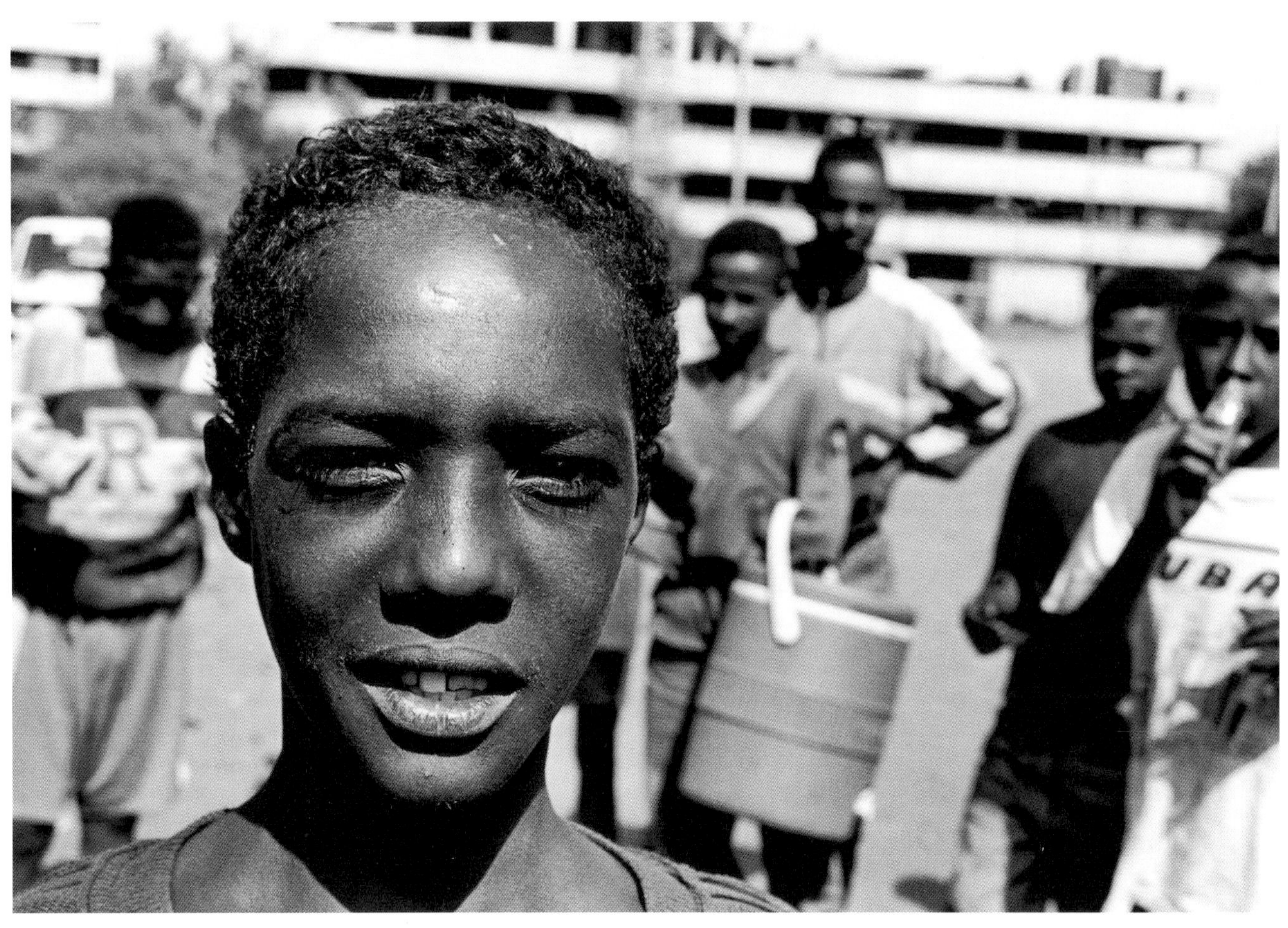

34 **MUSA ASEFA**

STREET KID, FOOTBALL STADIUM, ADDIS ABABA, ETHIOPIA

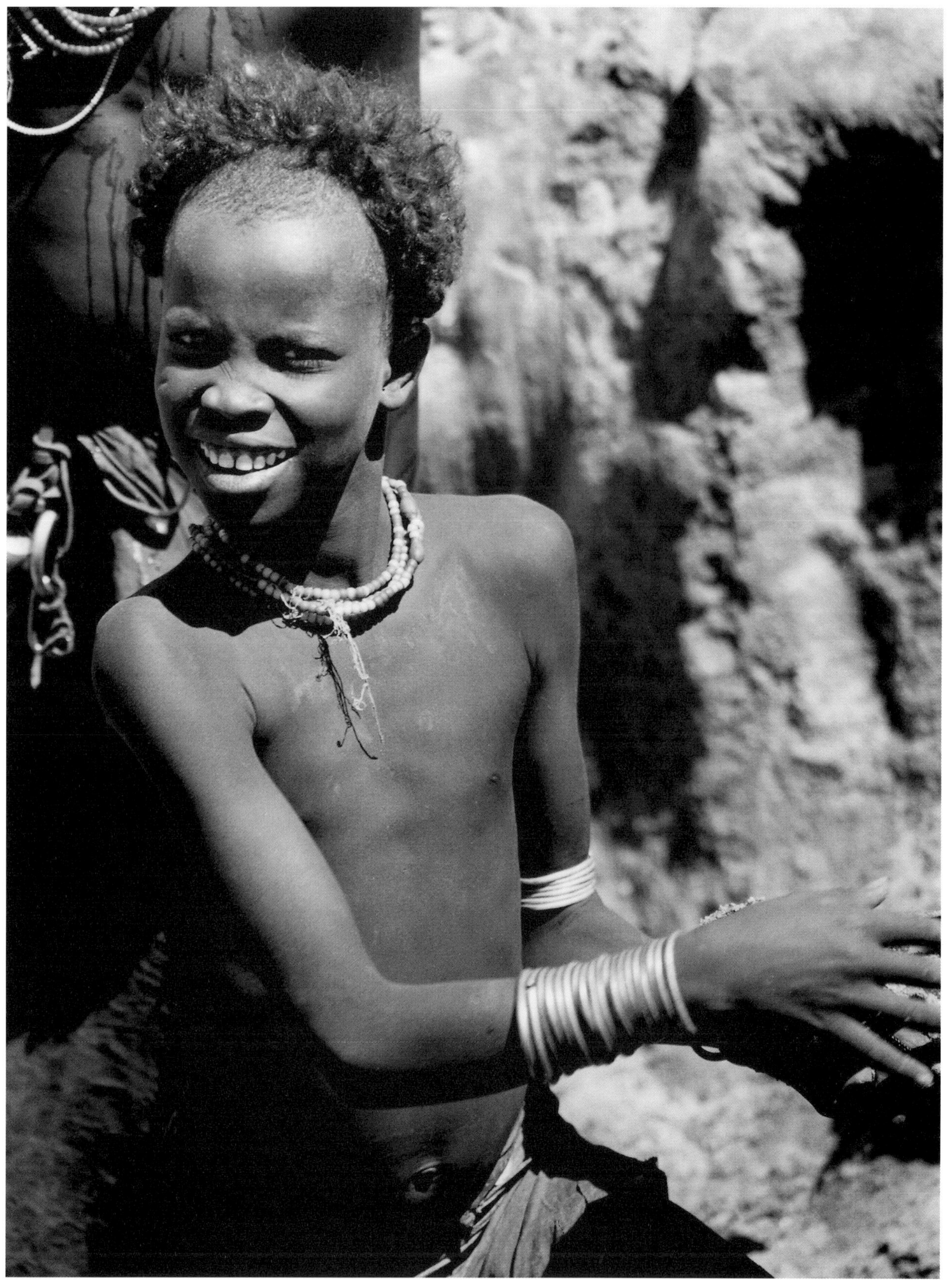

35 **EREK**

DAASANACH TRIBE, GAMO – GOFA,

ETHIOPIA

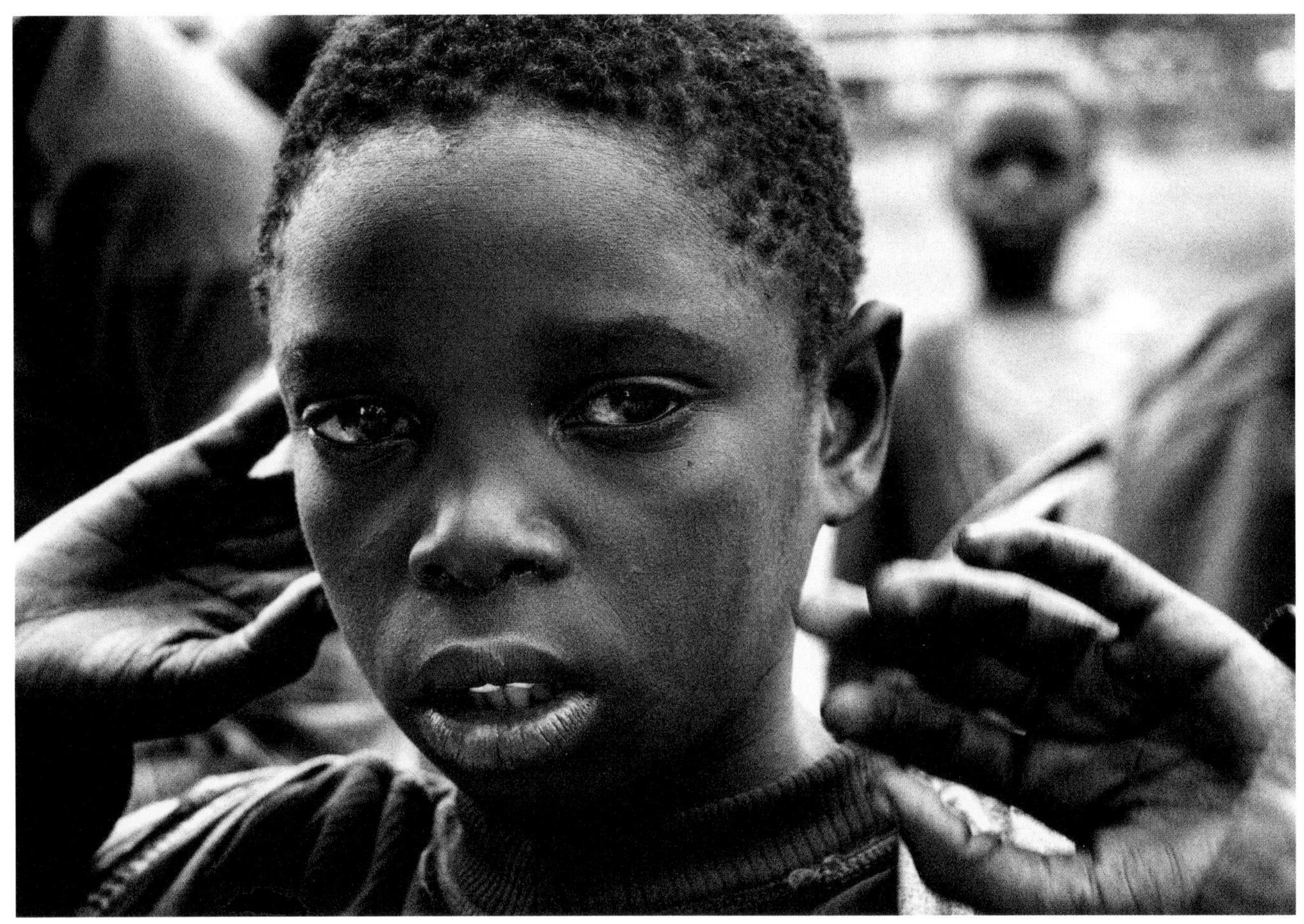

36 **JOHN MWANGI**

GLUE SNIFFING STREET KID, NAIROBI,

KENYA

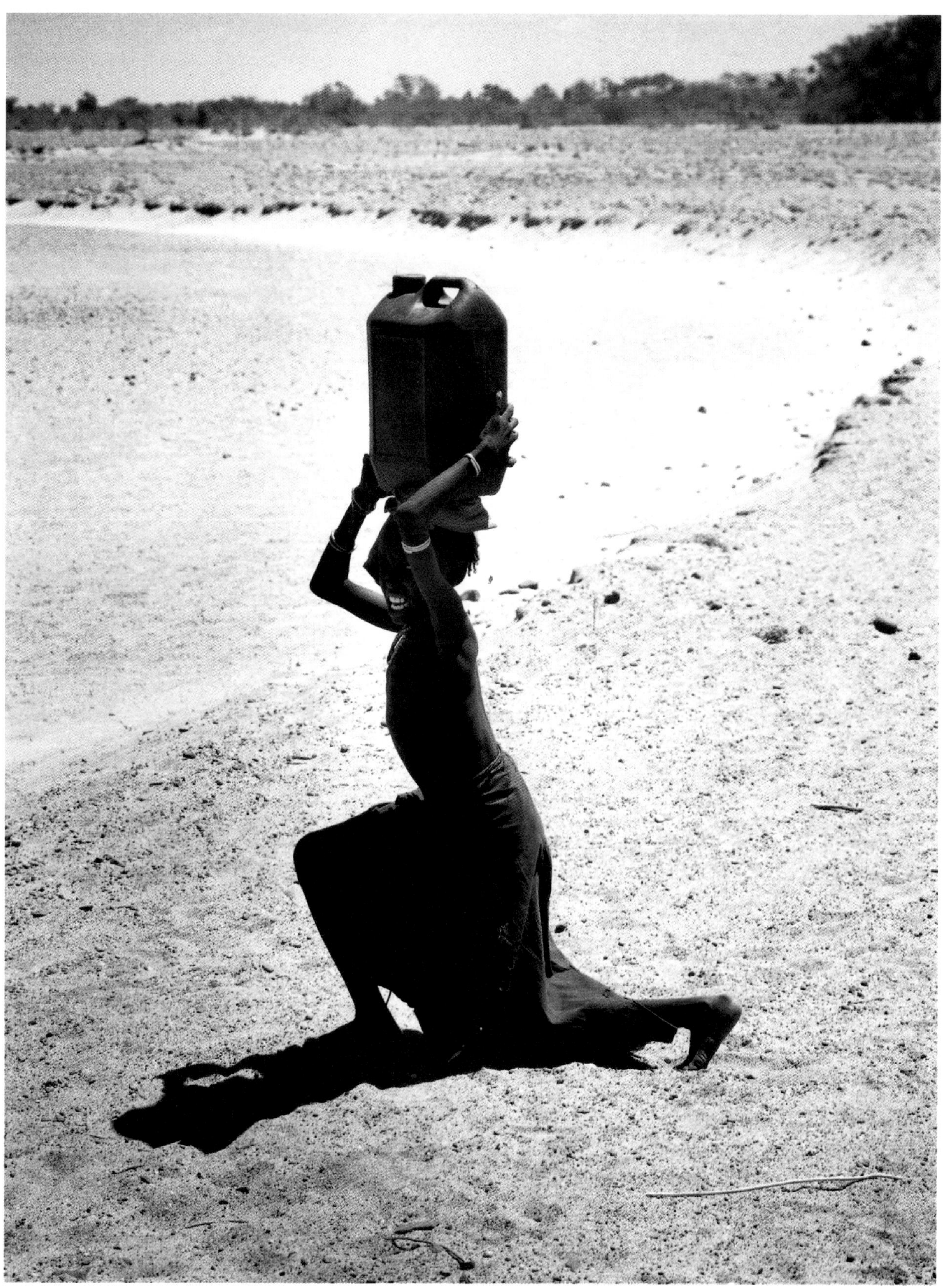

37 **NAKWAR**

DAASANACH TRIBE, GAMO – GOFA,

ETHIOPIA

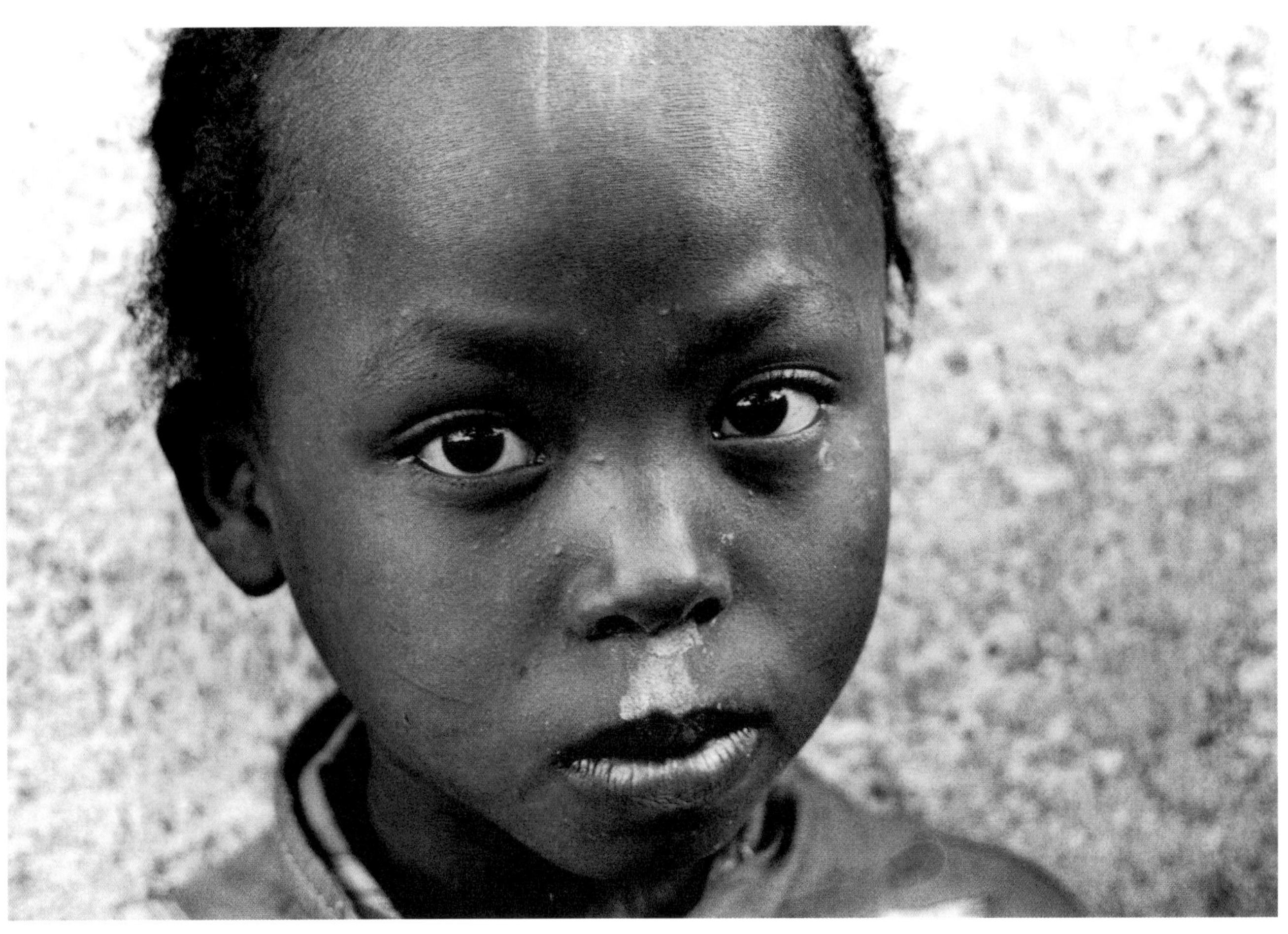

38 **AGNES NJERA**

DAGORETTI CORNER STREET CHILDRENS PROJECT, NAIROBI,

KENYA

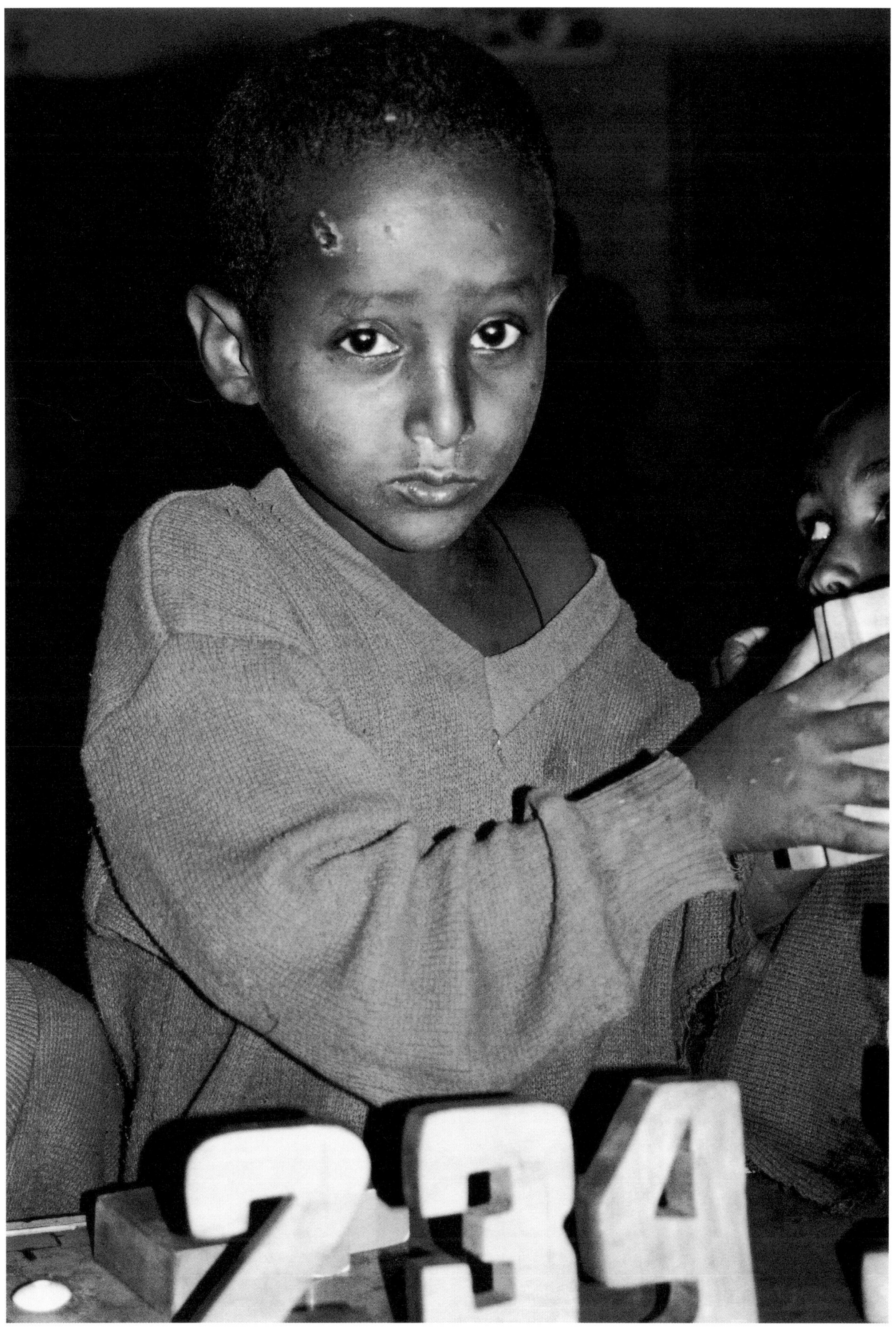

39 **YONAS GIZAW**

GOAL STREET CHILDRENS PROJECT, WOREDA 21, KEBELE 13, ADDIS ABABA, ETHIOPIA

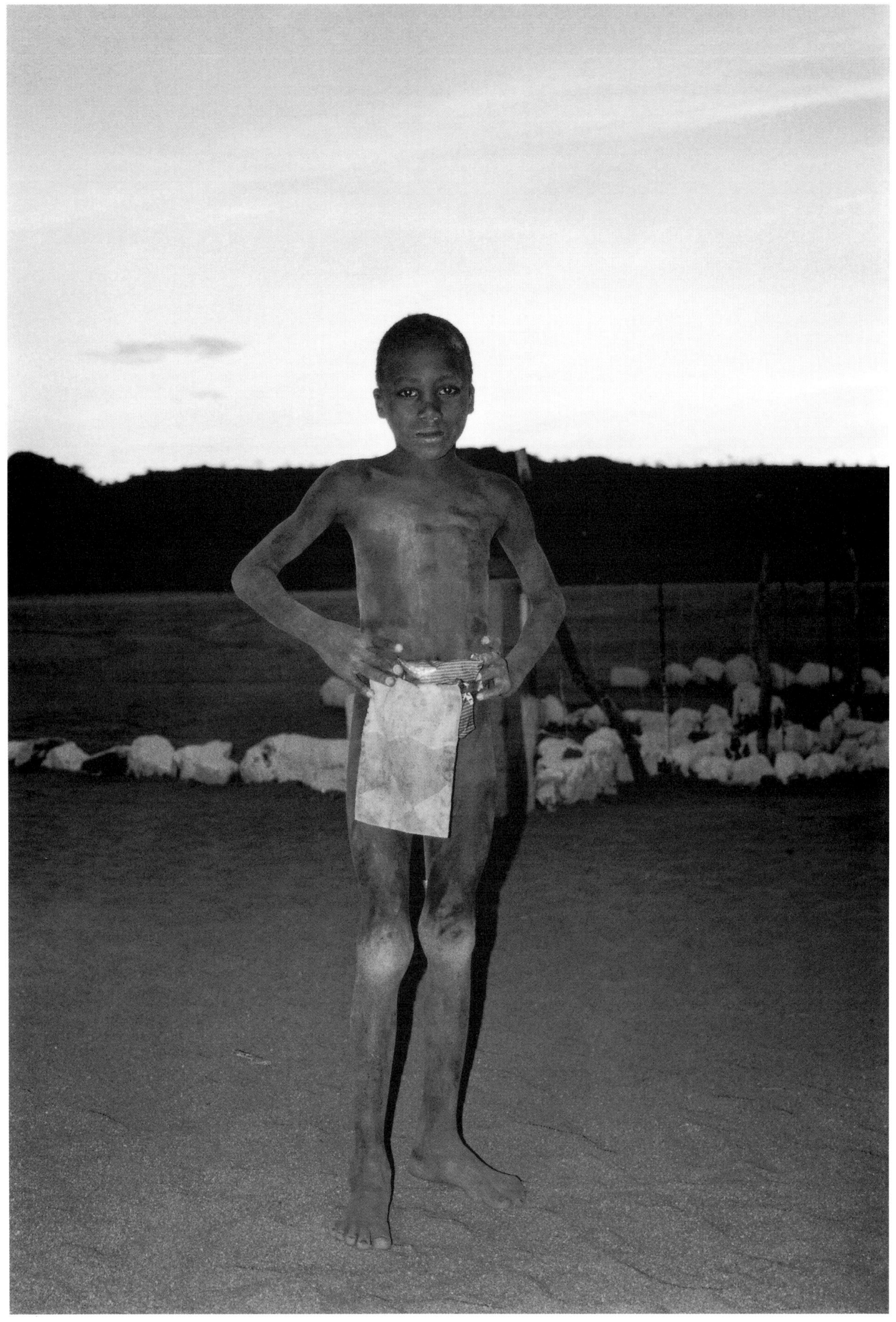

40 **MANFRED TJIHOZU**

MIDDLE OF THE DESERT, DAMARALAND,

NAMIBIA

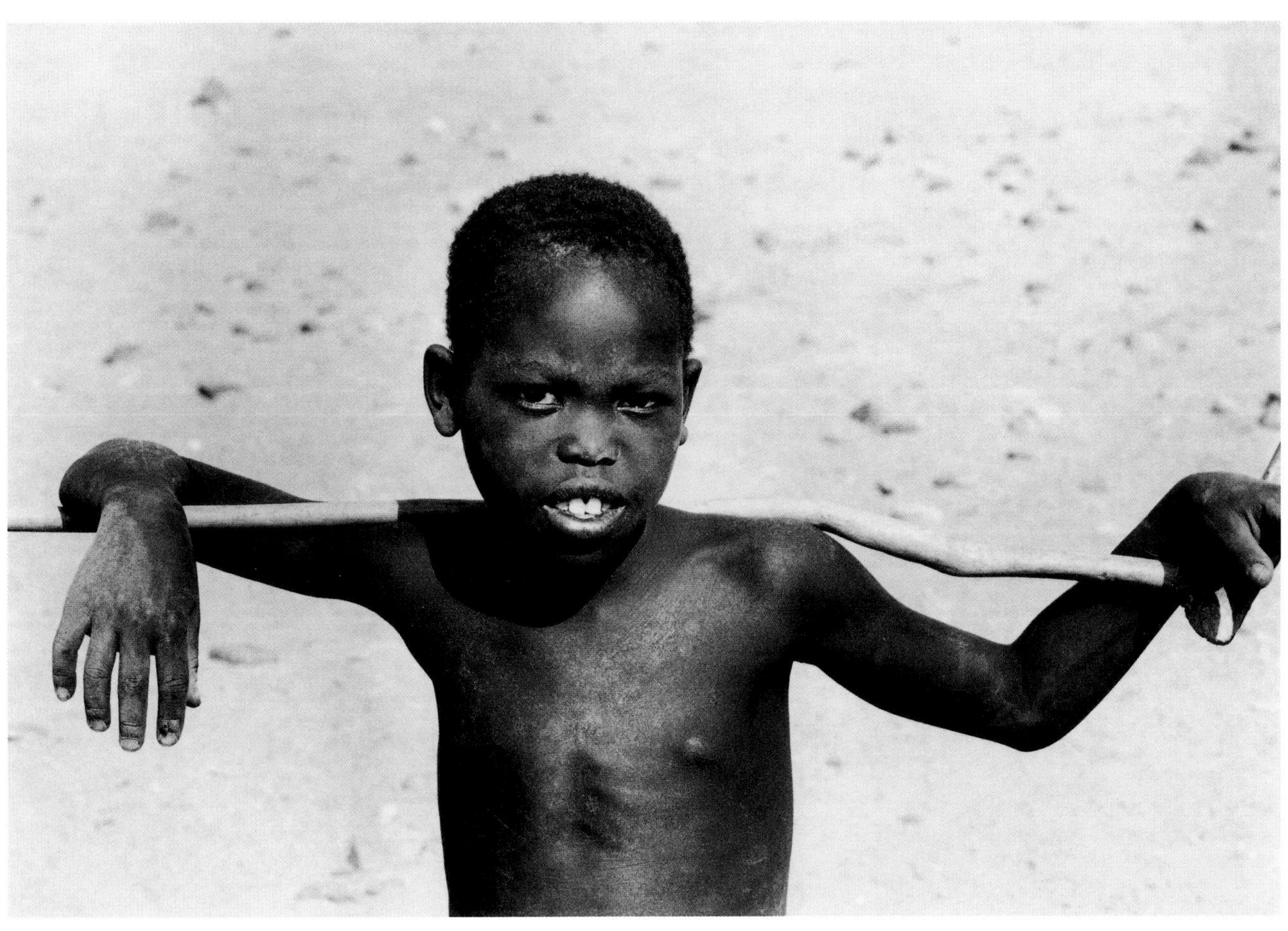

41 **JOSEPH**

TURKANA TRIBE, LOKALALEI, WEST TURKANA, RIFT VALLEY PROVINCE, KENYA

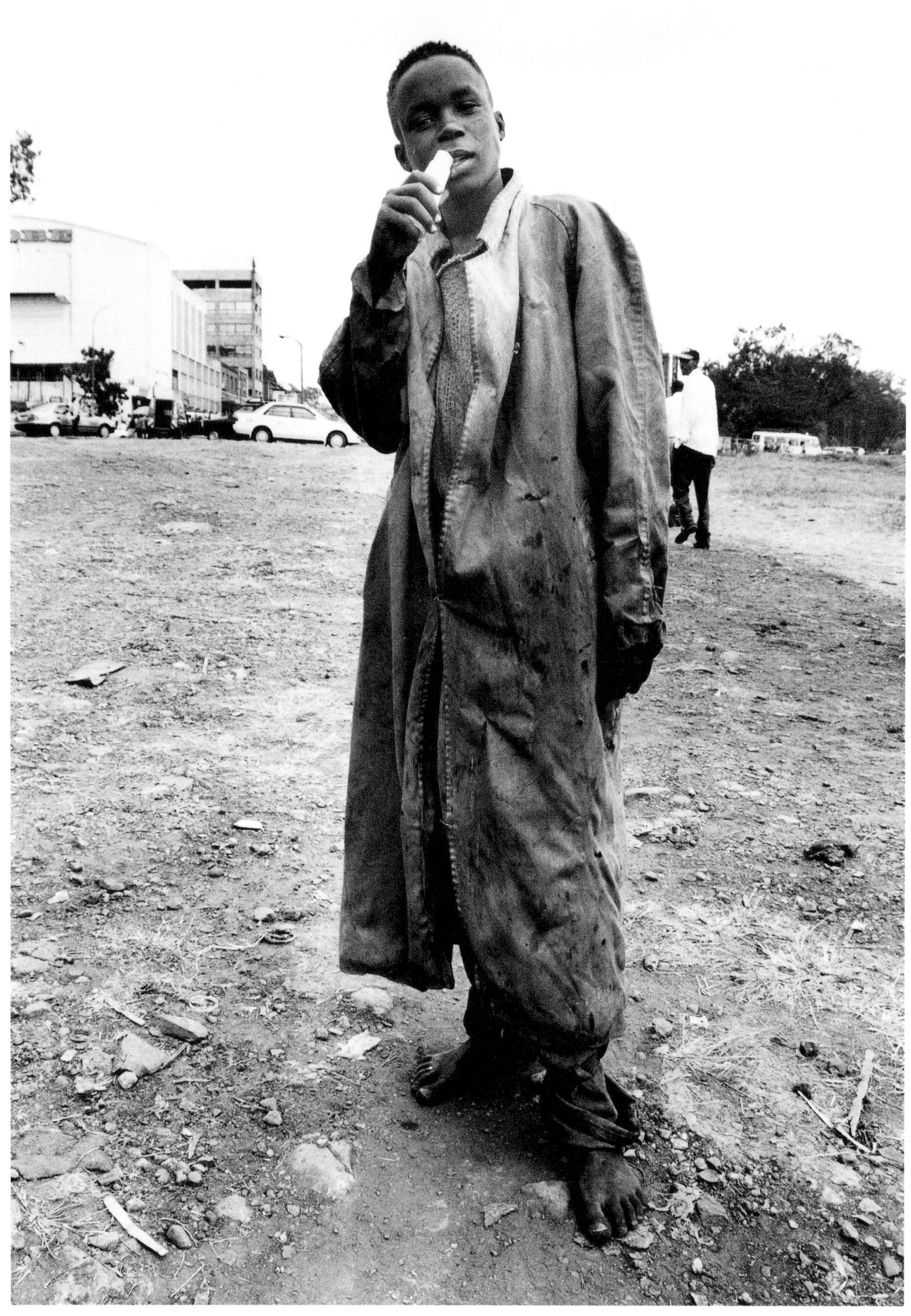

42 **SAMUEL MUSYOKA**

GLUE SNIFFING STREET KID, NAIROBI,

KENYA

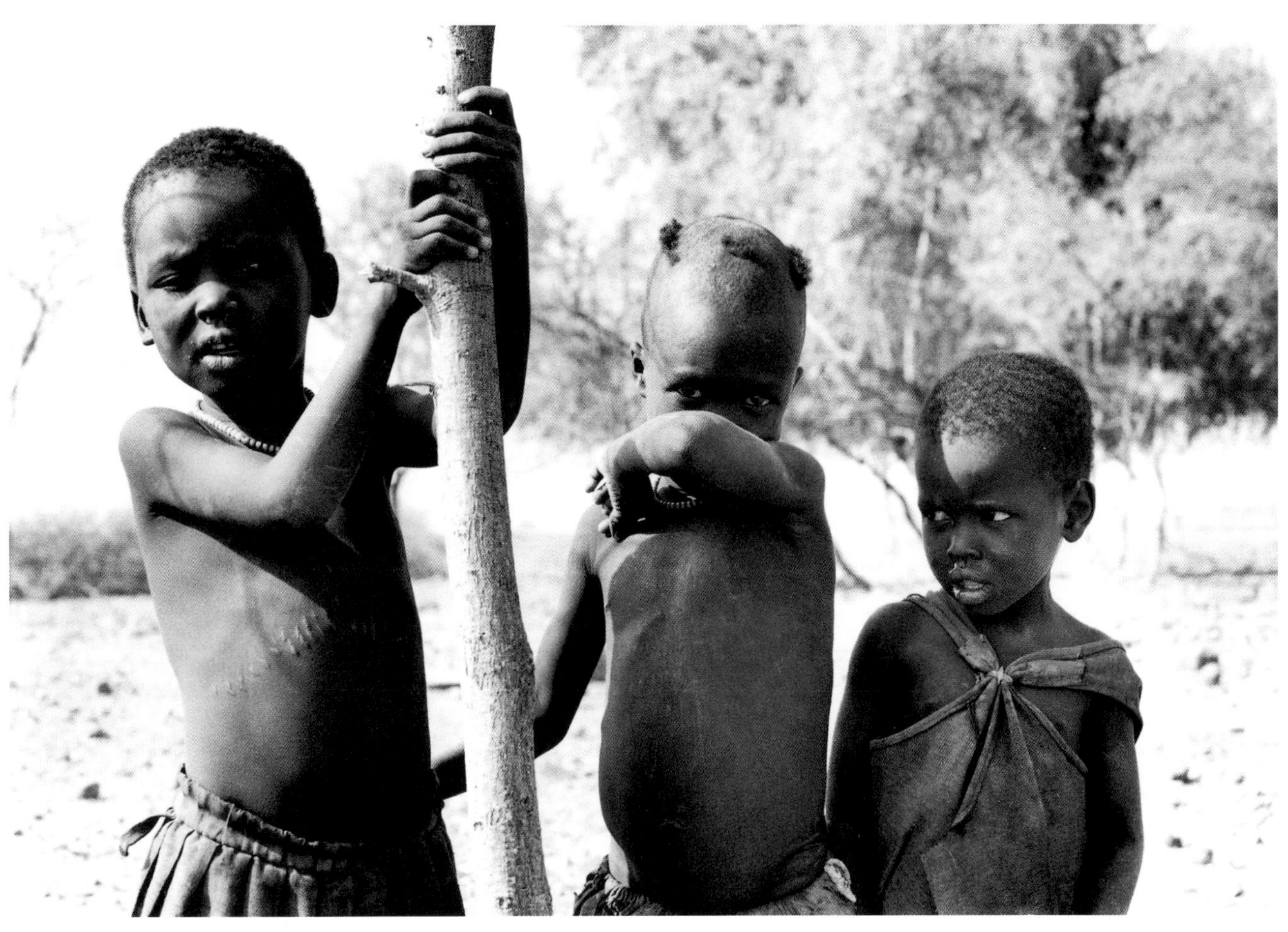

43 **TOANID ACHUKAI, EDAPAL EKWAKOL & REBECCA EKWAKOL**

TURKANA TRIBE, LOKALALEI, WEST TURKANA, RIFT VALLEY PROVINCE,

KENYA

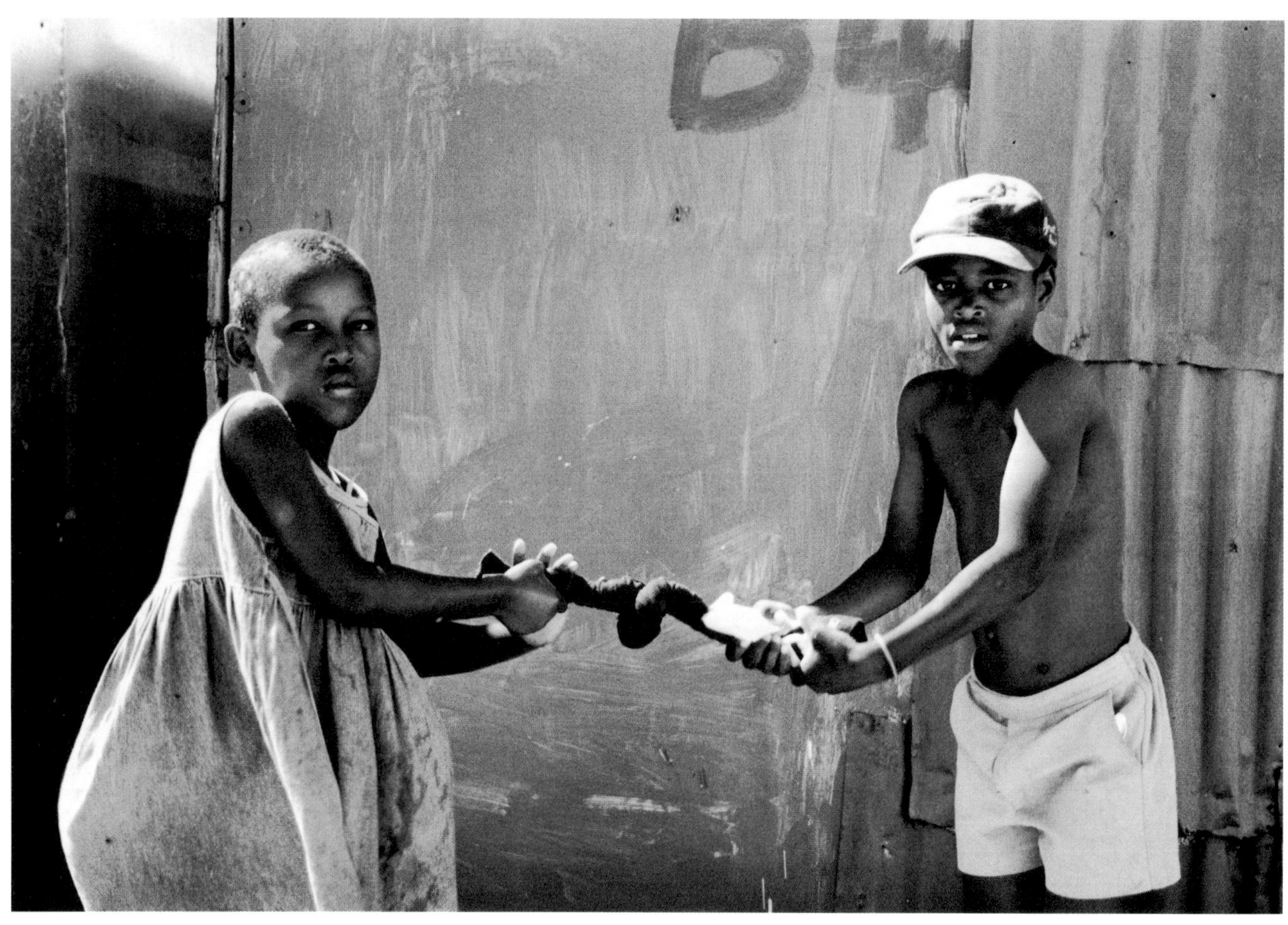

44 **ZIMKHITHA & YANGA**

LANGA TOWNSHIP, CAPE FLATS, WESTERN CAPE PROVINCE,

SOUTH AFRICA

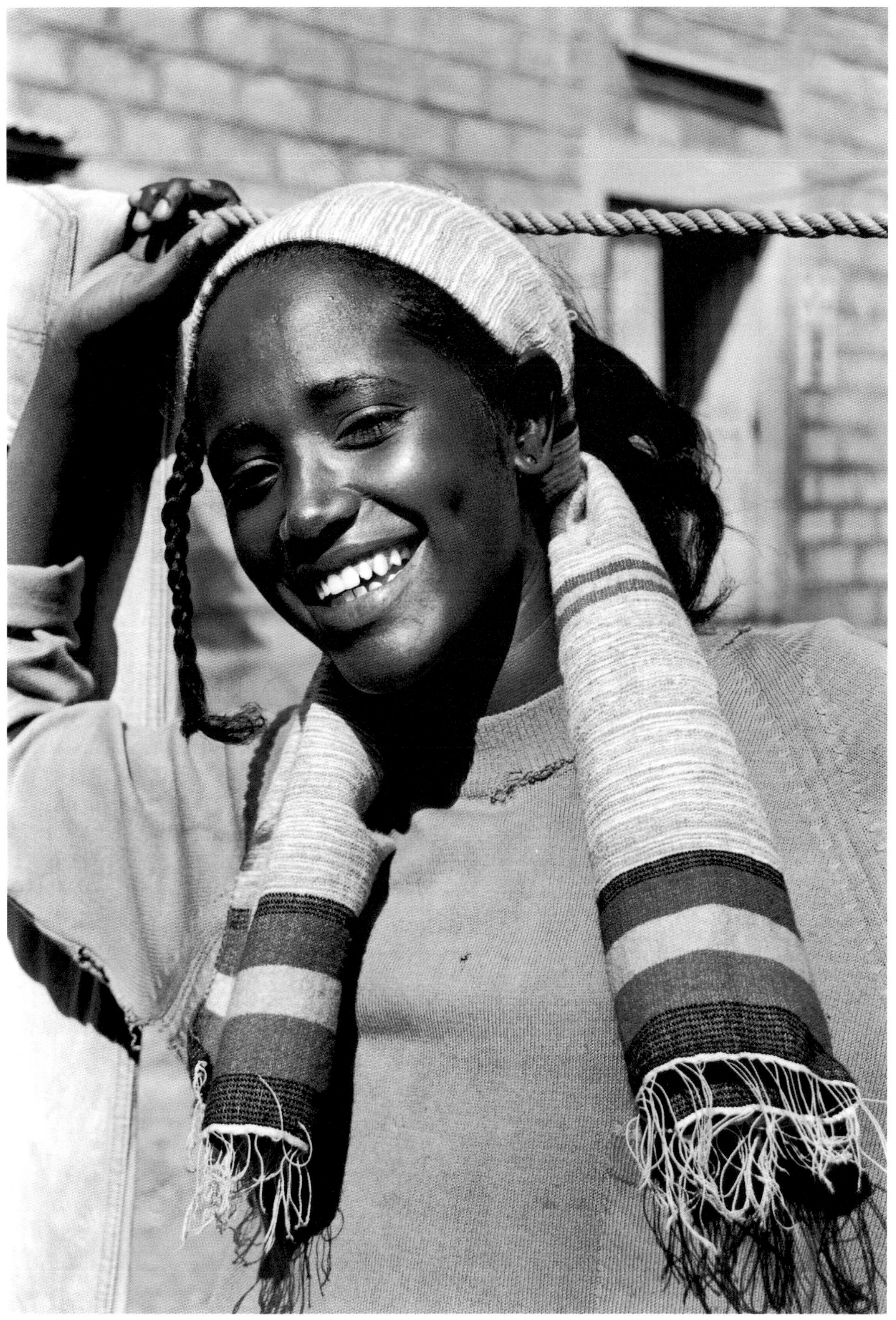

45 **ABERASH LEGESSE**

GOAL STREET CHILDRENS PROJECT, WOREDA 21, KEBELE 13, ADDIS ABABA, ETHIOPIA

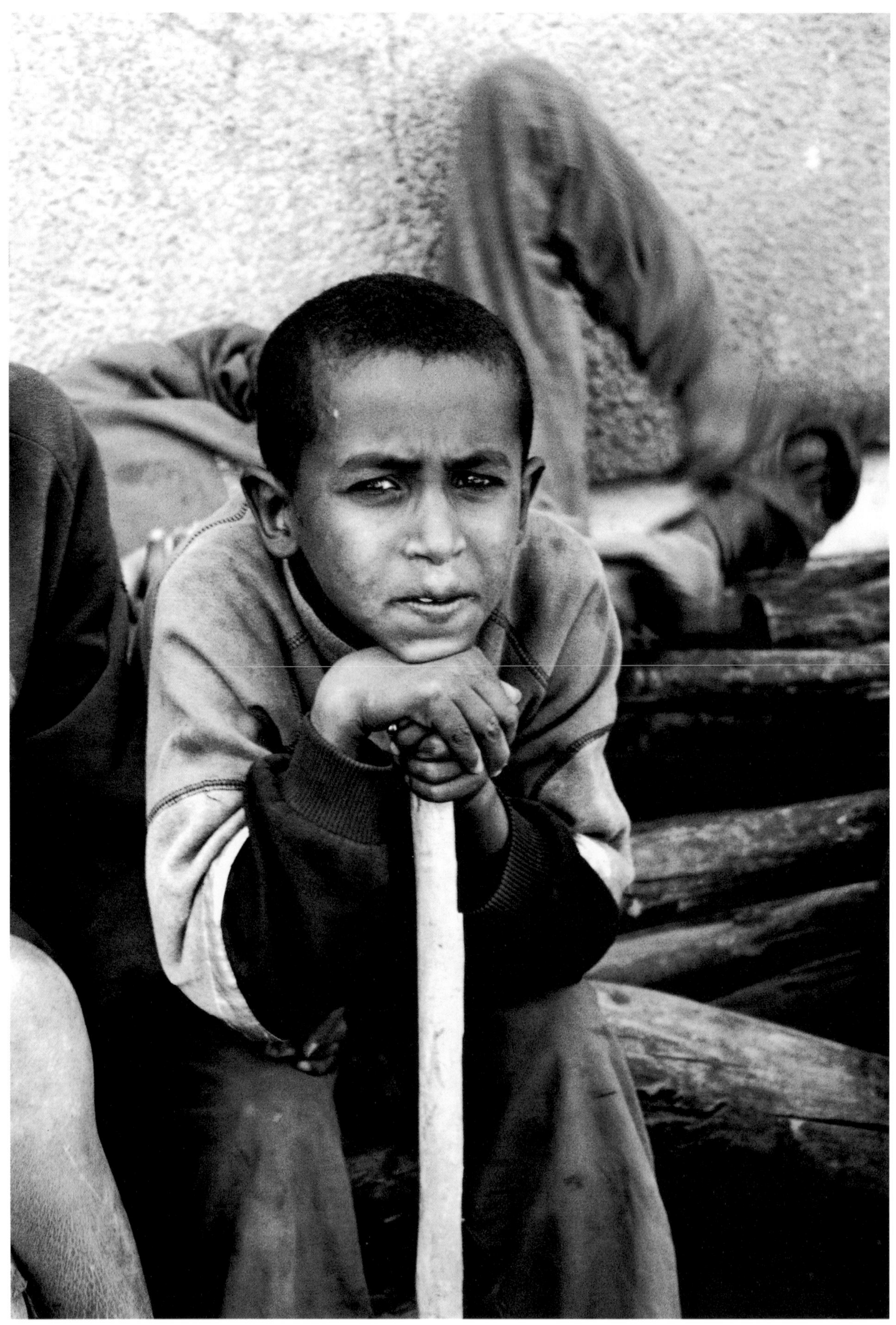

46 **MITIKU MEHERETE**

GOAL STREET CHILDRENS PROJECT, WOREDA 21, KEBELE 13, ADDIS ABABA, ETHIOPIA

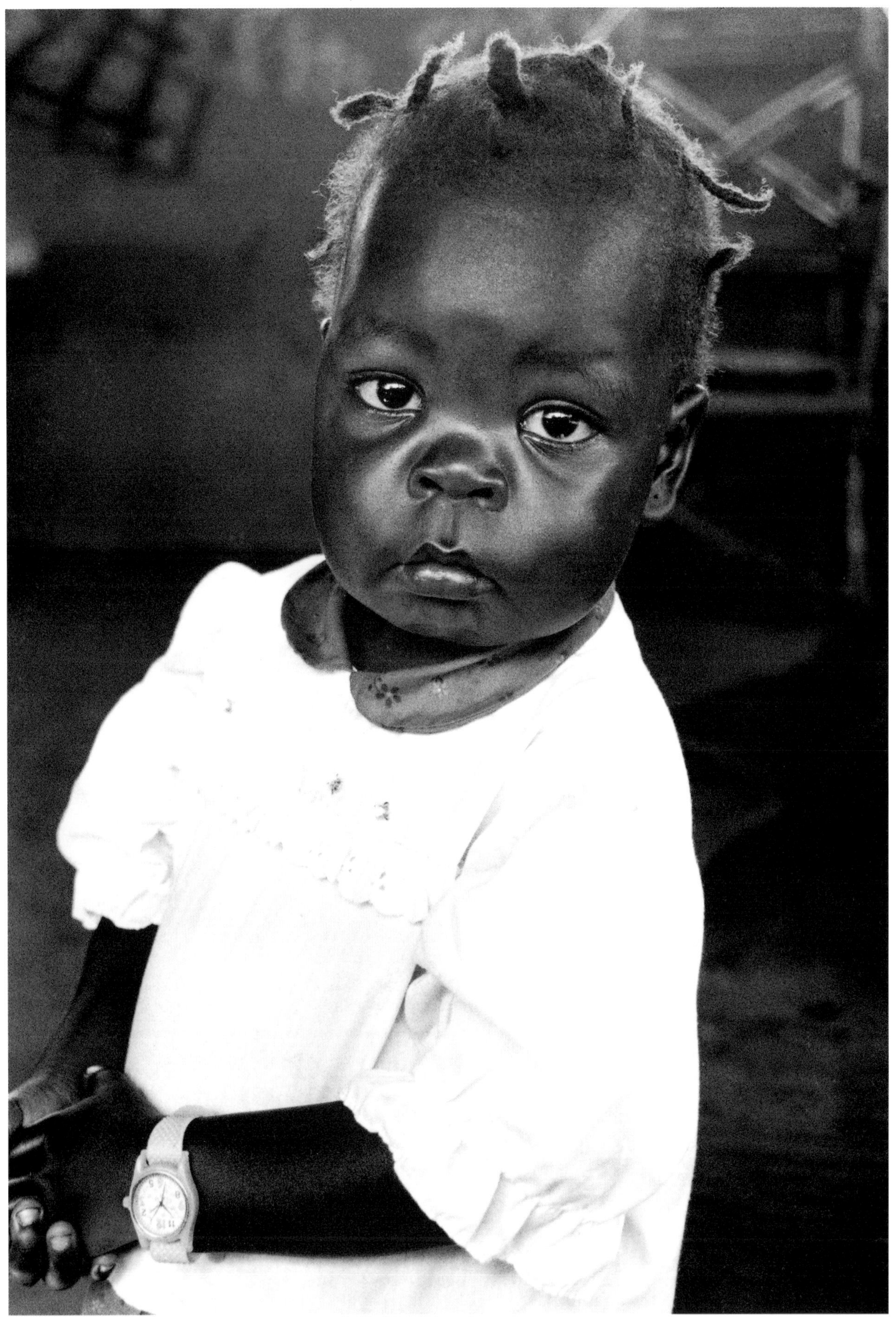

47 **SHARIYA BISO**

BUJUGALI FALLS, NILE RIVER, JINJA,

UGANDA

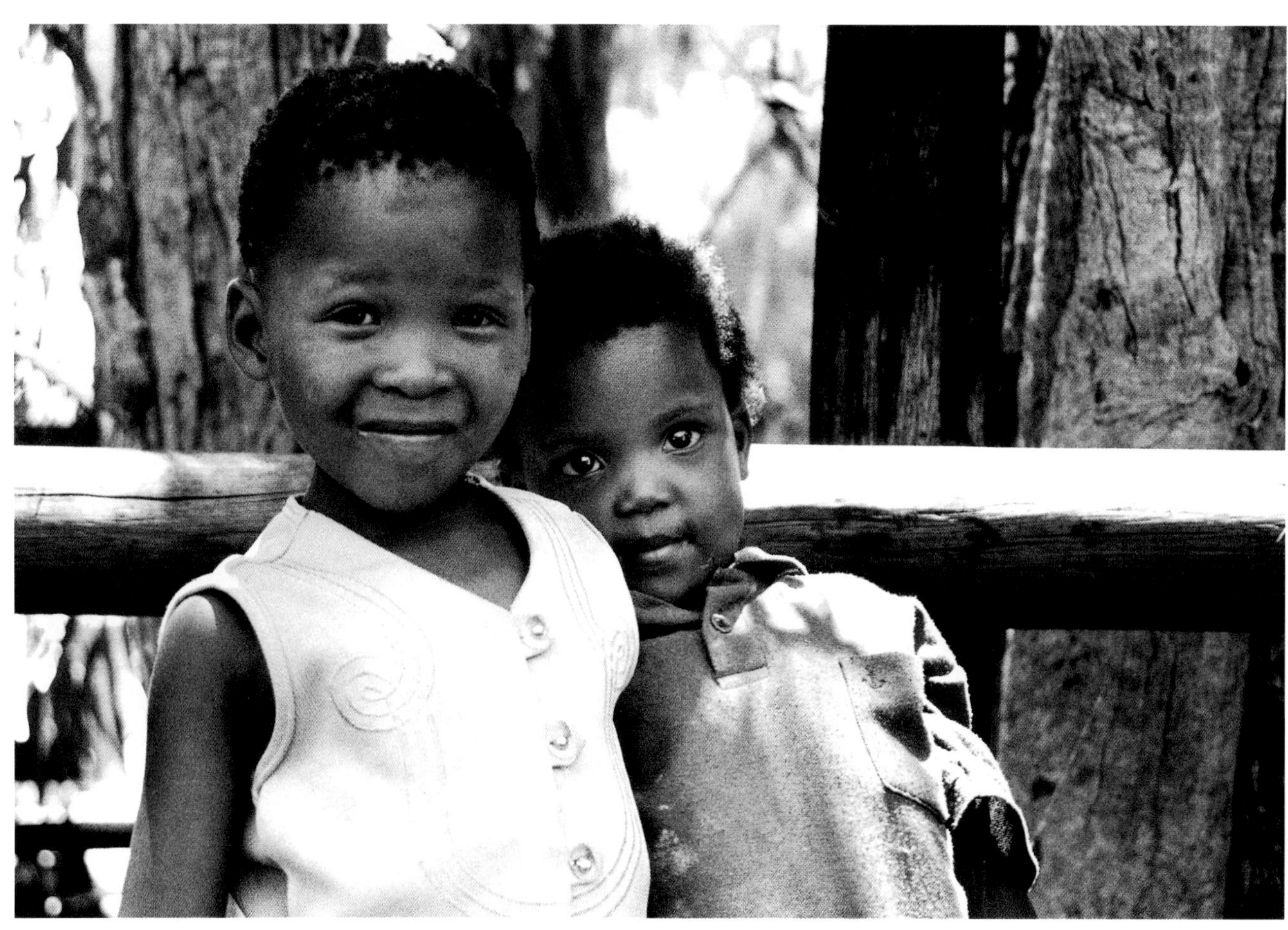

48 **JESSICA & LUCINDA VAN SCHALKWYK**

KIMBERLEY, NORTHERN CAPE PROVINCE,

SOUTH AFRICA

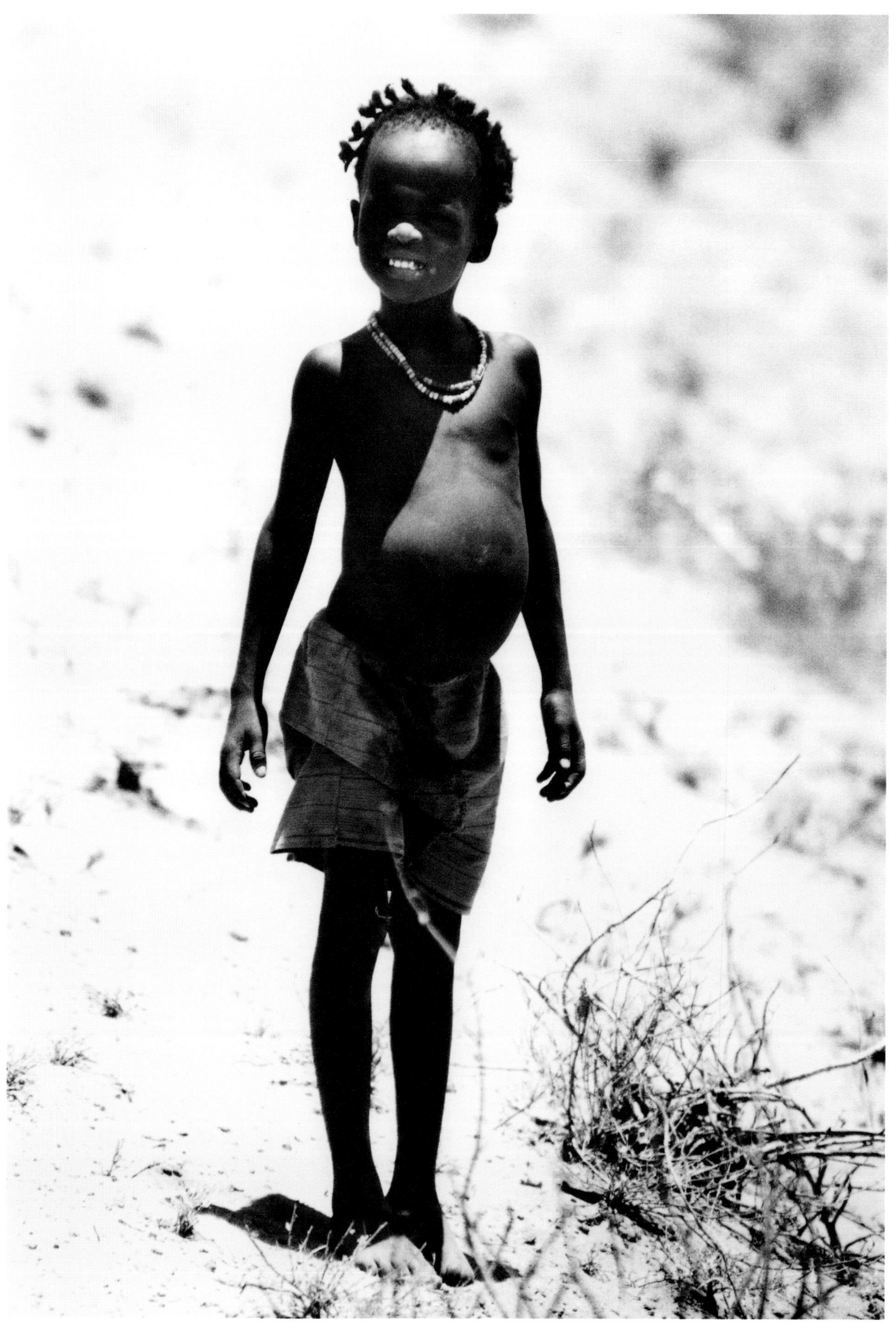

49 **KORINYANG**

DAASANACH TRIBE, GAMO – GOFA,

ETHIOPIA

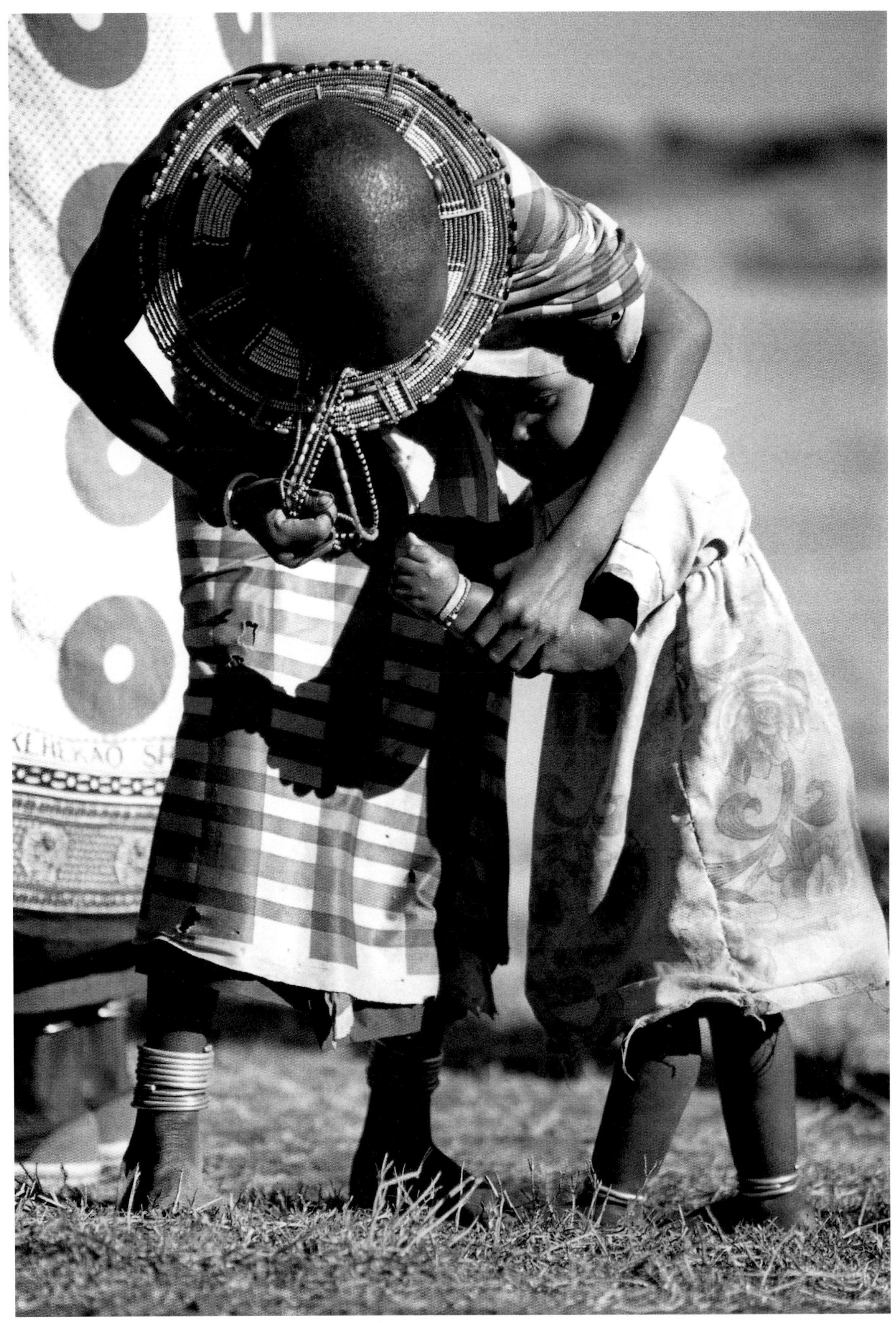

50 **ESIANKIKI O ENKERAI**

MAASAI WEDDING, LOITA HILLS, MORIJO,

KENYA

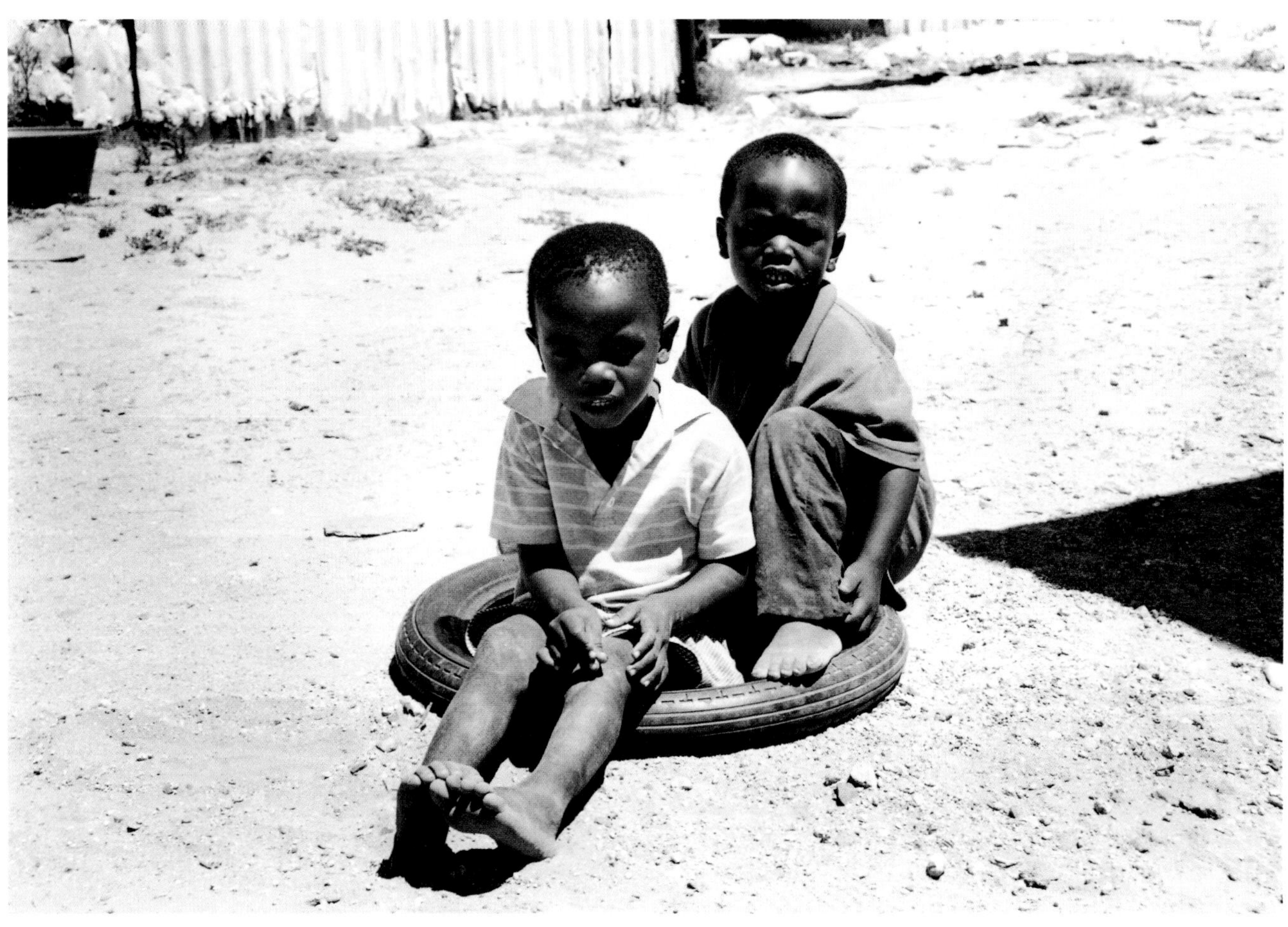

51 **AMAKHWENKWE**

KHAYELITSHA TOWNSHIP, CAPE FLATS, WESTERN CAPE PROVINCE,

SOUTH AFRICA

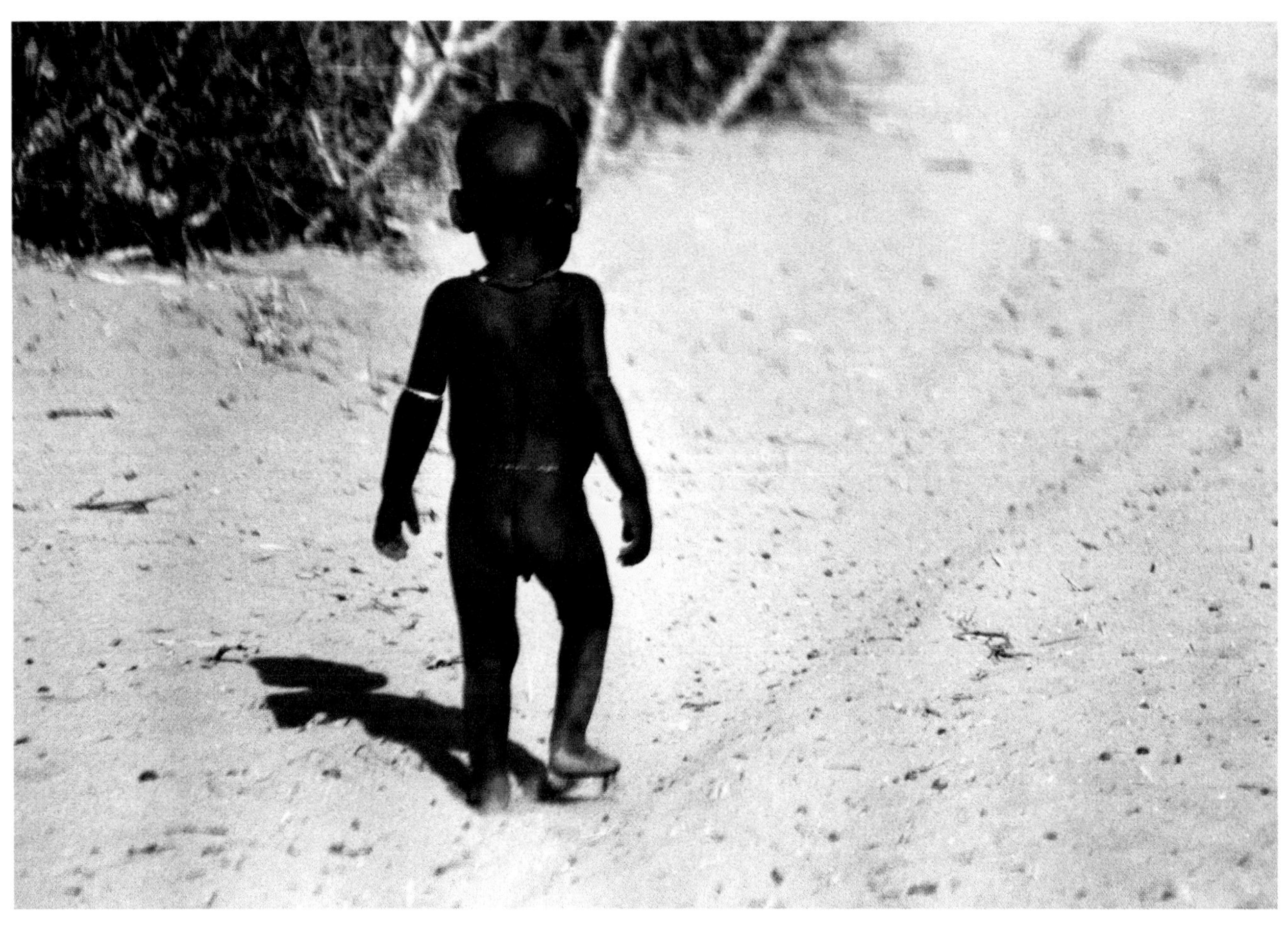

52 **NAKWAN**

TURKANA TRIBE, ILERET, MARSABIT DISTRICT, EASTERN PROVINCE,

KENYA

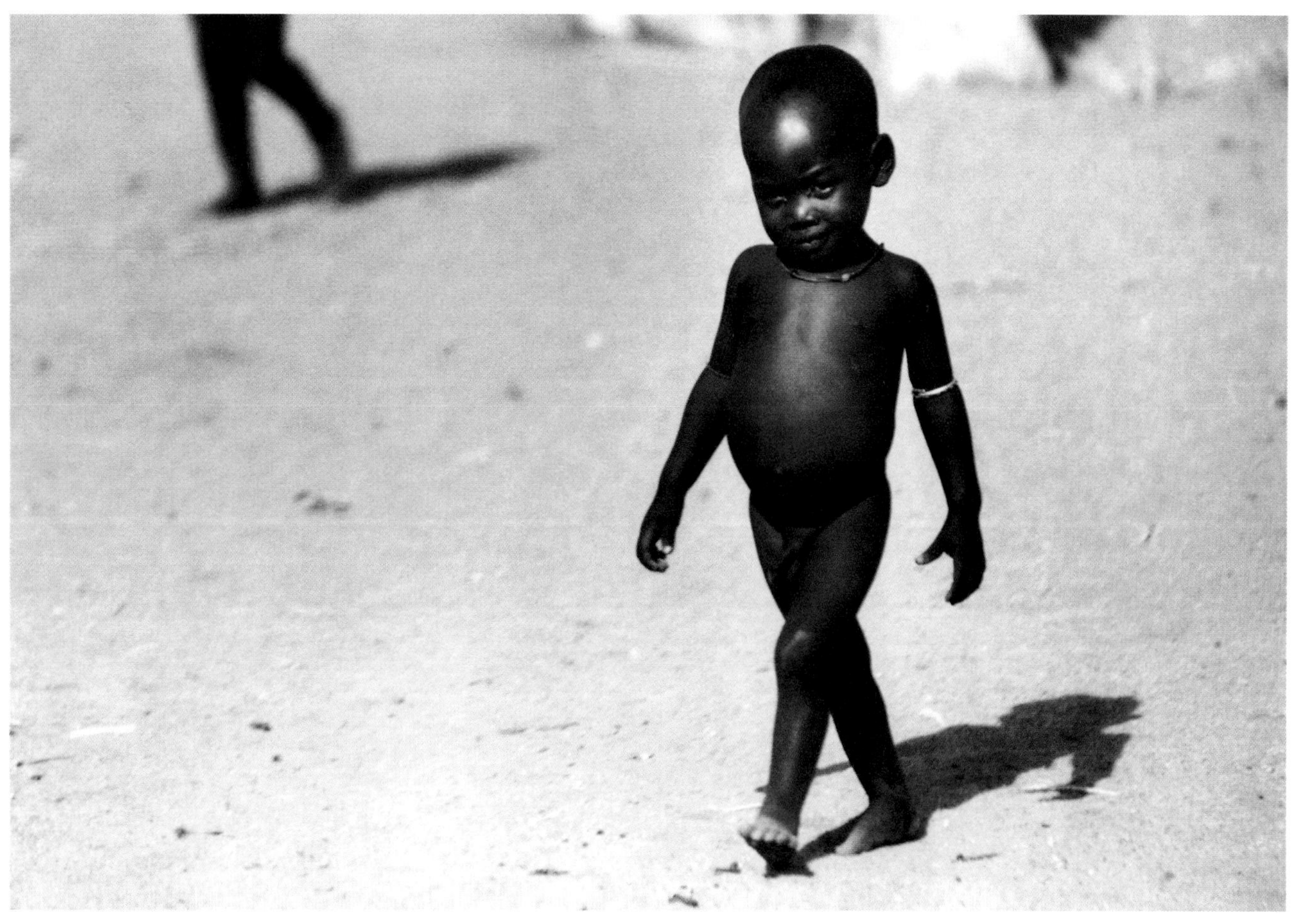

53 **NAKWAN**

TURKANA TRIBE, ILERET, MARSABIT DISTRICT, EASTERN PROVINCE, KENYA

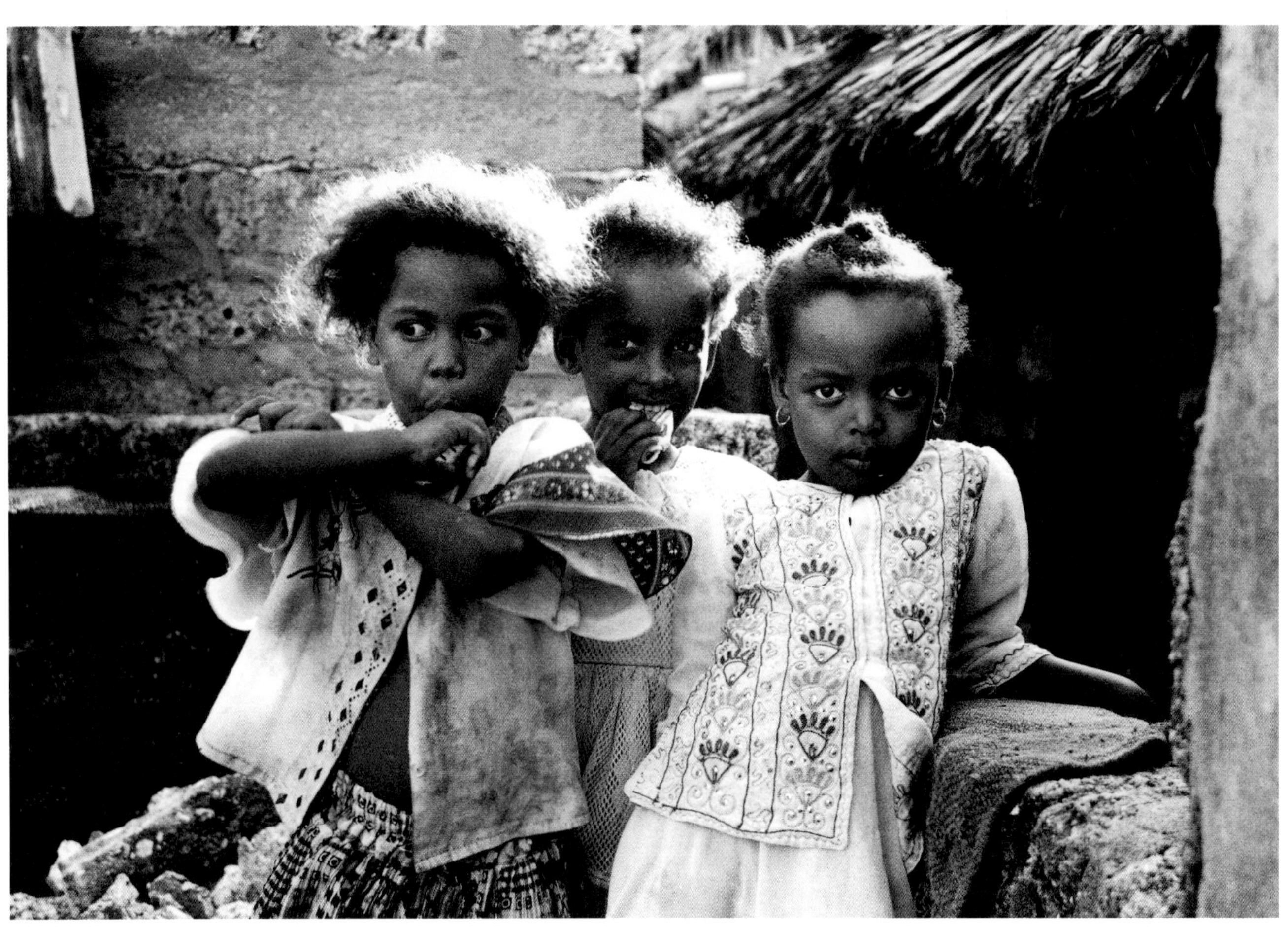

54 **NAHIDA, ALYA & SADIA**

LAMU TOWN, LAMU ISLAND,

KENYA

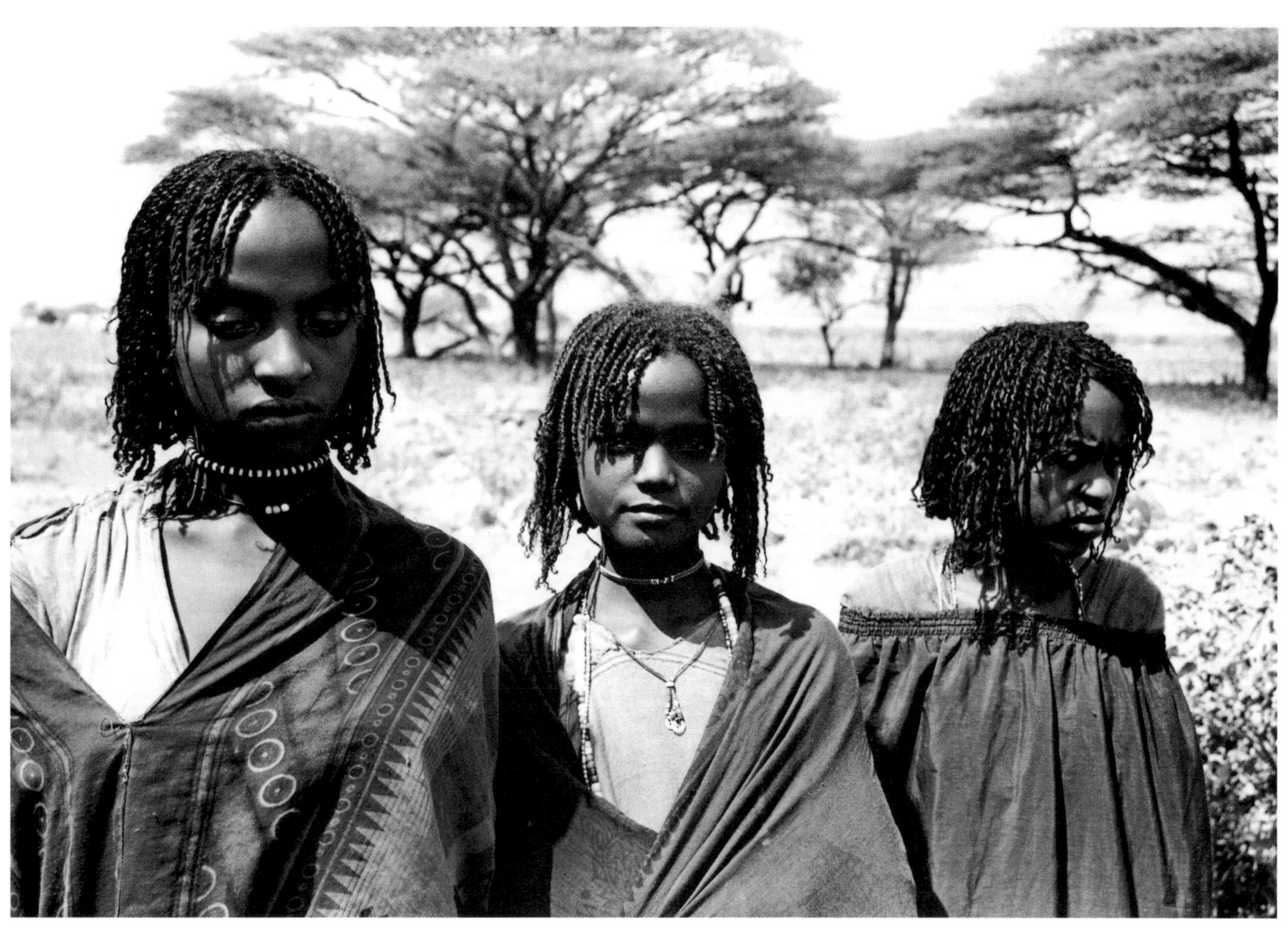

55 **HACKO ROBA, GELE JICCO & GUYE ROBA**

KEREYOU TRIBE, DHEBITY, METAHARA, EAST-SHOWA,

ETHIOPIA

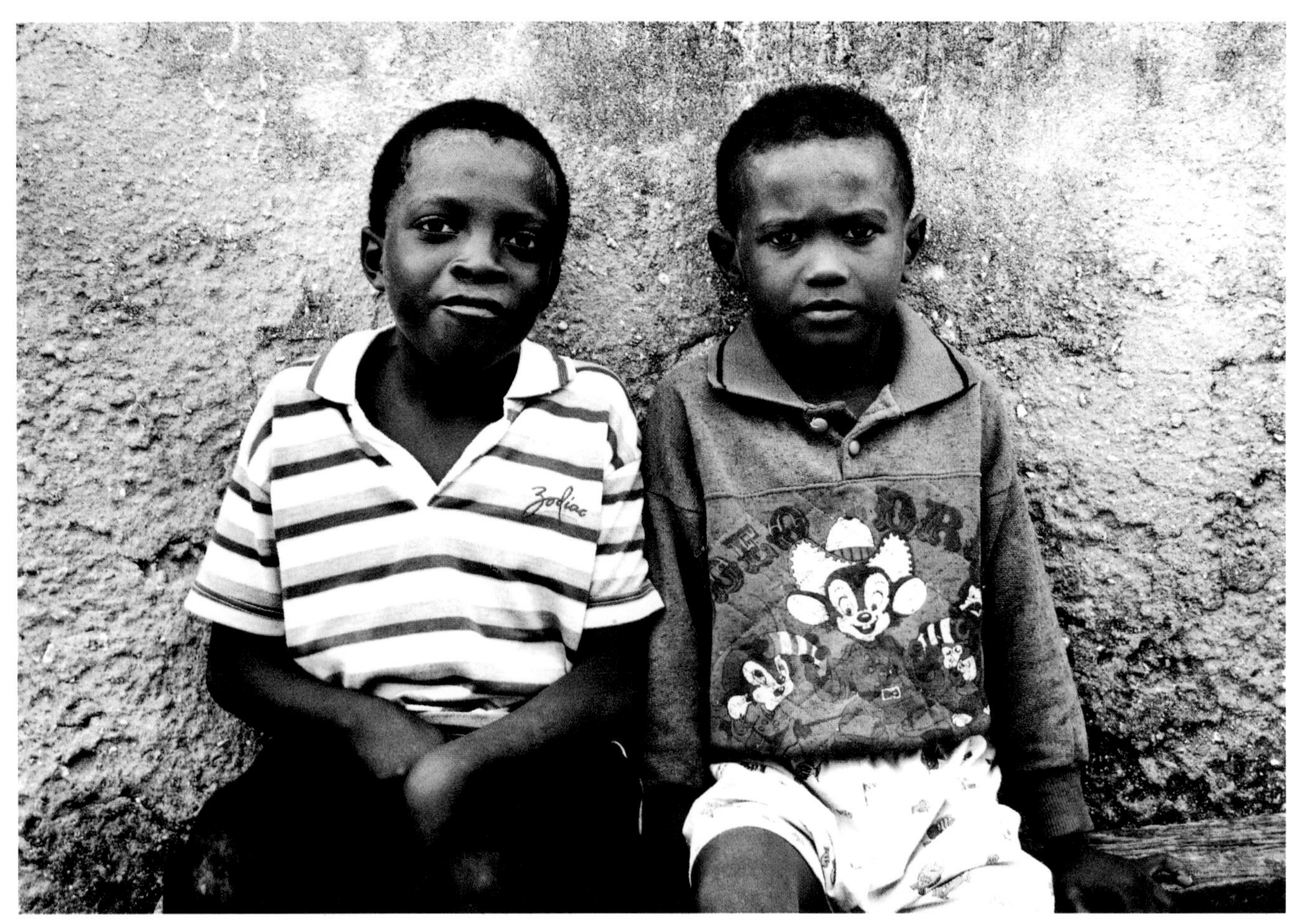

56 **KADARI & MOHAMMED**

LAMU TOWN, LAMU ISLAND,

KENYA

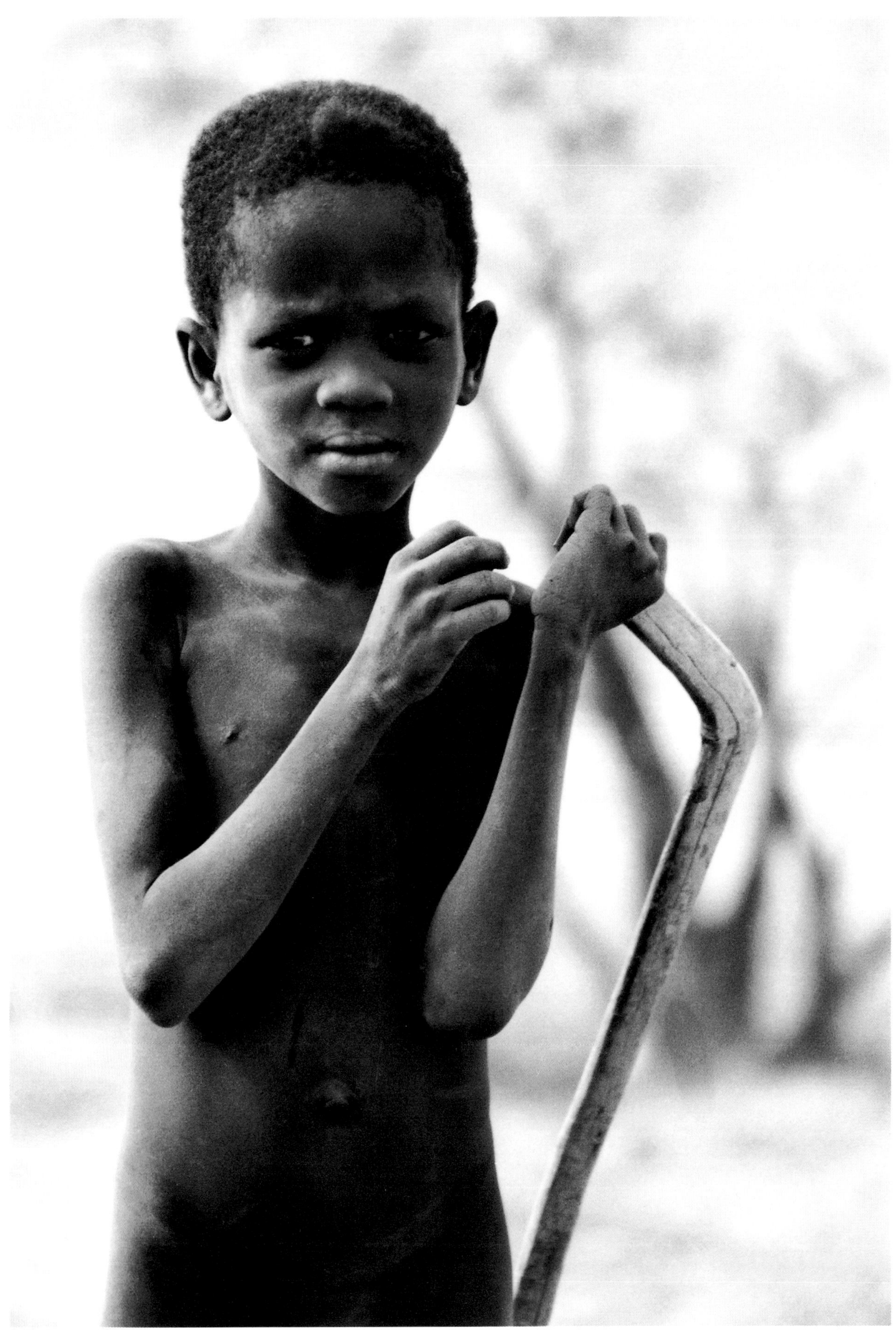

57 **ASHI**

TURKANA TRIBE, ILERET, MARSABIT DISTRICT, EASTERN PROVINCE,

KENYA

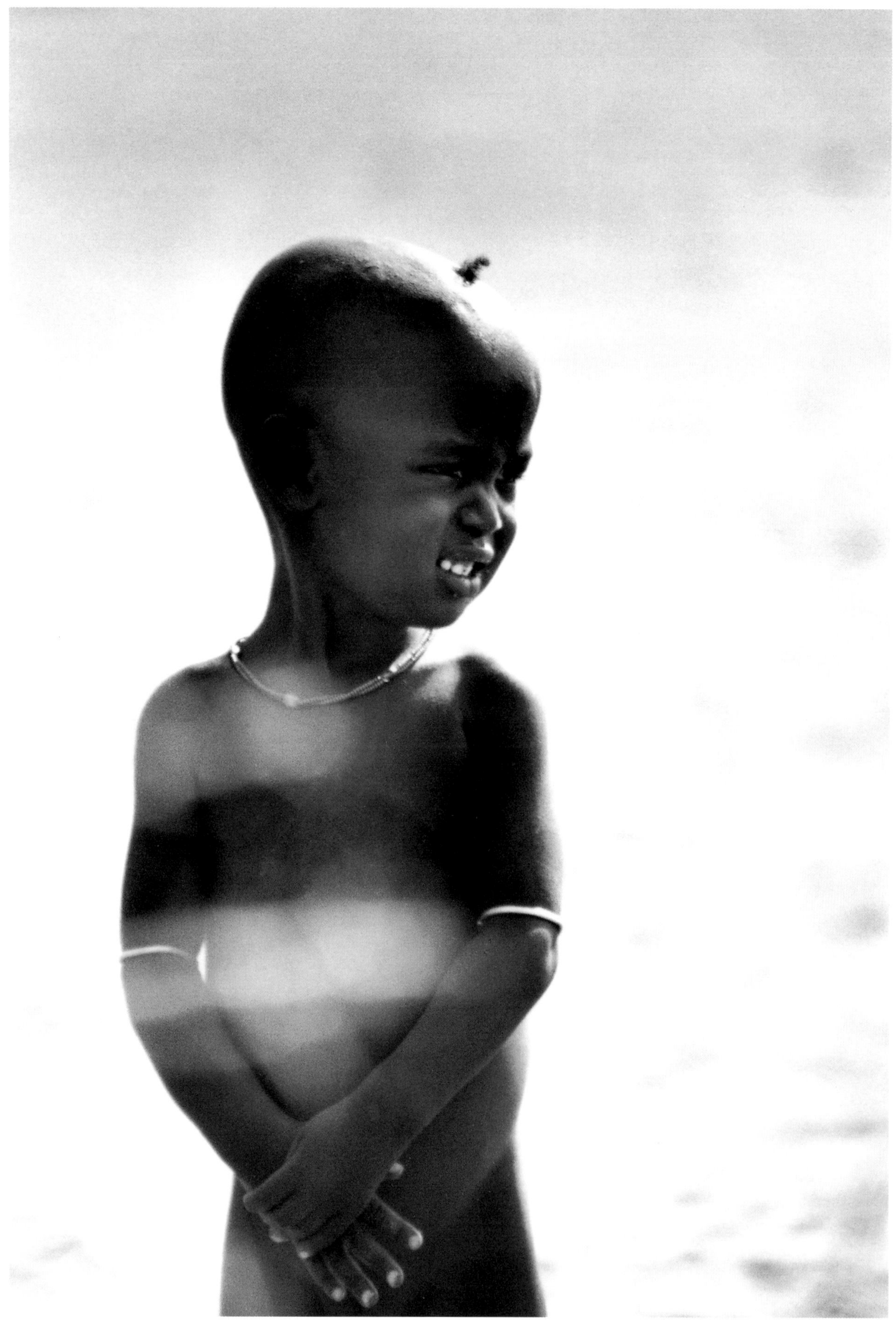

58 **IDEA NIICI**

TURKANA TRIBE, ILERET, MARSABIT DISTRICT, EASTERN PROVINCE,

KENYA

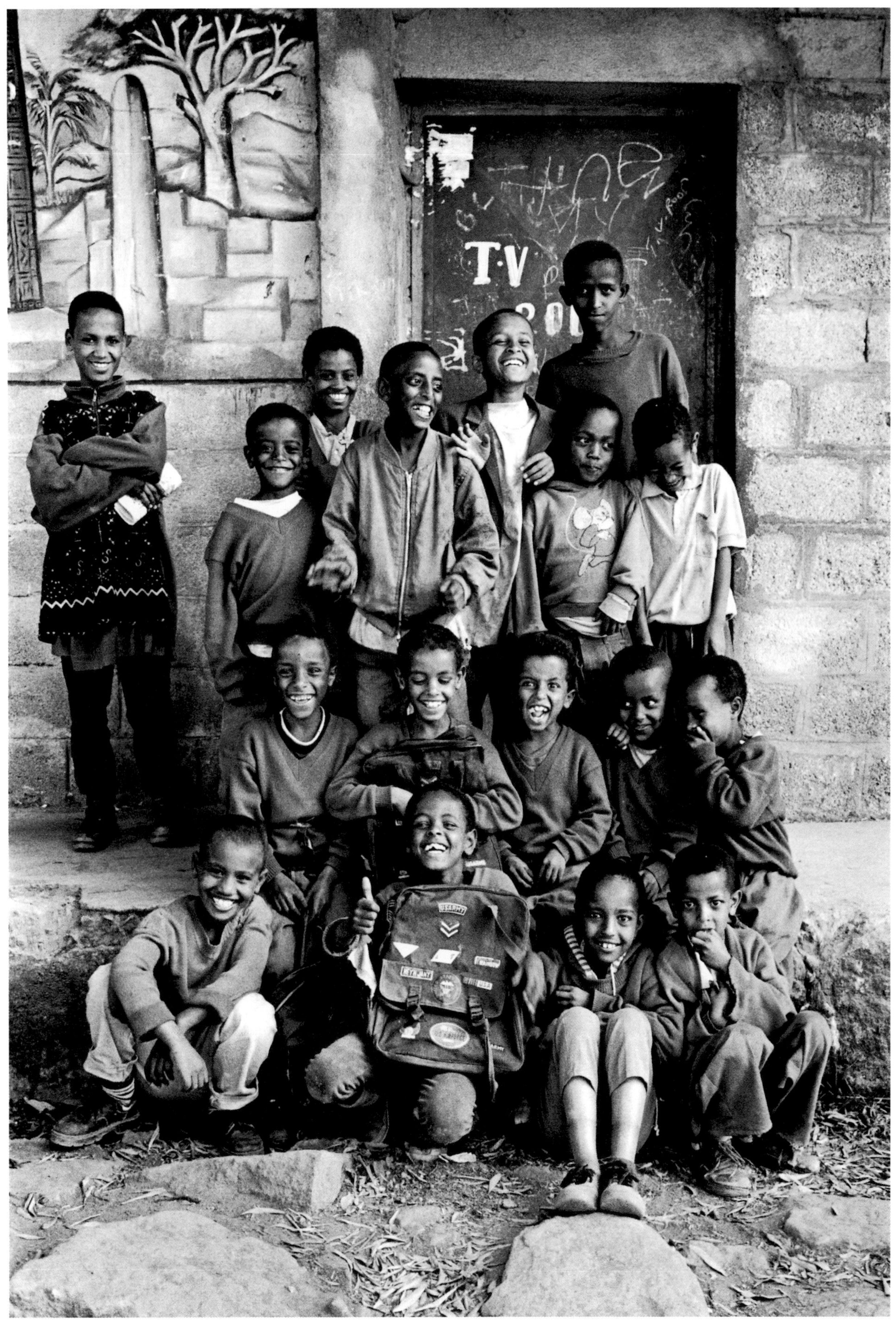

59 **SCHOOL CHILDREN**

SALAM BIRR ELEMENTARY SCHOOL, WOREDA 24, KEBELE 9, ADDIS ABABA, ETHIOPIA

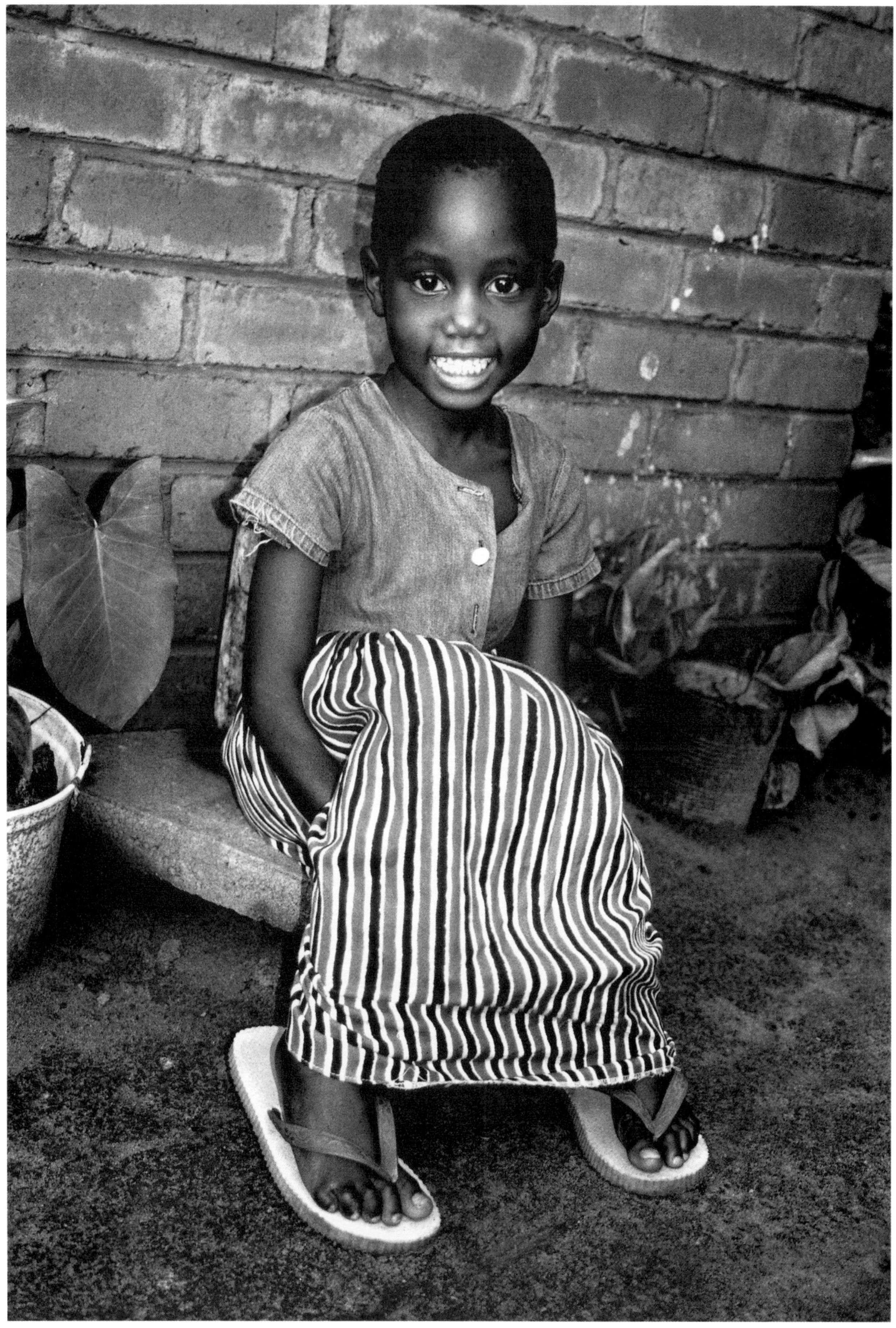

60 **LAURA MABHENA**

CHINOTIMBA TOWNSHIP, MATABELELAND NORTH,

ZIMBABWE

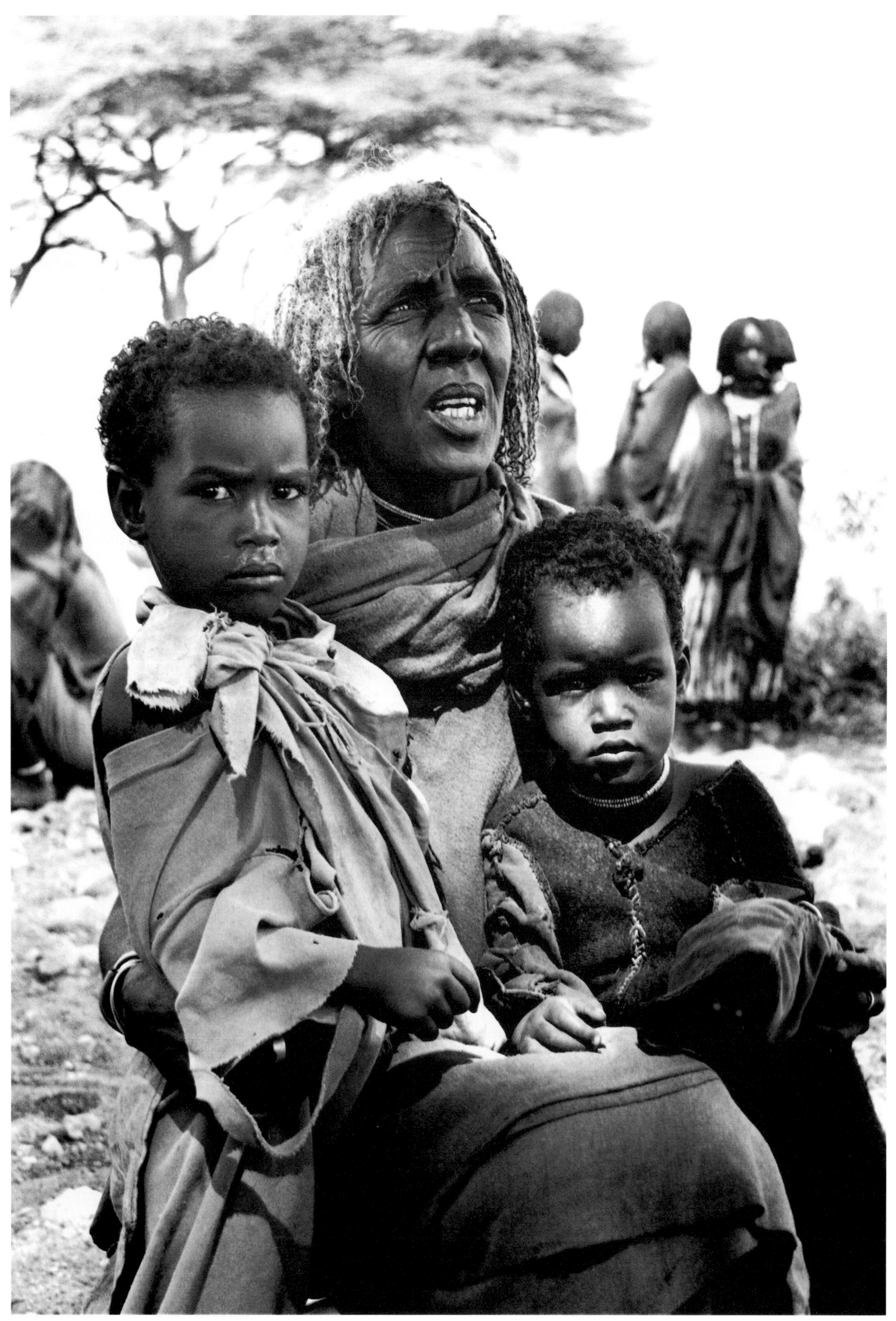

61 **AYANTU JICCO, BEUITE TEDECHO & BERITE KUBI**

KEREYOU TRIBE, DHEBITY, METAHARA, EAST-SHOWA,

ETHIOPIA

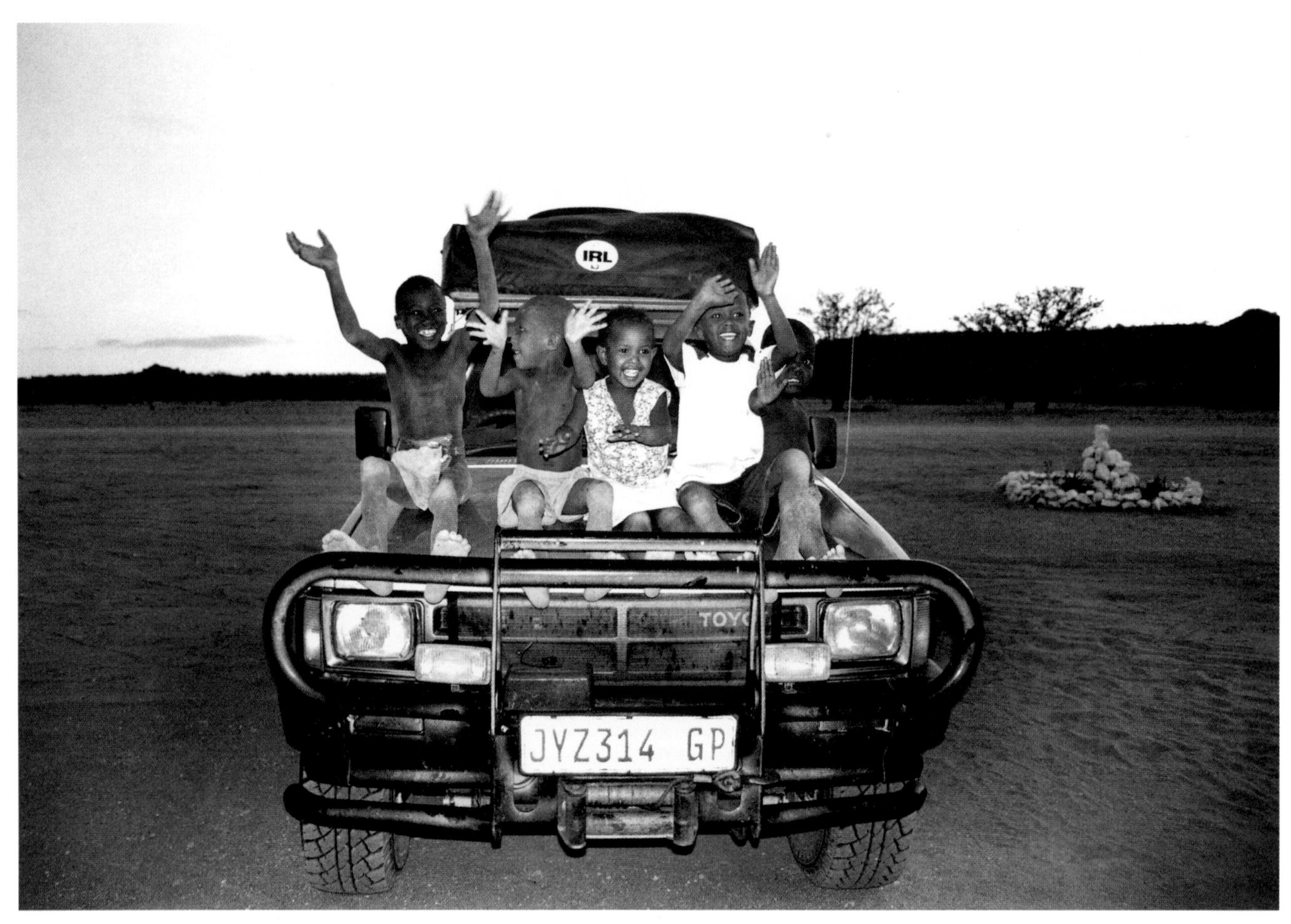

62 MANFRED, STEVEN, CHINESTONE, IVEN & BENET

MIDDLE OF THE DESERT, DAMARALAND,

NAMIBIA

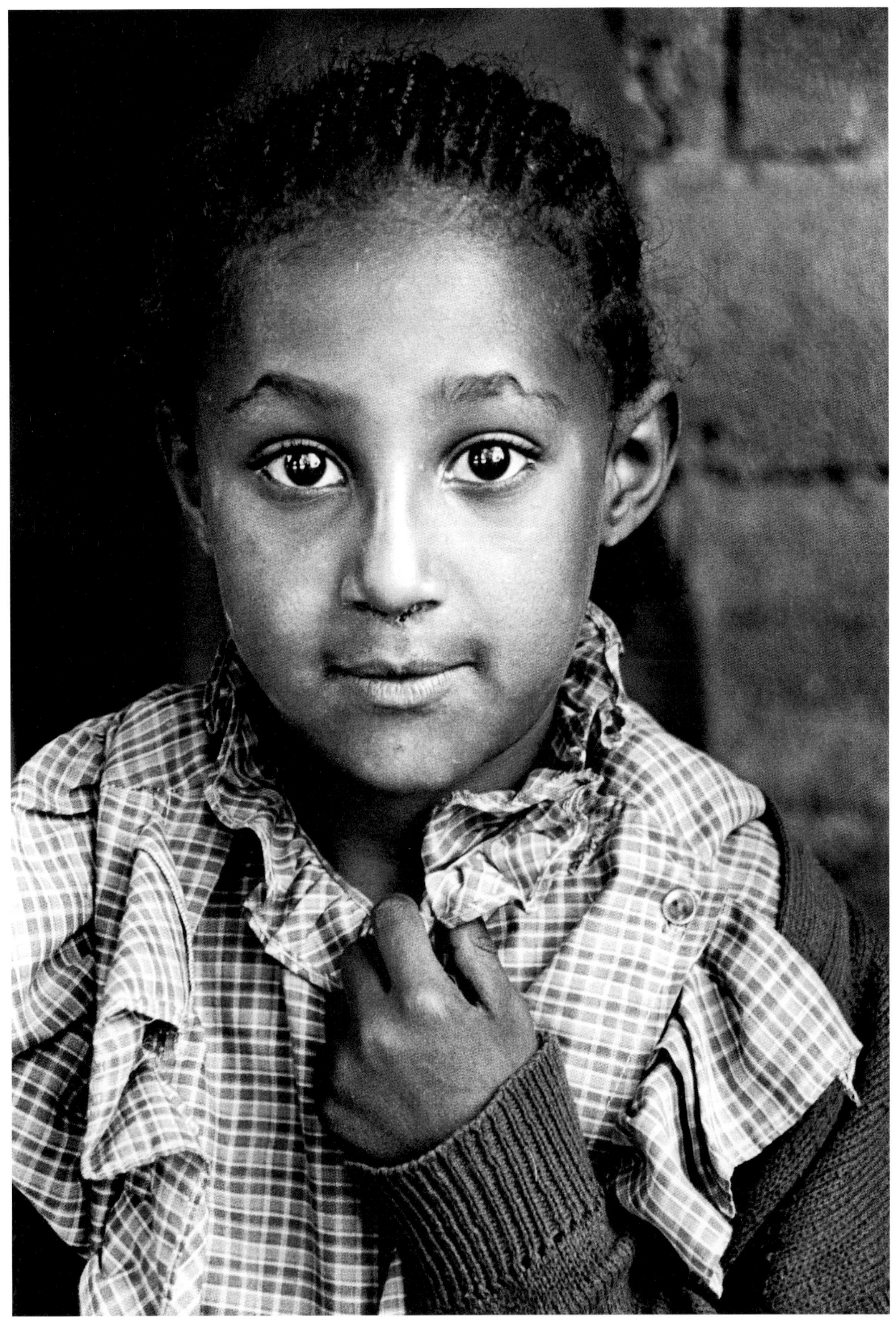

63 **ELSABET AMARA**

SALAM BIRR ELEMENTARY SCHOOL, WOREDA 24, KEBELE 9, ADDIS ABABA, ETHIOPIA

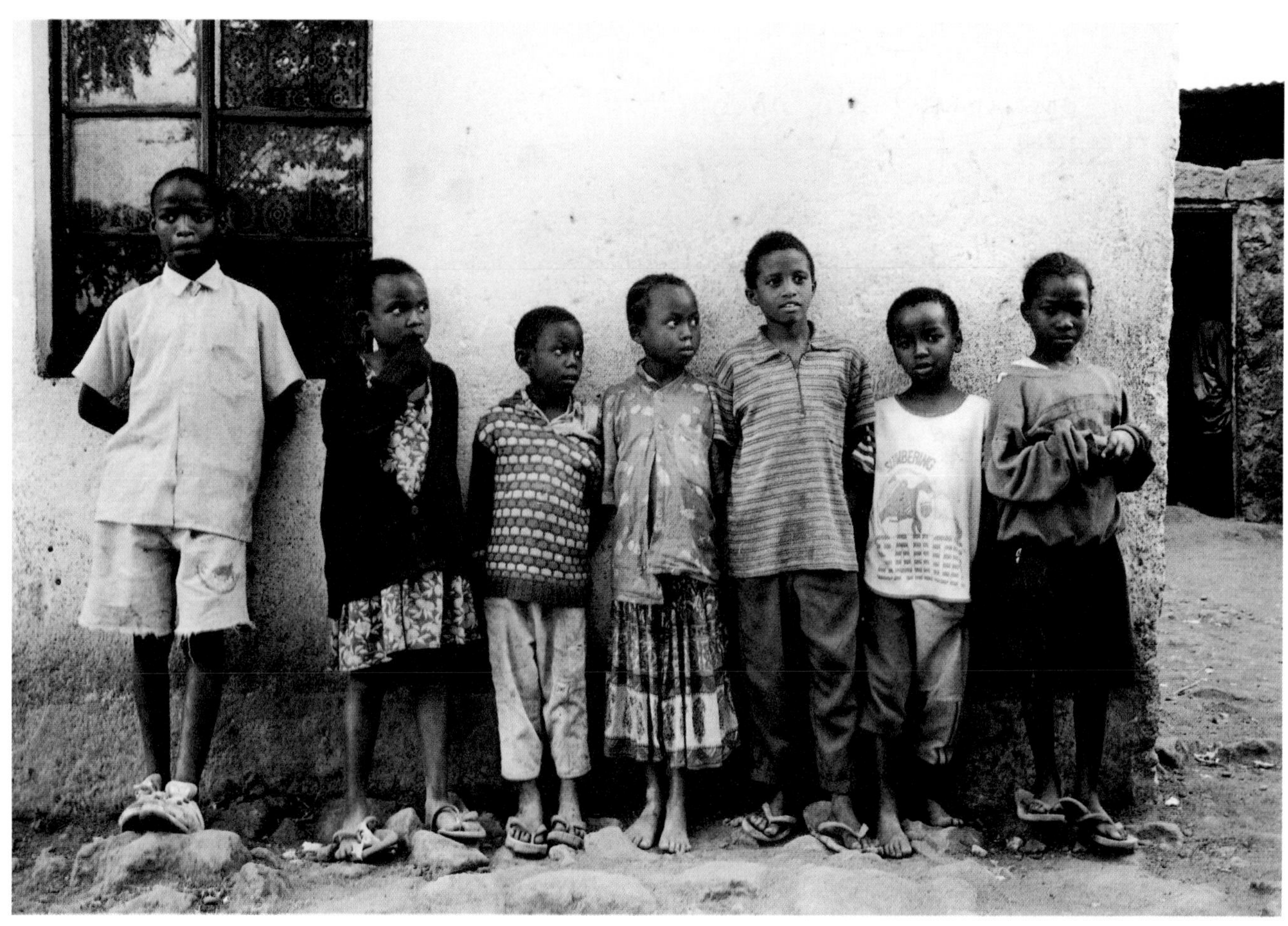

64 **PHILIP MBURU, SUSAN WANGOI, JOSEPH MWANGI, AGNES NJERA, SIMON IGESA, MWANGI MACHARIA & ELIZABETH WANJIRU**

DAGORETTI CORNER STREET CHILDRENS PROJECT, NAIROBI, KENYA

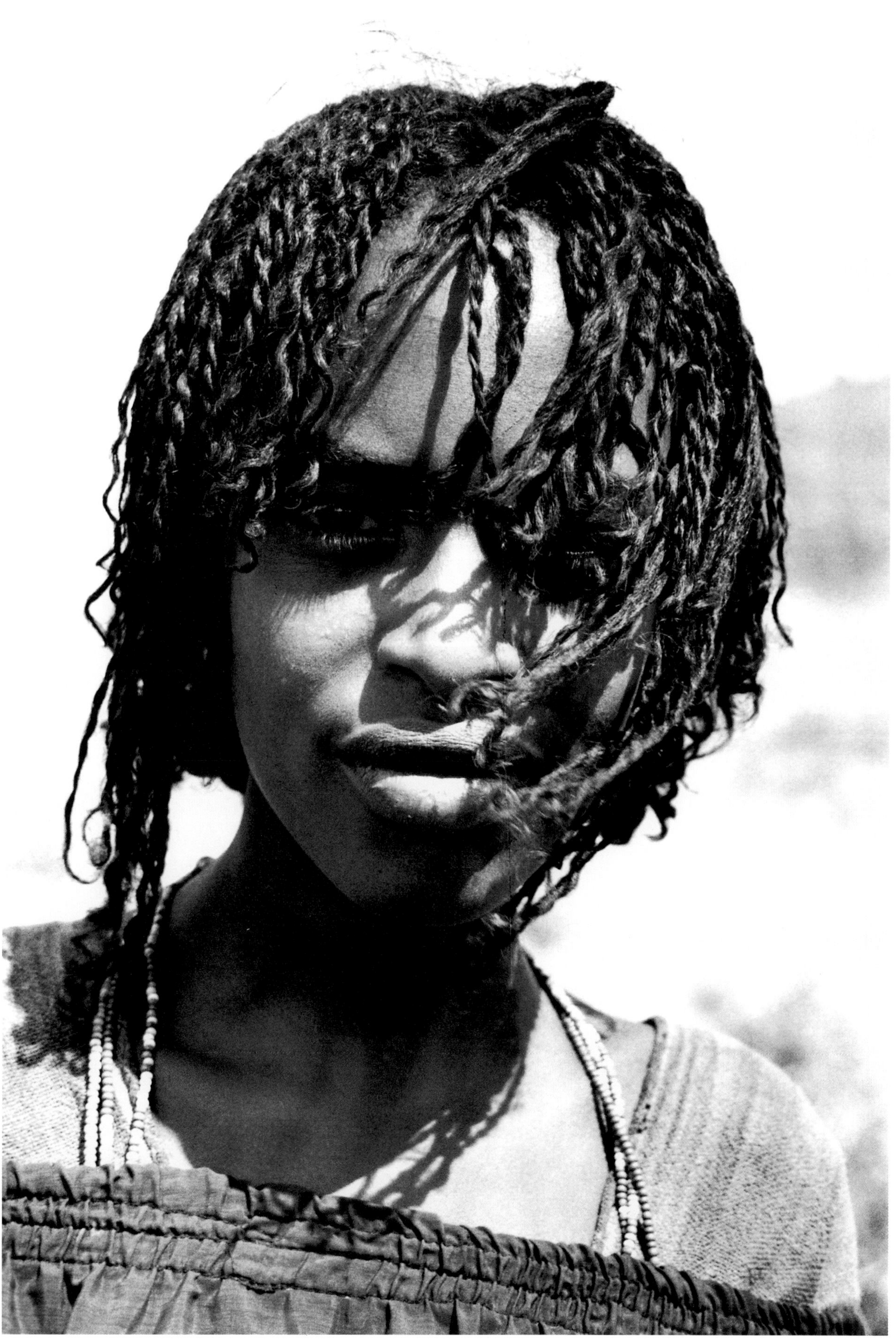

65 **GUYE ROBA**

KEREYOU TRIBE, DHEBITY, METAHARA, EAST-SHOWA,

ETHIOPIA

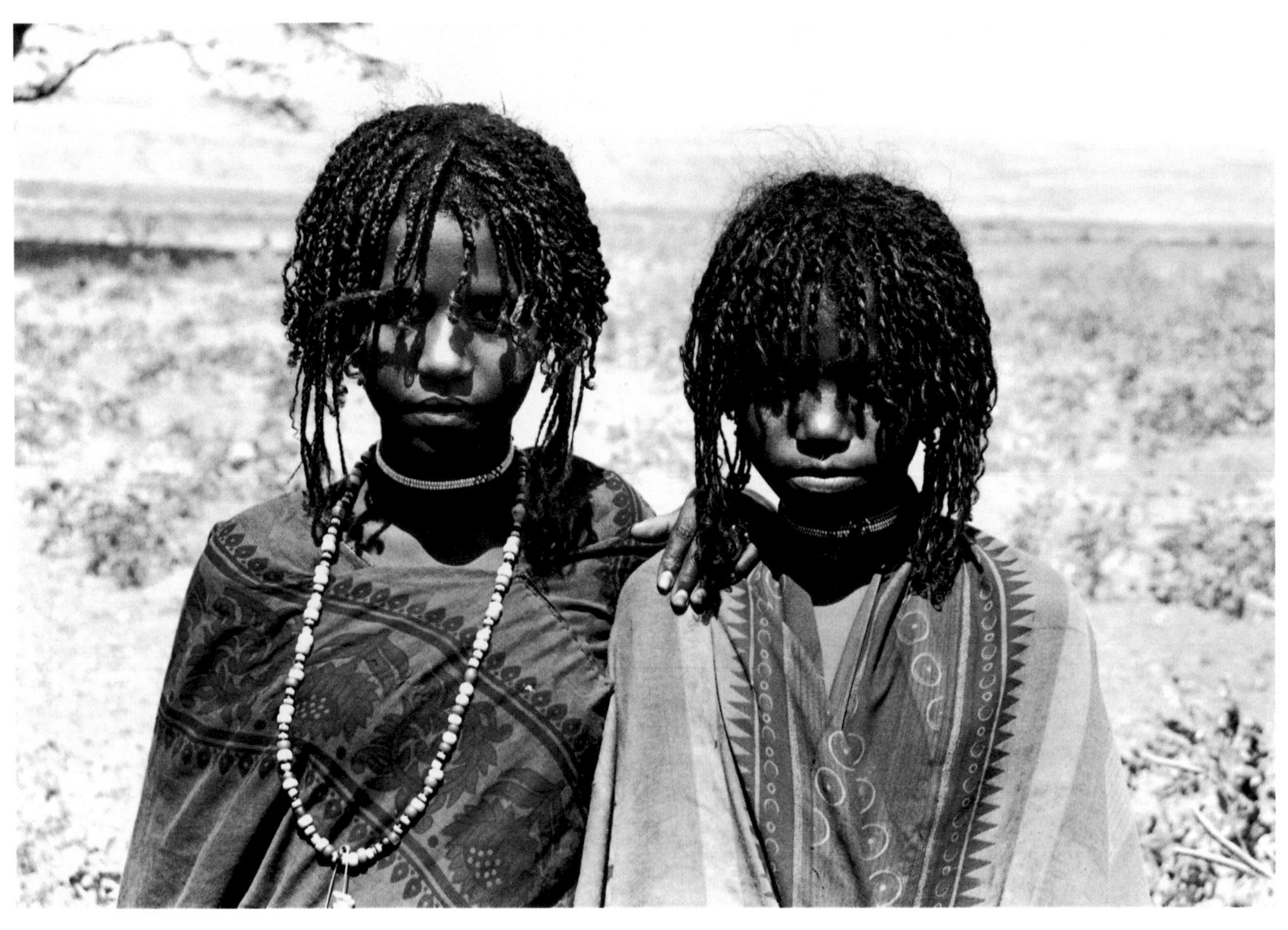

66 **HAWI HAWAS & HACK BORU**

KEREYOU TRIBE, DHEBITY, METAHARA, EAST-SHOWA,

ETHIOPIA

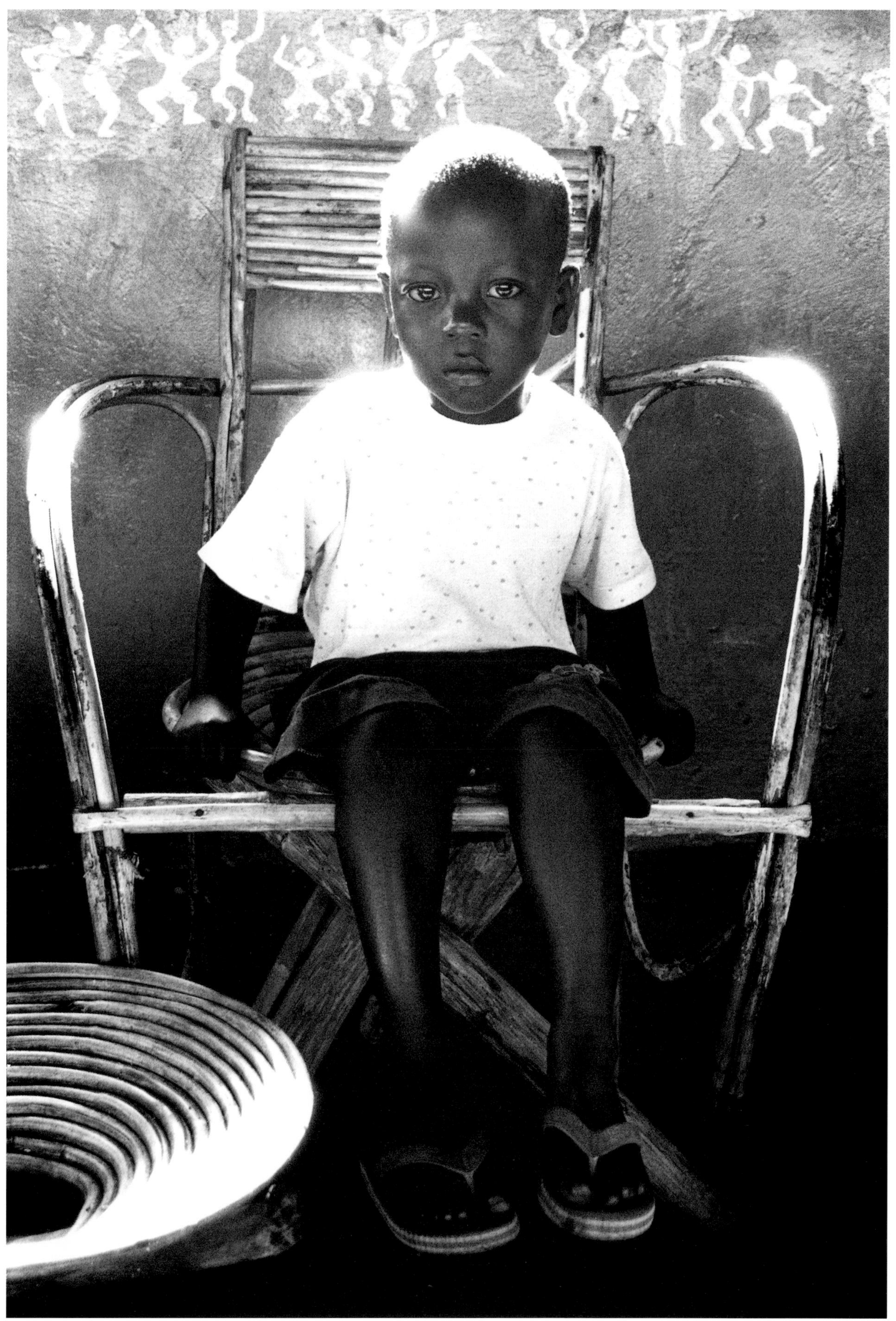

67 **ALEX BISO**

BUJUGALI FALLS, NILE RIVER, JINJA,

UGANDA

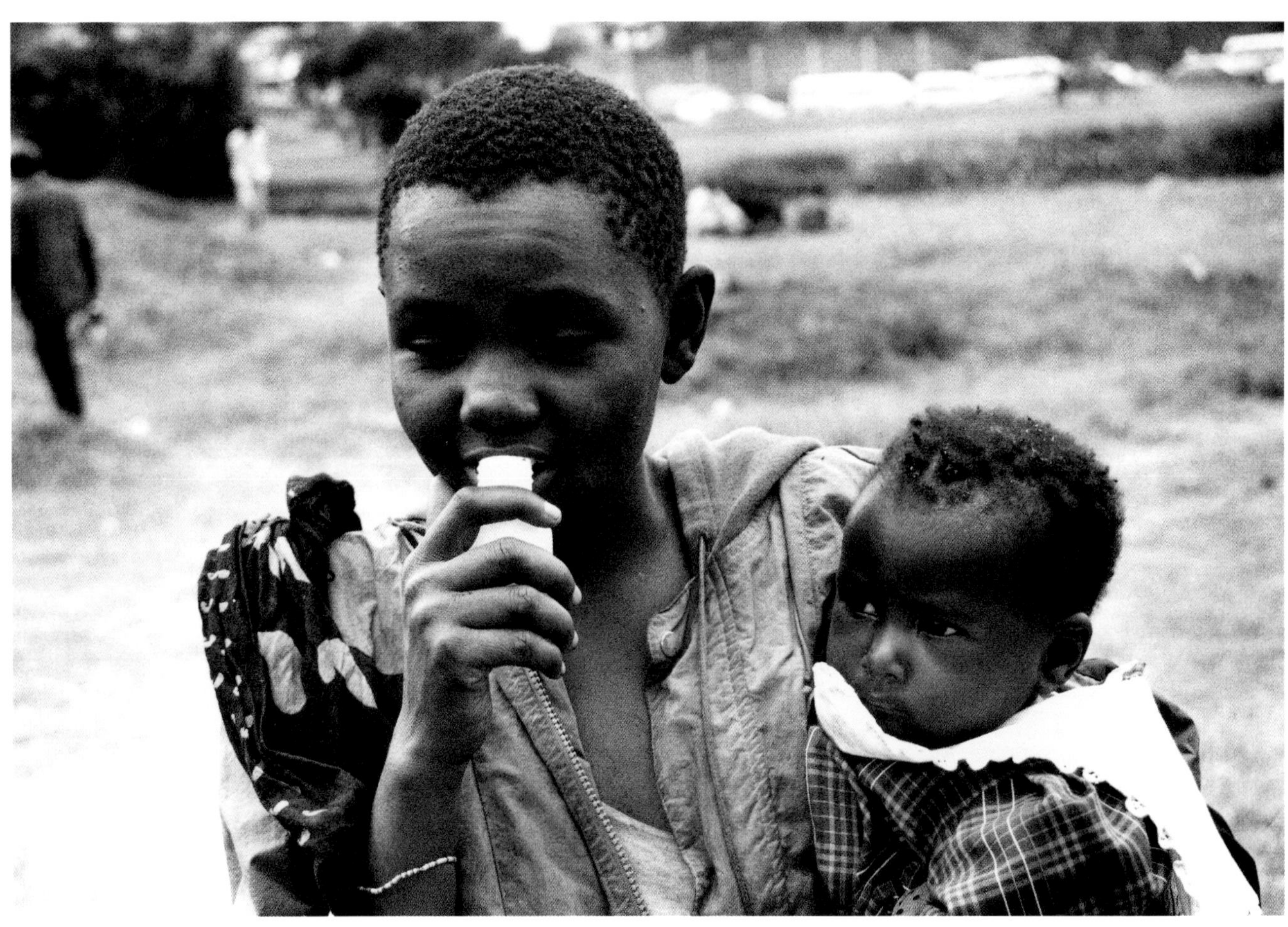

68 **GINA & ANASTASIA**

GLUE SNIFFING MOTHER & CHILD, NAIROBI,

KENYA

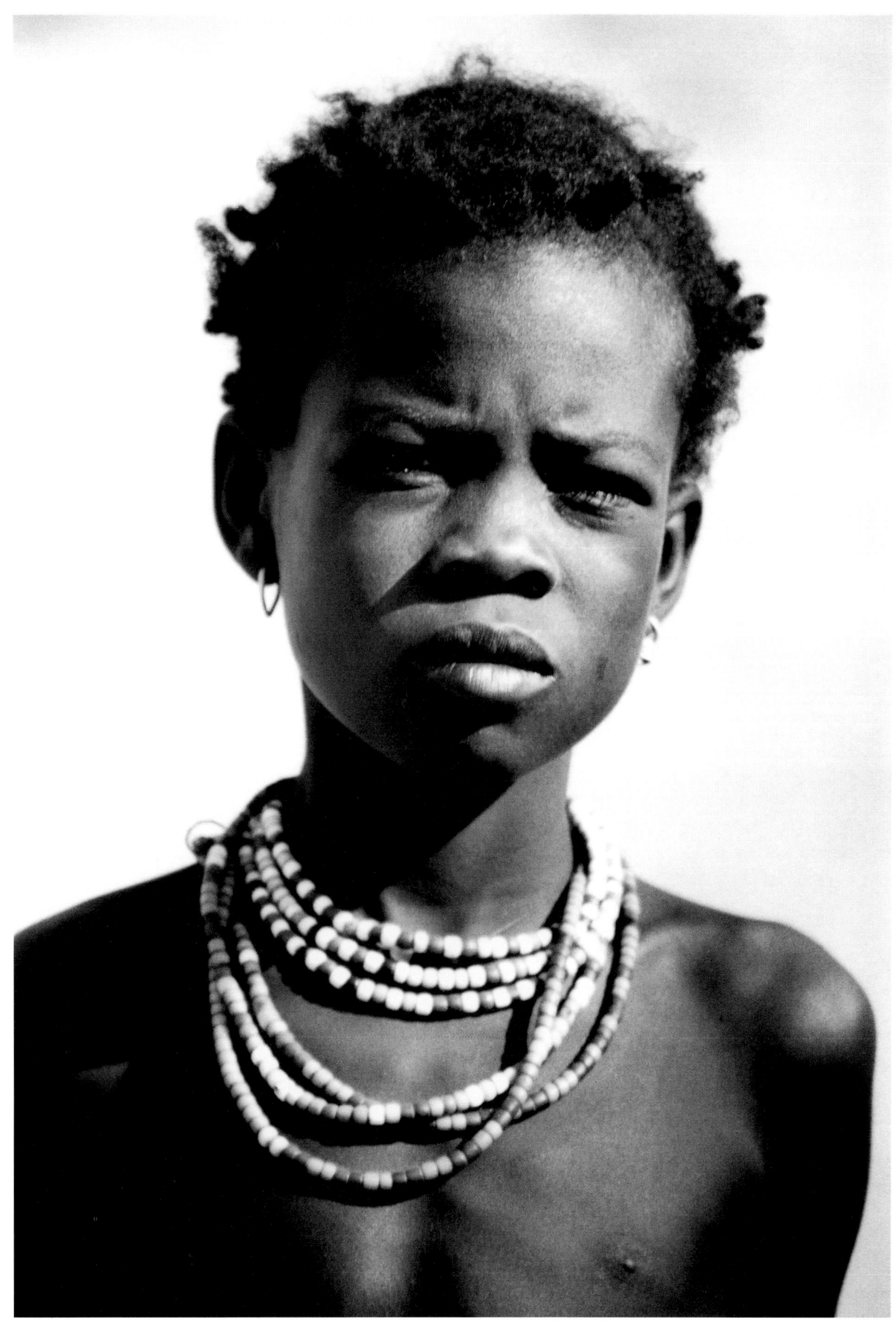

69 **EROHO**

DAASANACH TRIBE, GAMO – GOFA,

ETHIOPIA

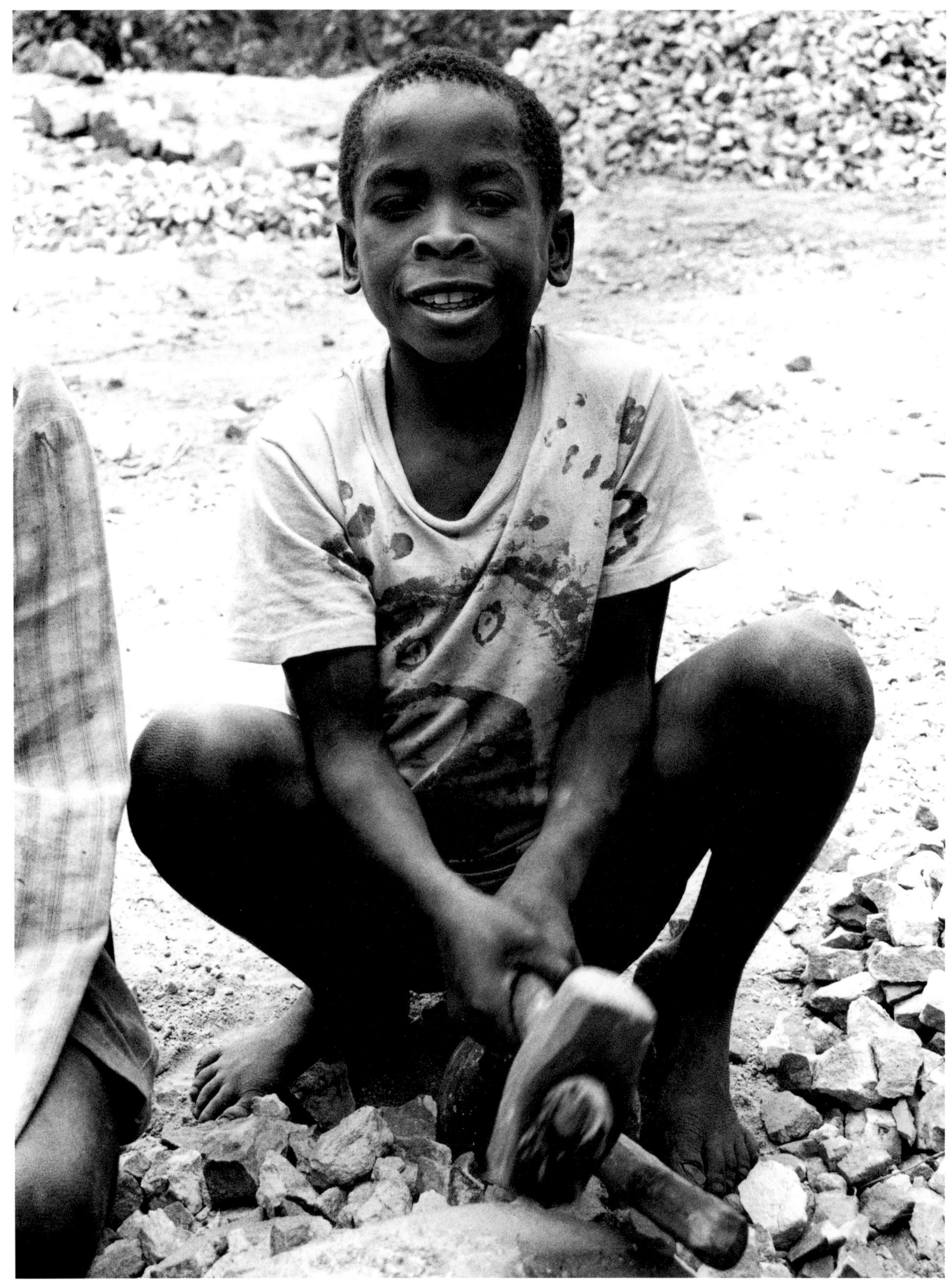

70 **ISAAC**

LAKE BUNYONYI ROAD, KABALE,

UGANDA

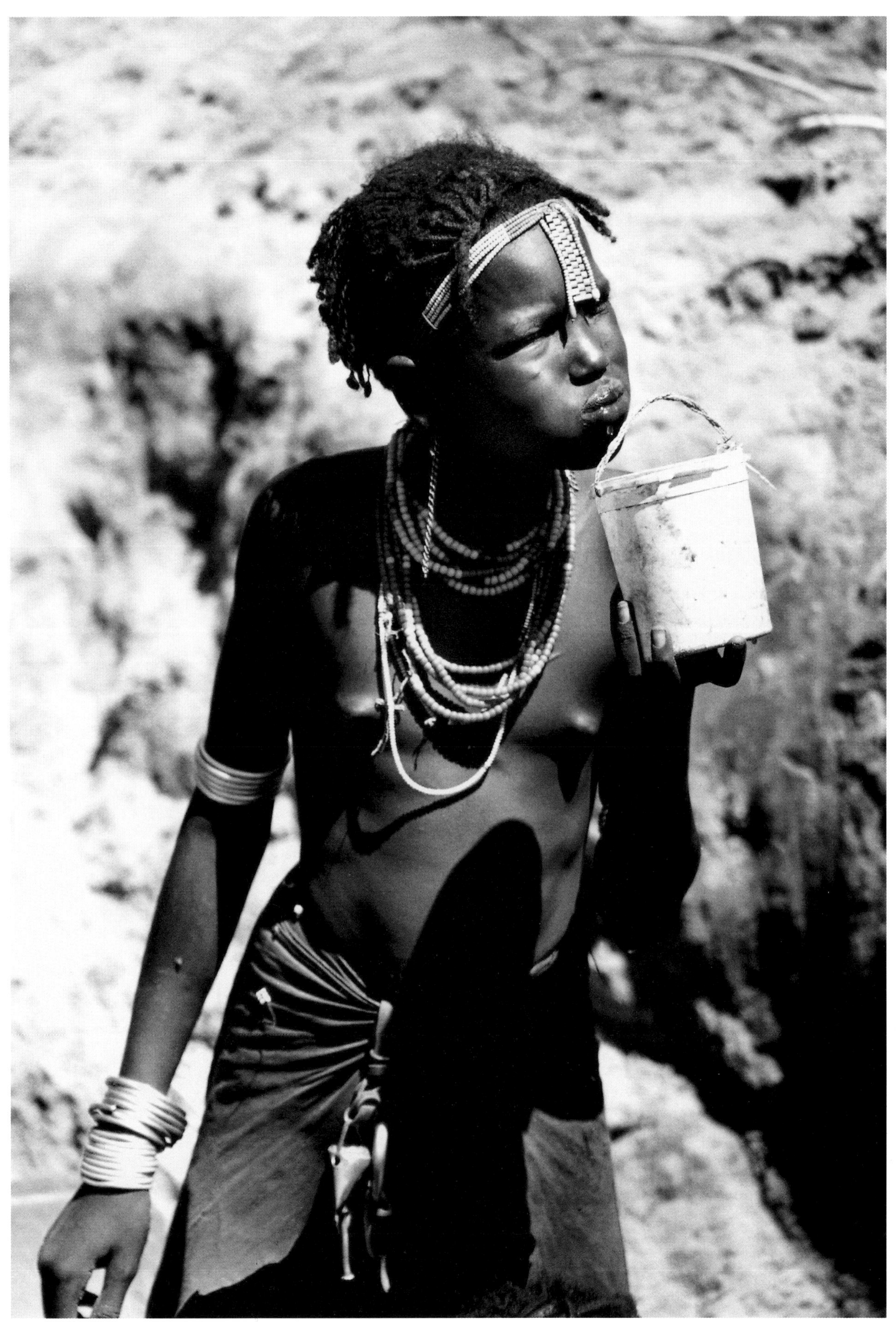

71 **AYALA**

DAASANACH TRIBE, GAMO – GOFA,

ETHIOPIA

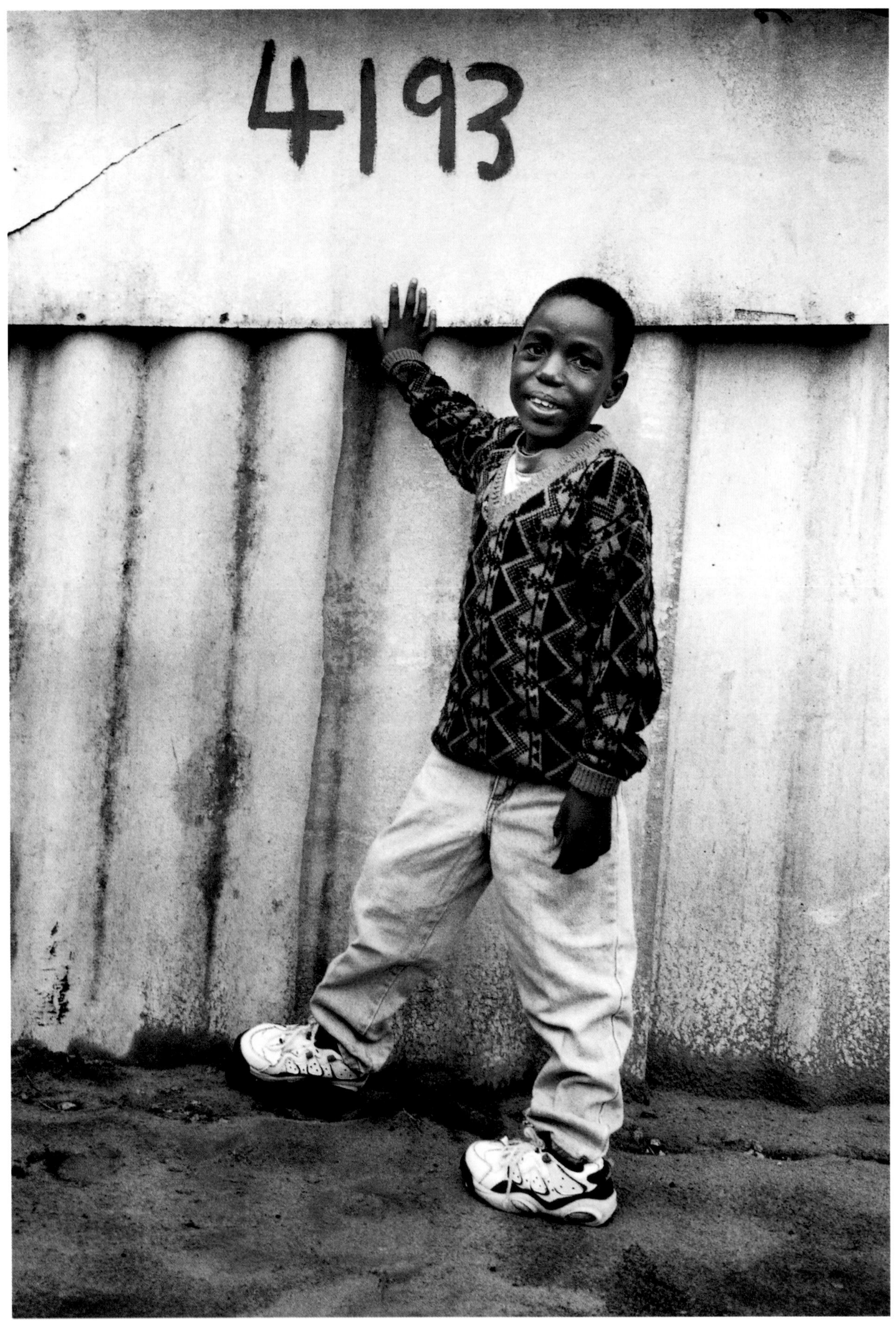

72 **PRIORITY NDEBELE**

CHINOTIMBA TOWNSHIP, MATABELELAND NORTH,

ZIMBABWE

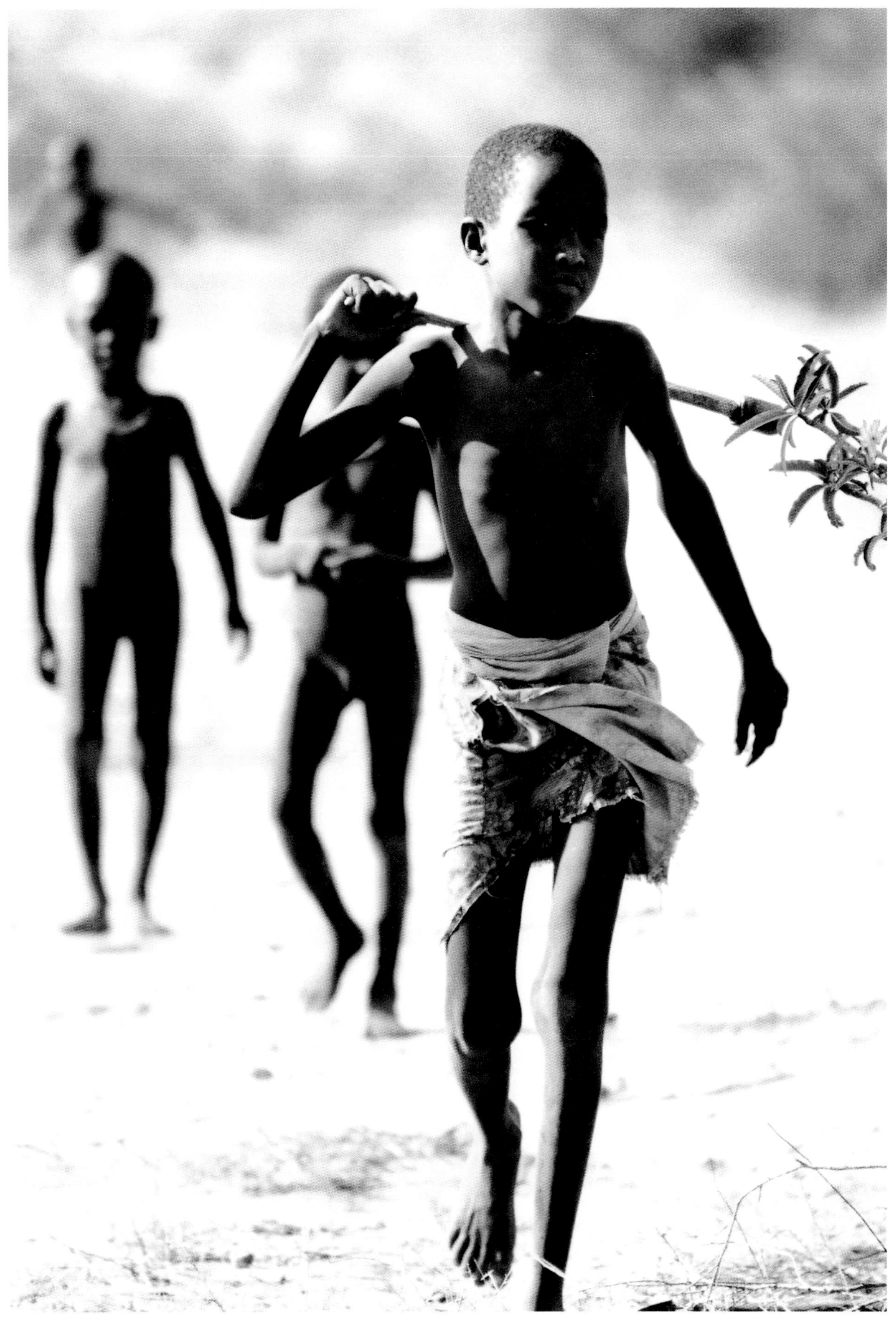

73 **EDEA IOSORKIT**

TURKANA TRIBE, ILERET, MARSABIT DISTRICT, EASTERN PROVINCE,

KENYA

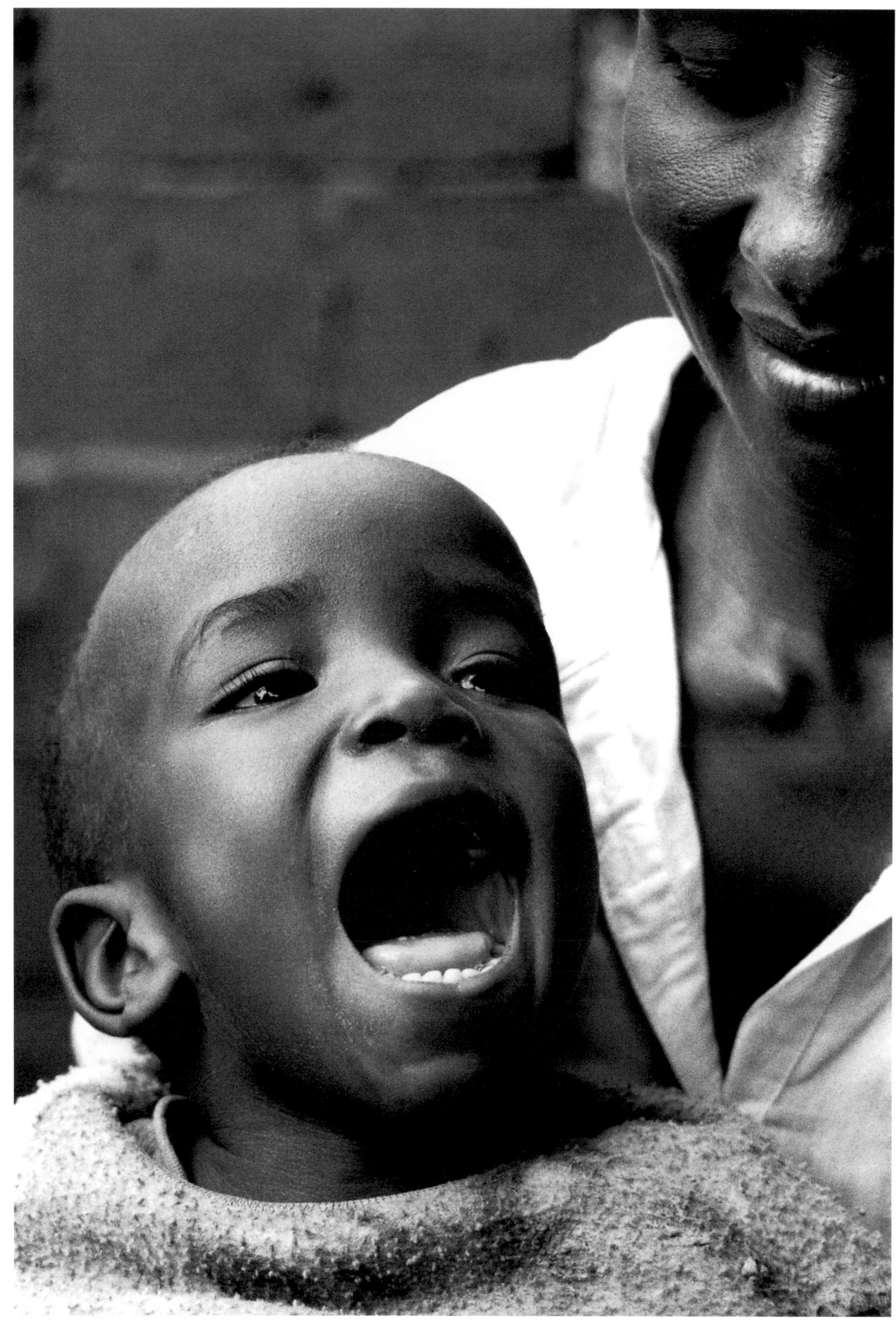

74 **MAJAHANA NGWENYA**

CHINOTIMBA TOWNSHIP, MATABELELAND NORTH,

ZIMBABWE

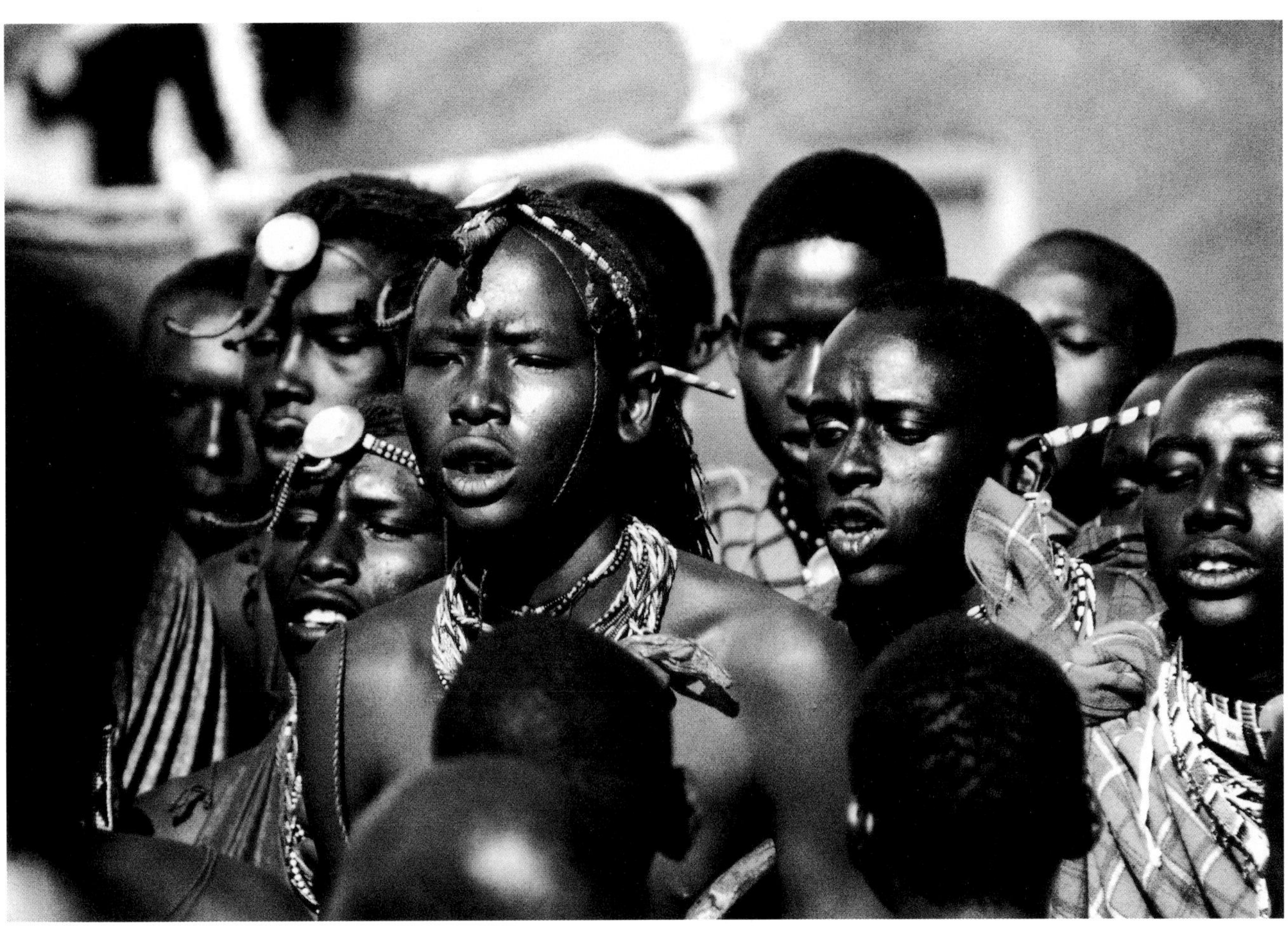

75 **OLGOLMONI**

MAASAI WEDDING, LOITA HILLS, MORIJO,

KENYA

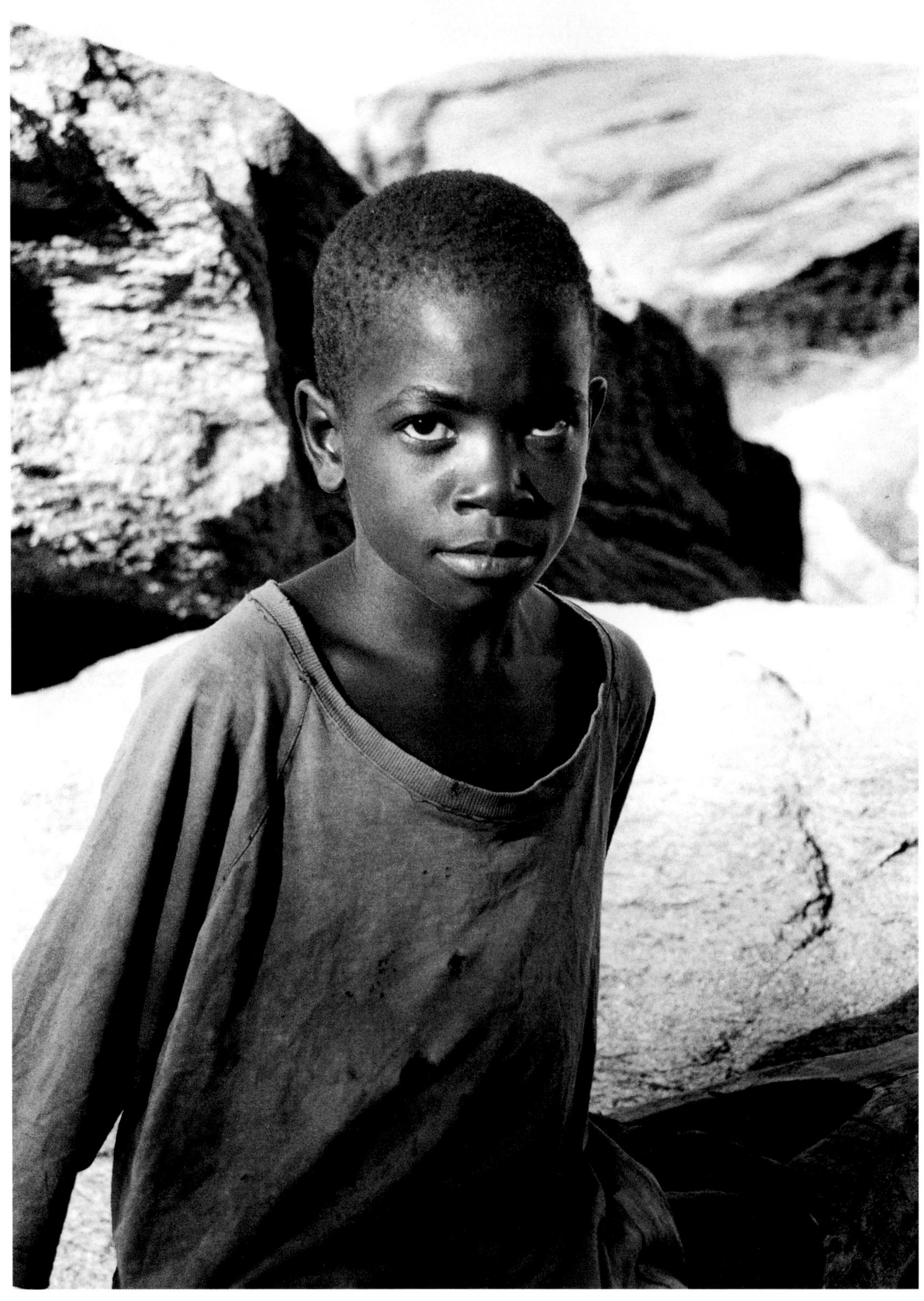

76 **MALUMBO SAKA**

NKATHA BAY, NORTHERN PROVINCE,

MALAWI

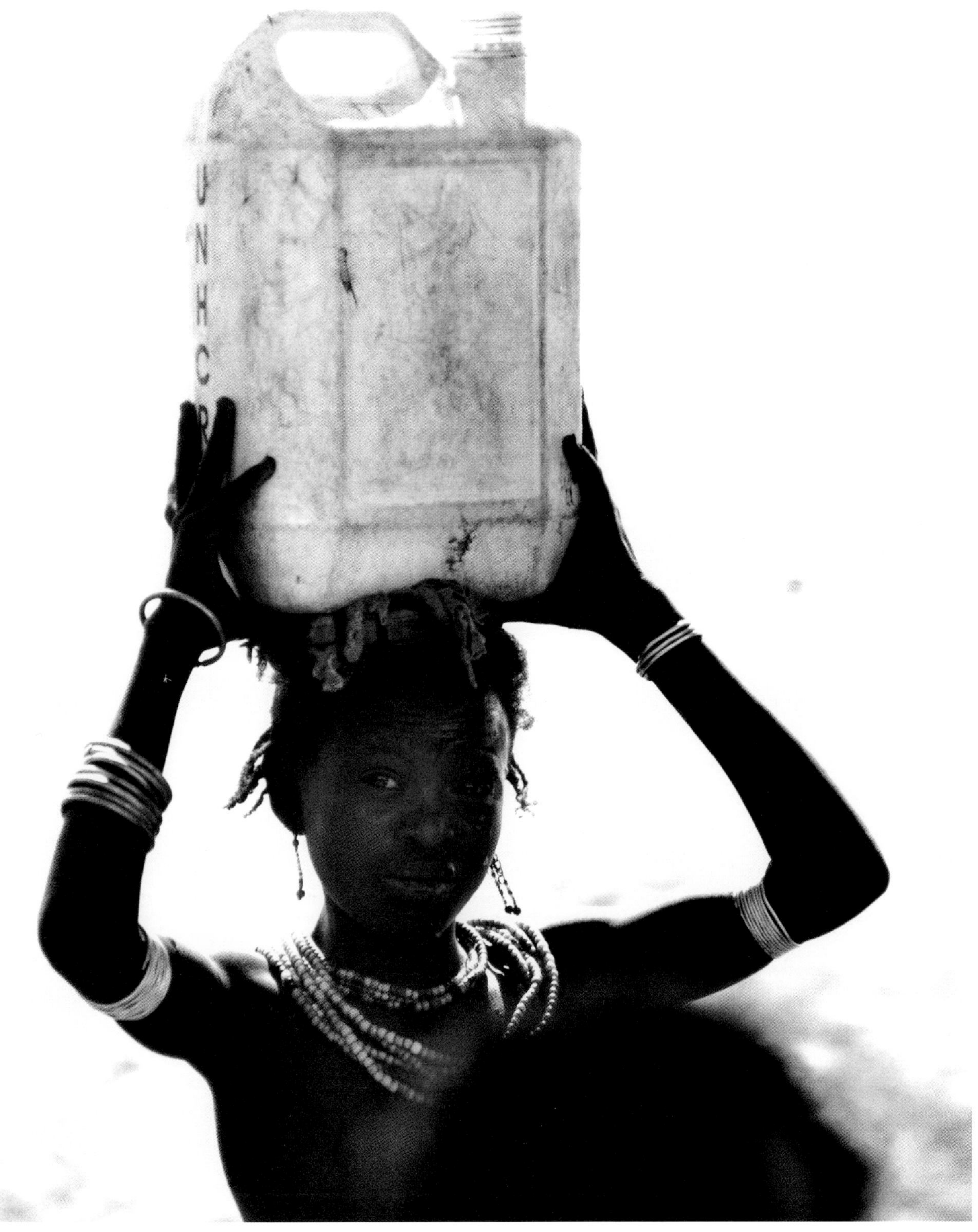

77 **TULU**

DAASANACH TRIBE, GAMO – GOFA,

ETHIOPIA

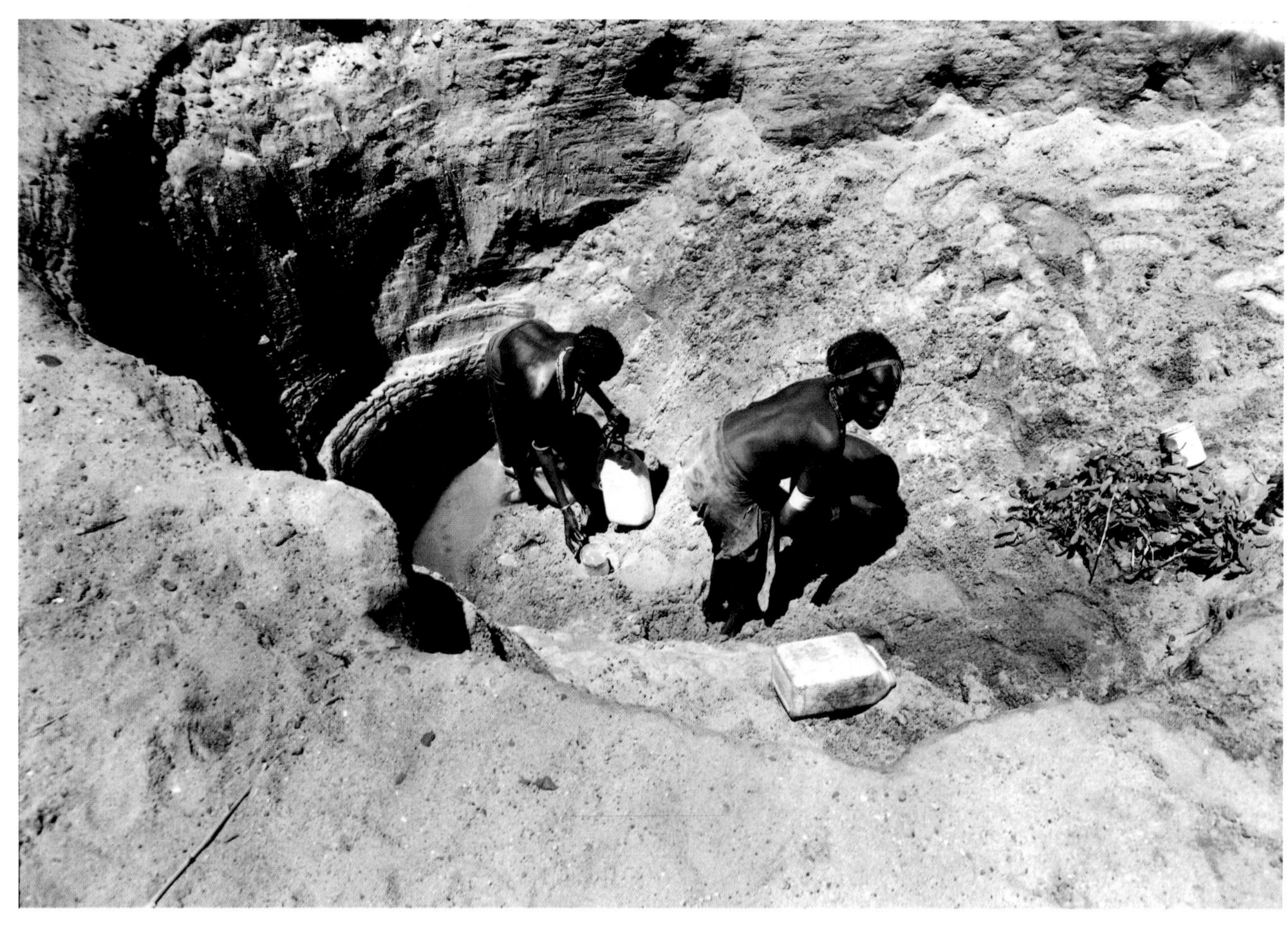

78 **APESE NASOROKIT**

DAASANACH TRIBE, GAMO – GOFA,

ETHIOPIA

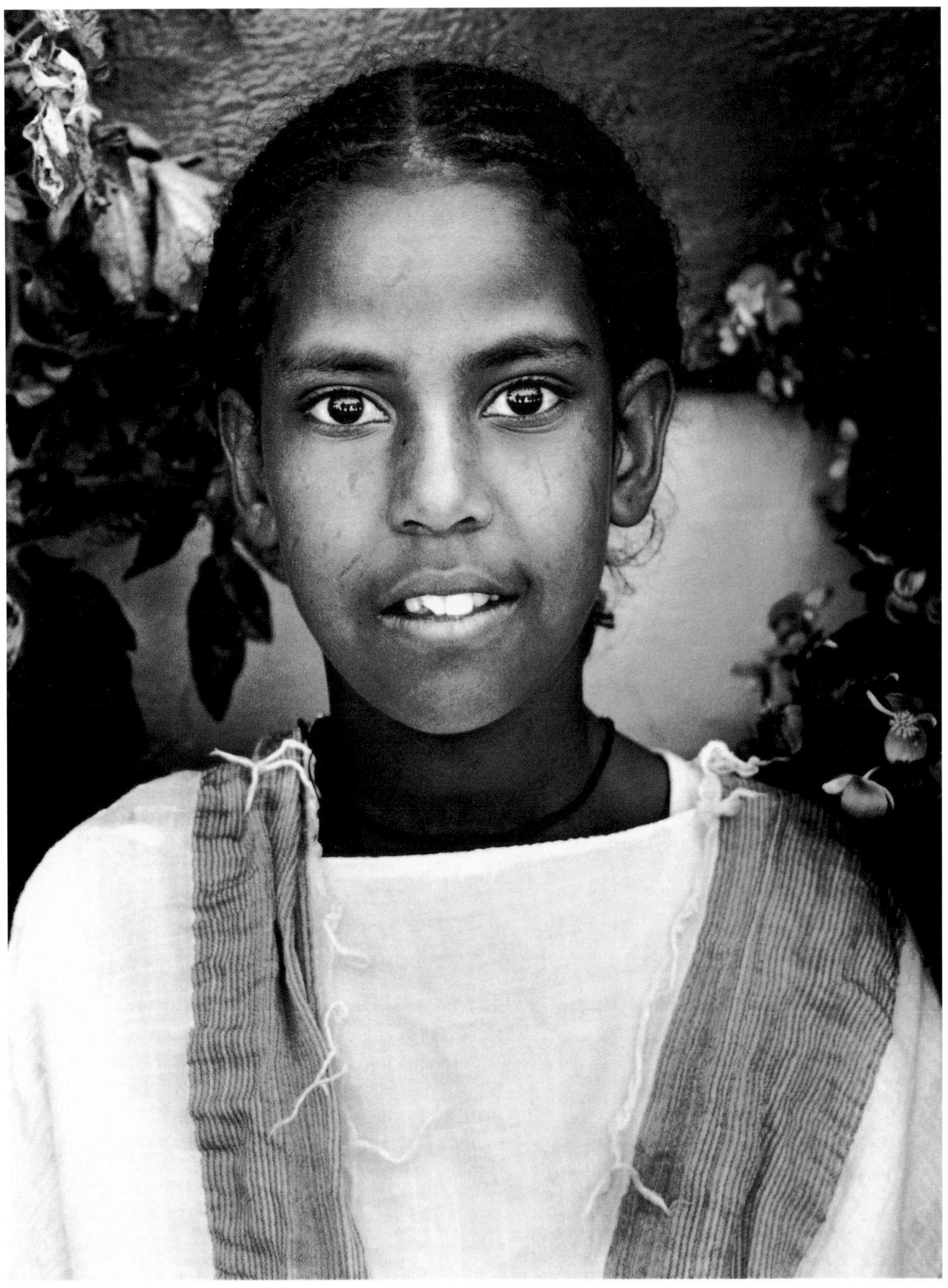

79 BETHLEHEM ANDEBERHANE

ABEBECH GOBENA ORPHANAGE & SCHOOL, ADDIS ABABA,

ETHIOPIA

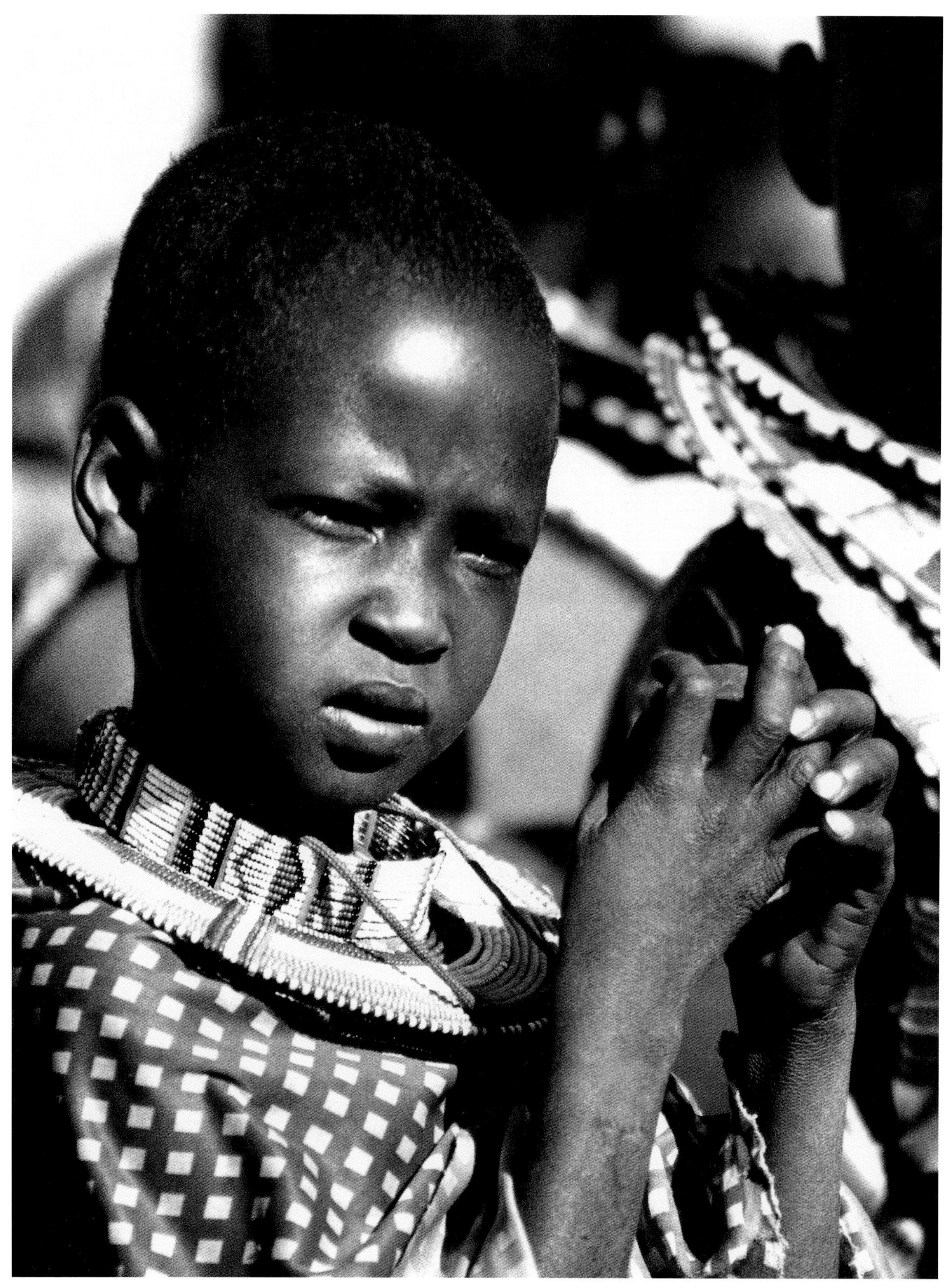

80 **ENTITO**

MAASAI WEDDING, LOITA HILLS, MORIJO,

KENYA

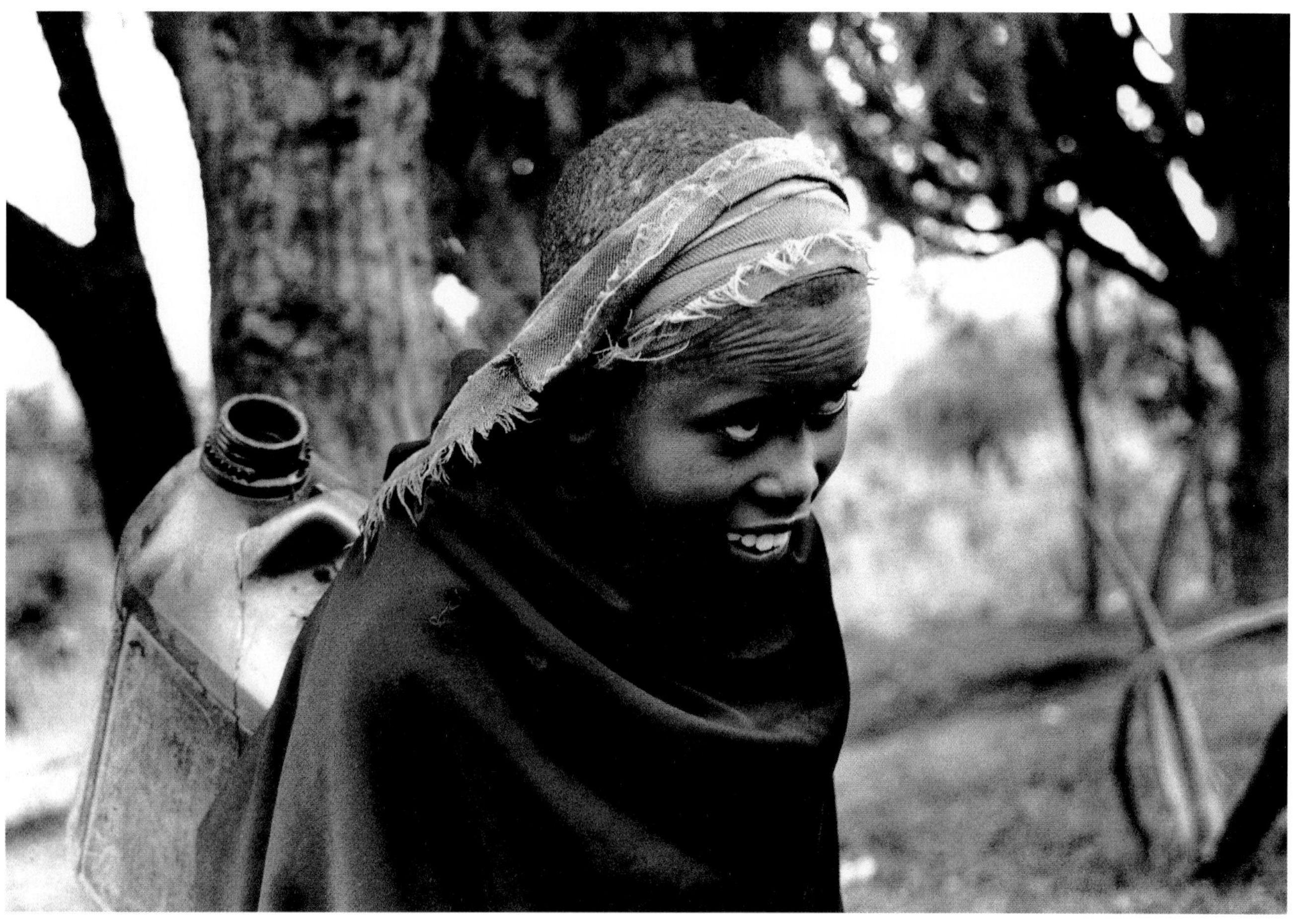

81 **KENNEDY LEKIREKICHO**

MARALAL, SAMBURU DISTRICT, RIFT VALLEY PROVINCE,

KENYA

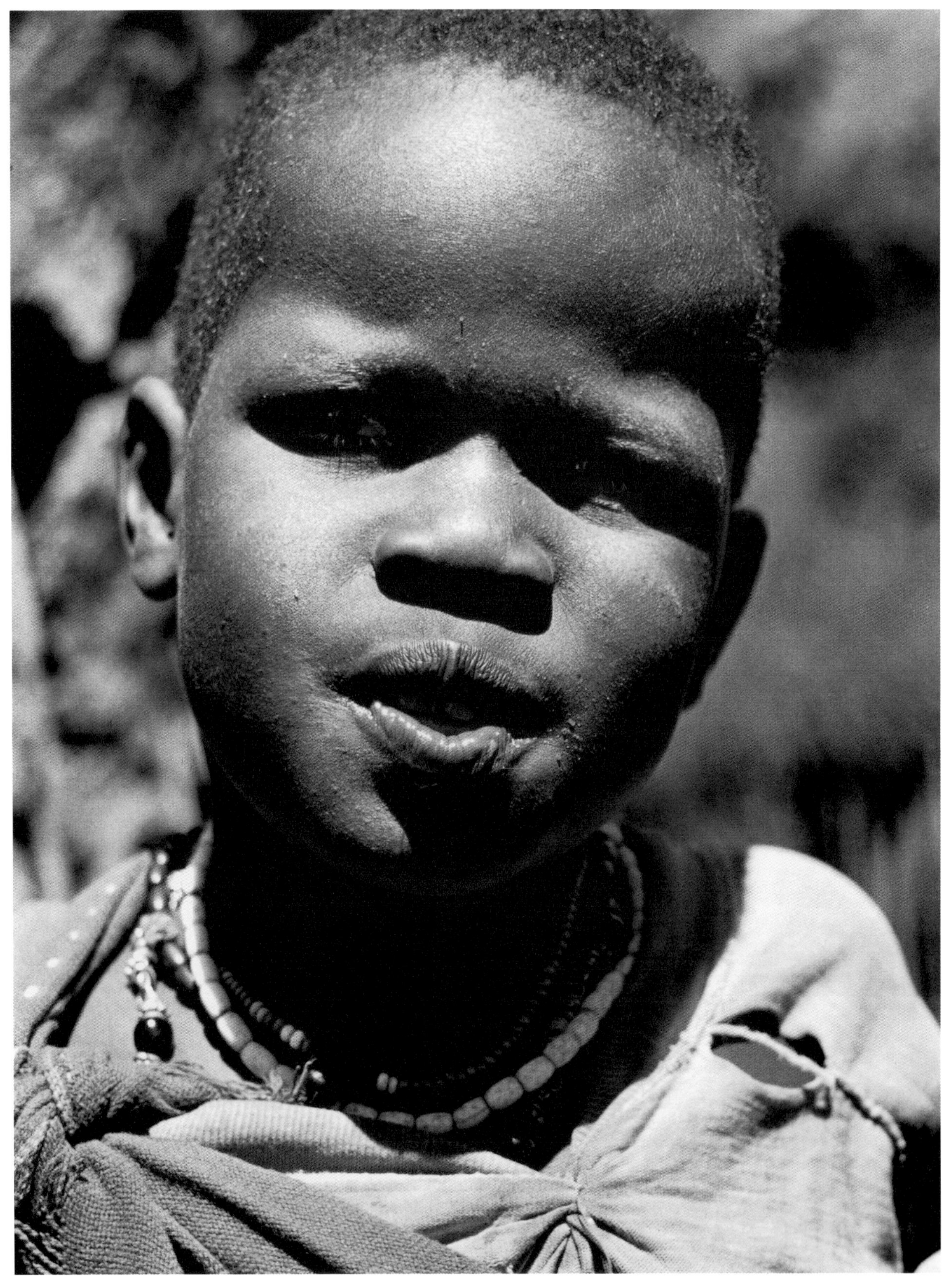

82 **KATOI MOKORA**

KANJIRO SENETO MAASAI BOMA, NGORONGORO,

TANZANIA

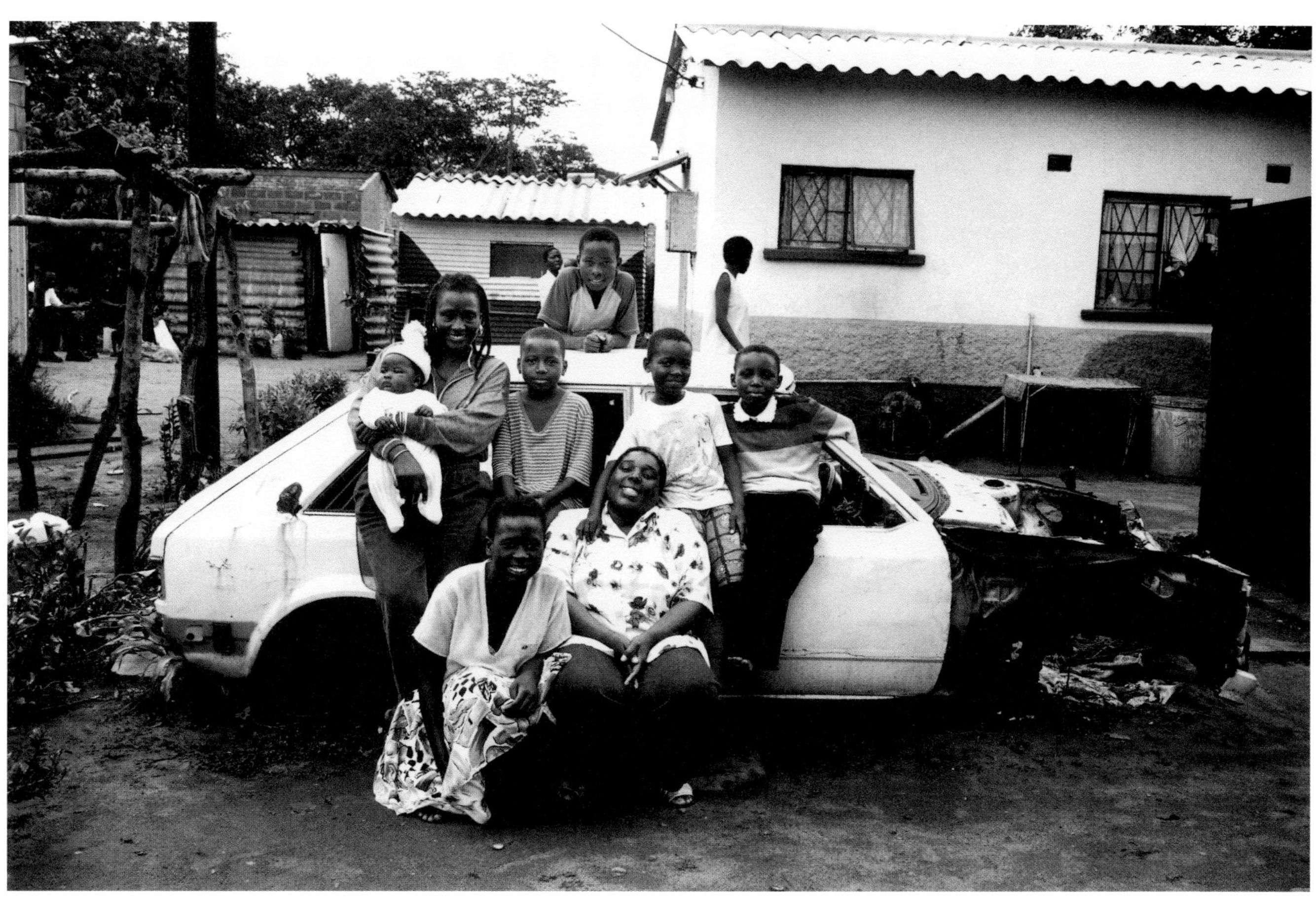

83 **VIOLET MOYO, MARGARET & FAMILY**

CHINOTIMBA TOWNSHIP, MATABELELAND NORTH,

ZIMBABWE

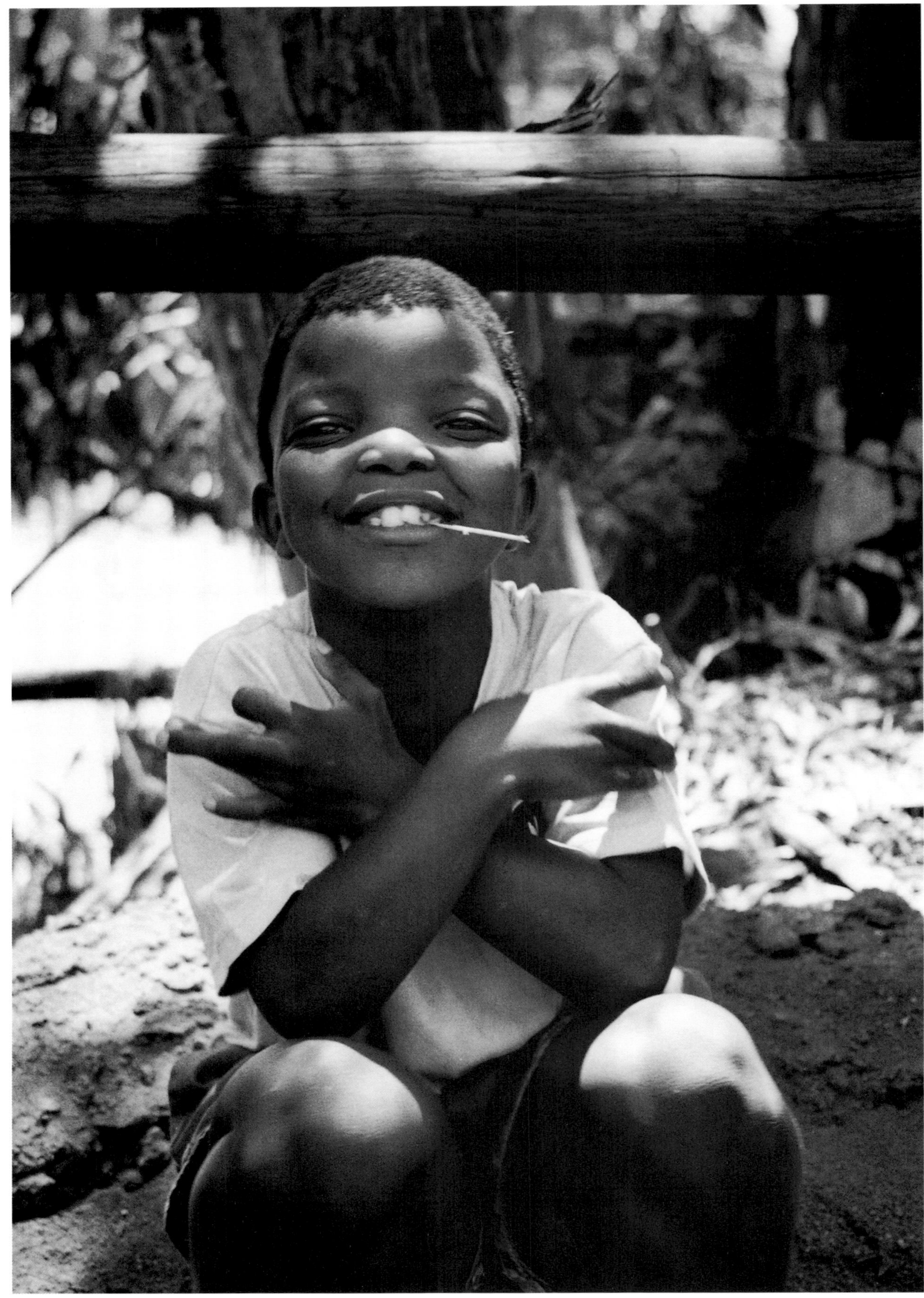

84 **JOSEPH VAN SCHALKWYK**

KIMBERLEY, NORTHERN CAPE PROVINCE,

SOUTH AFRICA

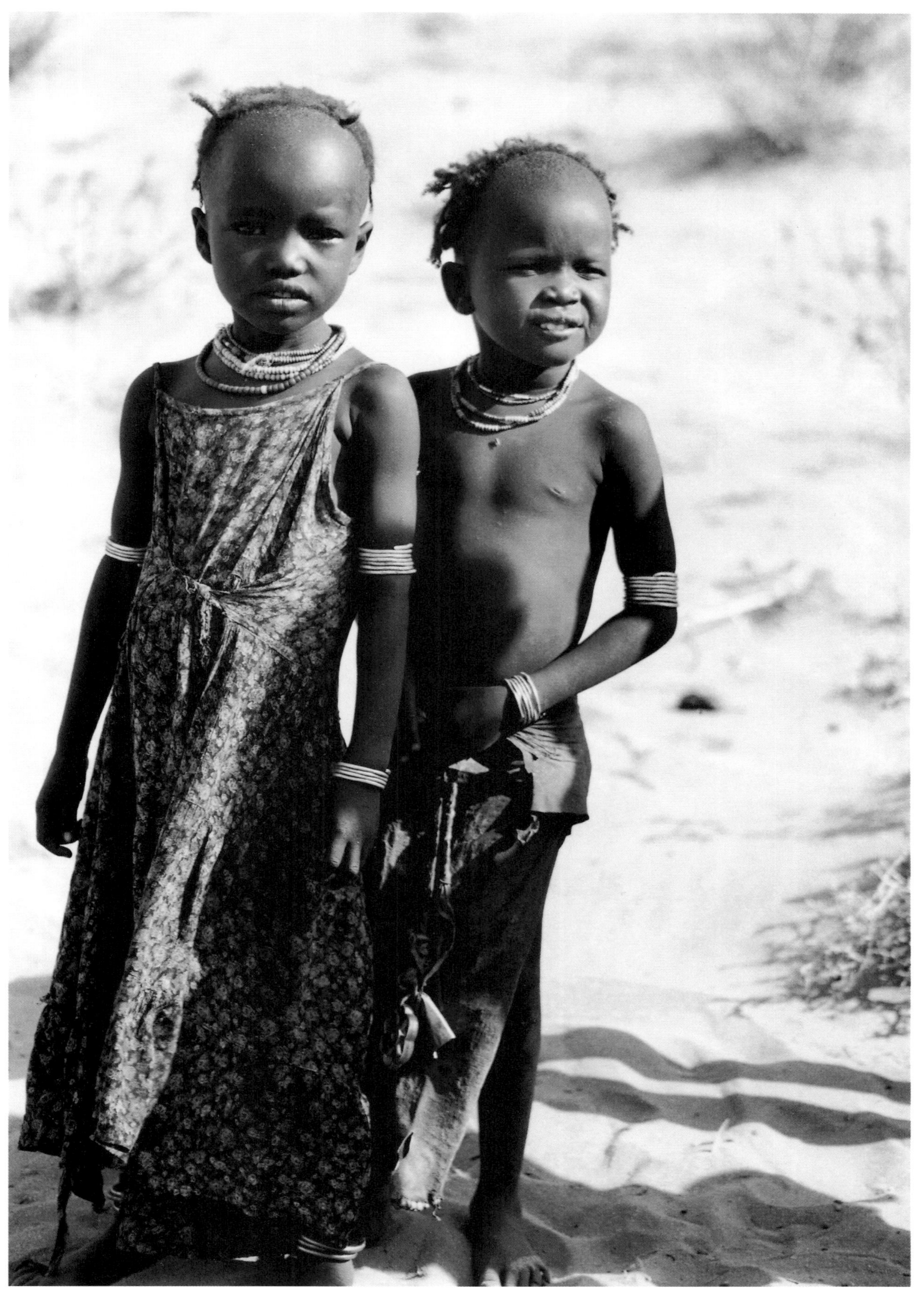

85 **ERRMI & NASSIA**

DAASANACH TRIBE, GAMO – GOFA,

ETHIOPIA

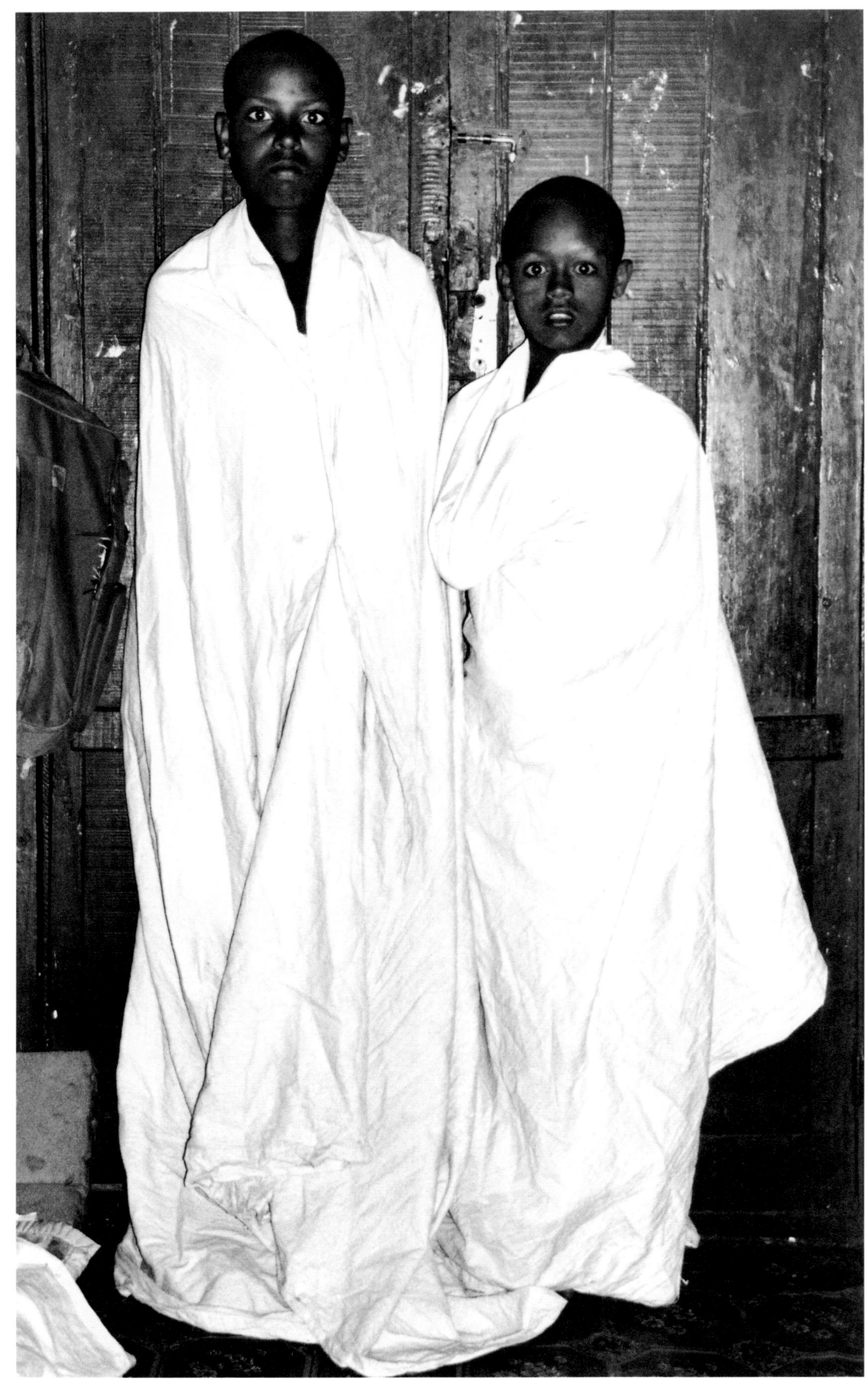

86 **SHEFERAW TESHOME & ABUBEKER MOHAMMED**

GOAL STREET CHILDRENS NIGHT SHELTER, WOREDA 21, KEBELE 13, ADDIS ABABA, ETHIOPIA

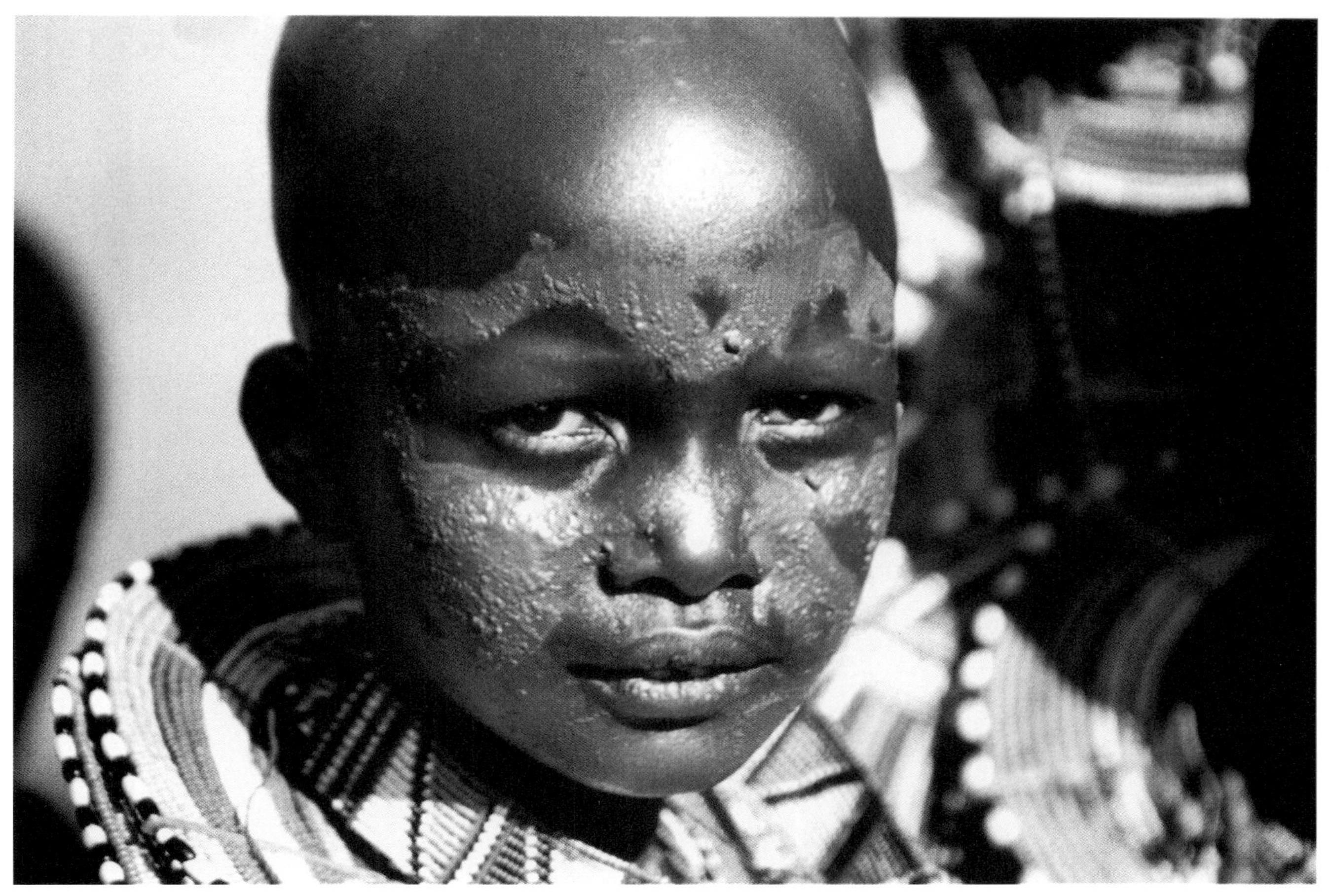

87 **PIRIAS**

MAASAI WEDDING, LOITA HILLS, MORIJO,

KENYA

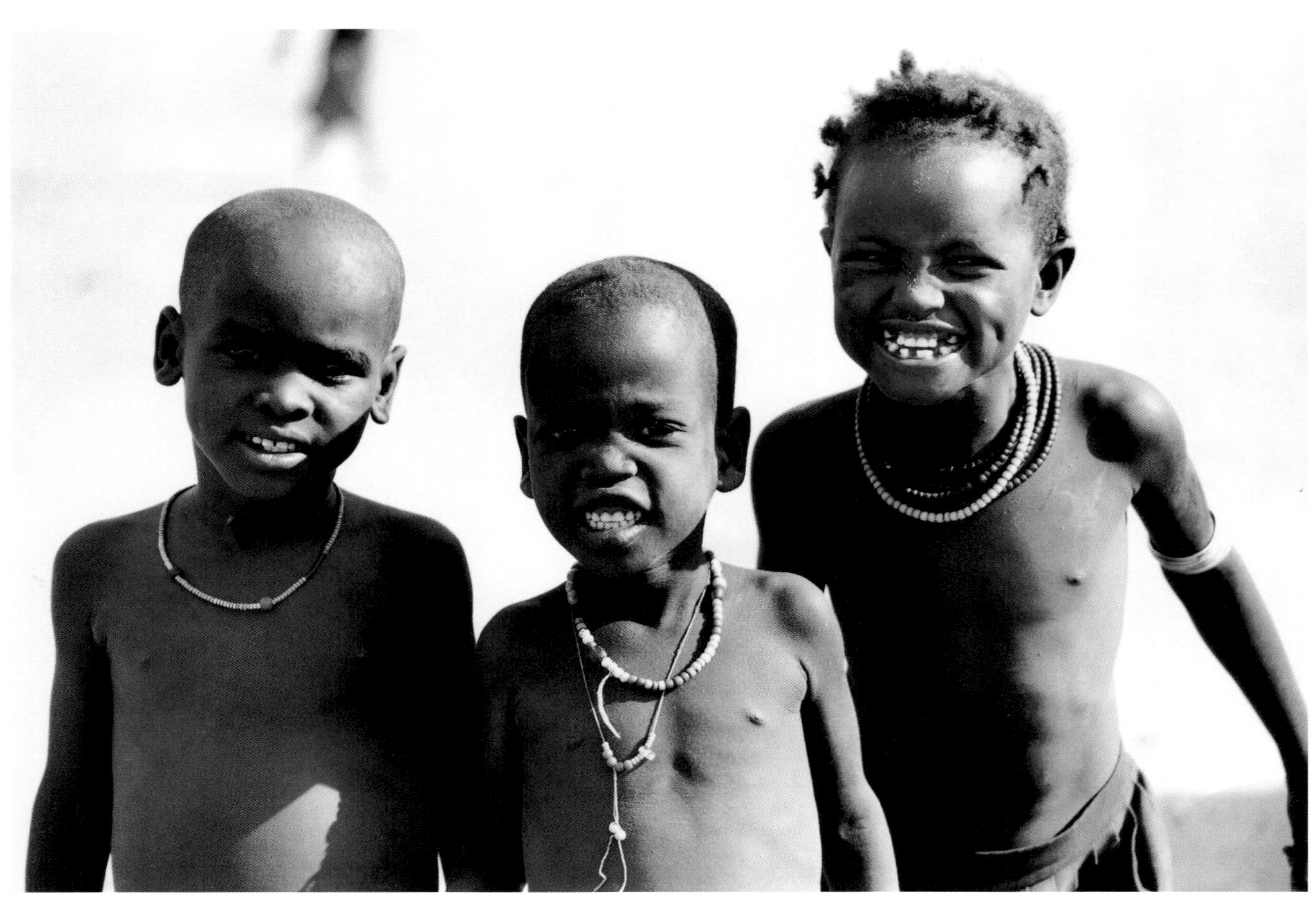

88 **DAASANACH CHILDREN**

DAASANACH TRIBE, GAMO – GOFA,

ETHIOPIA

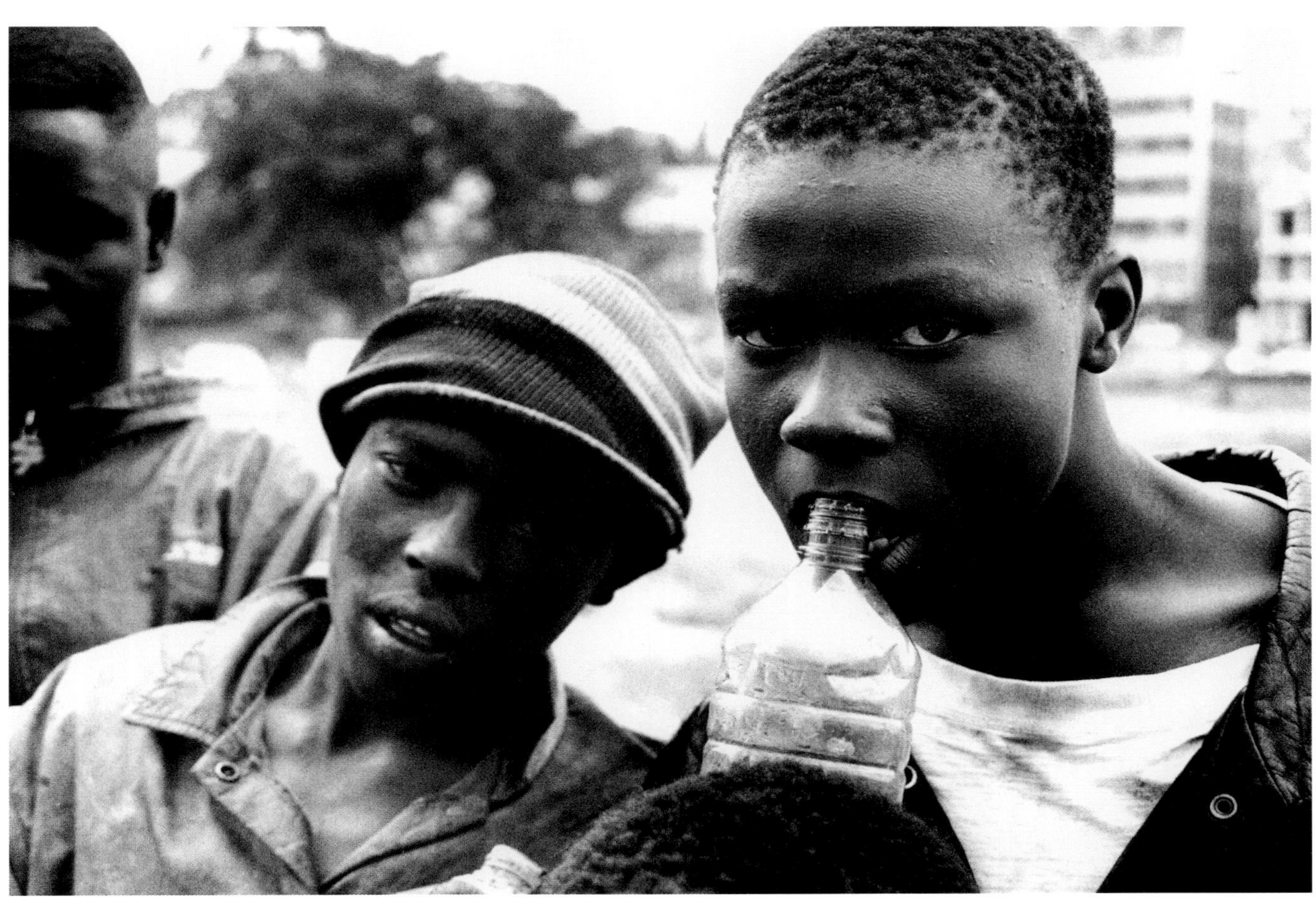

89 **MICHAEL MUIRURI & JOHN**

GLUE SNIFFING STREET KIDS, NAIROBI,

KENYA

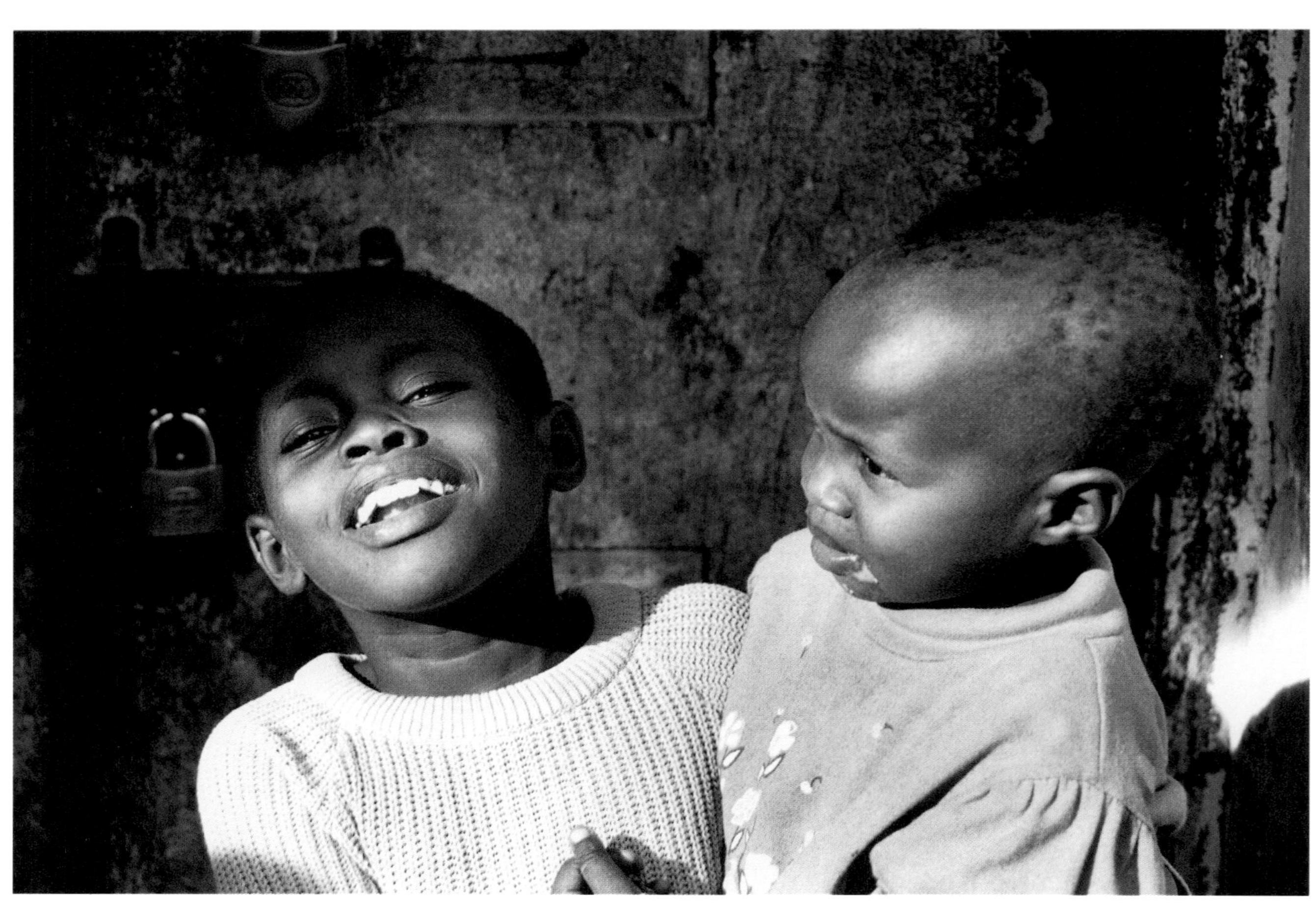

90 **MAMA NA MTOTO**

LAMU TOWN, LAMU ISLAND,

KENYA

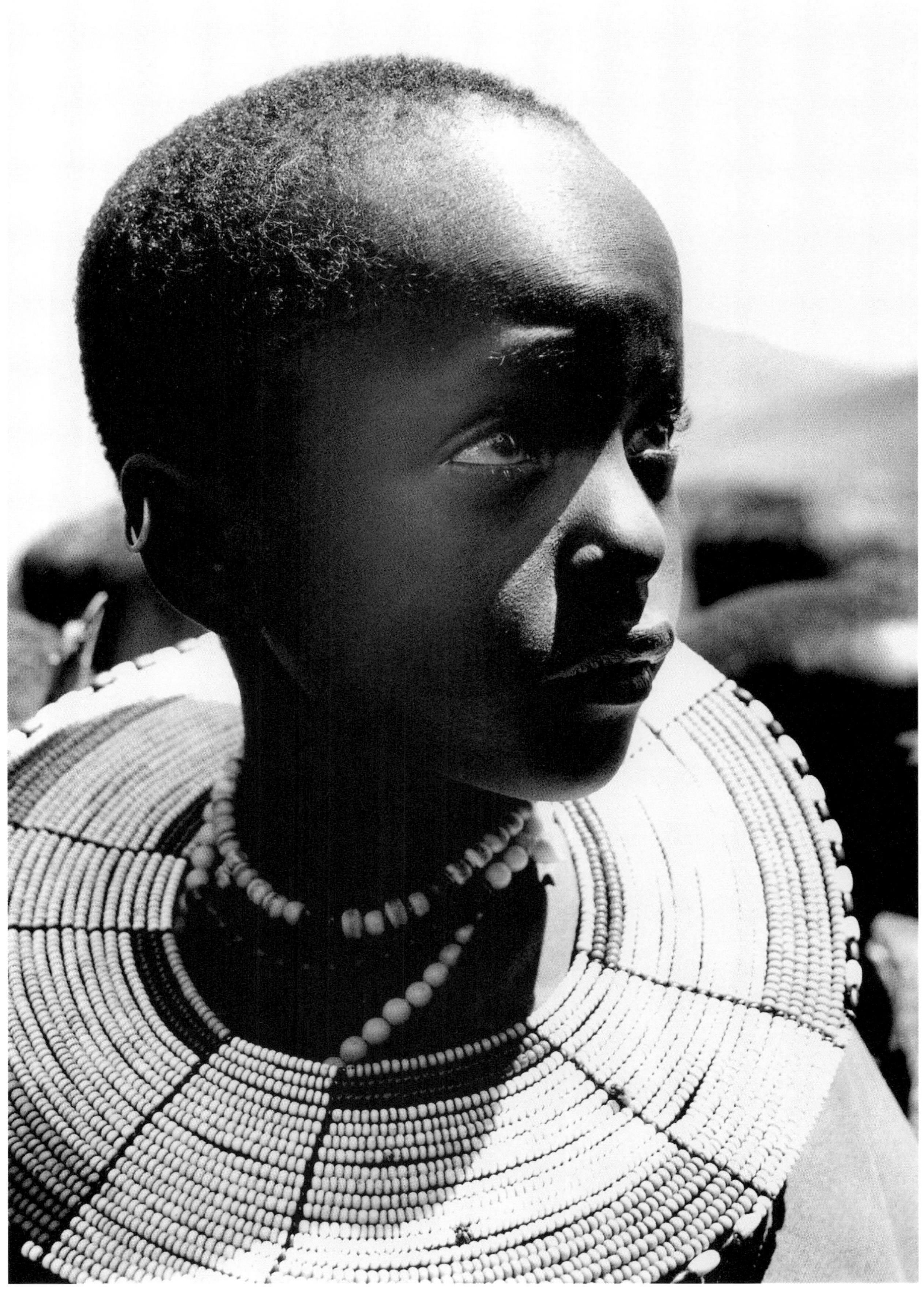

91 **KITAYAIT ALEKARI**

KANJIRO SENETO MAASAI BOMA, NGORONGORO,

TANZANIA

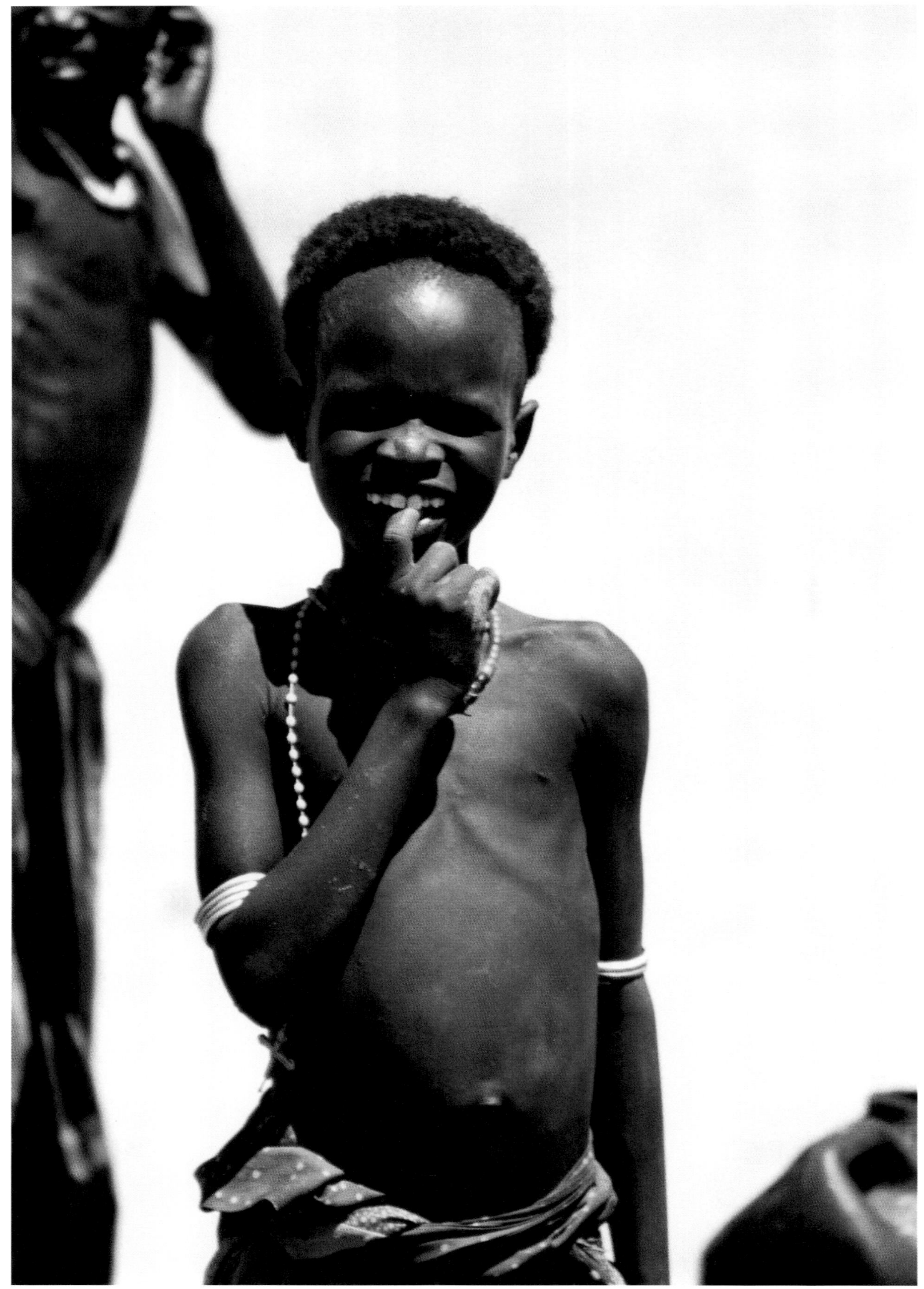

92 **LOBOCH**

DAASANACH TRIBE, GAMO – GOFA,

ETHIOPIA

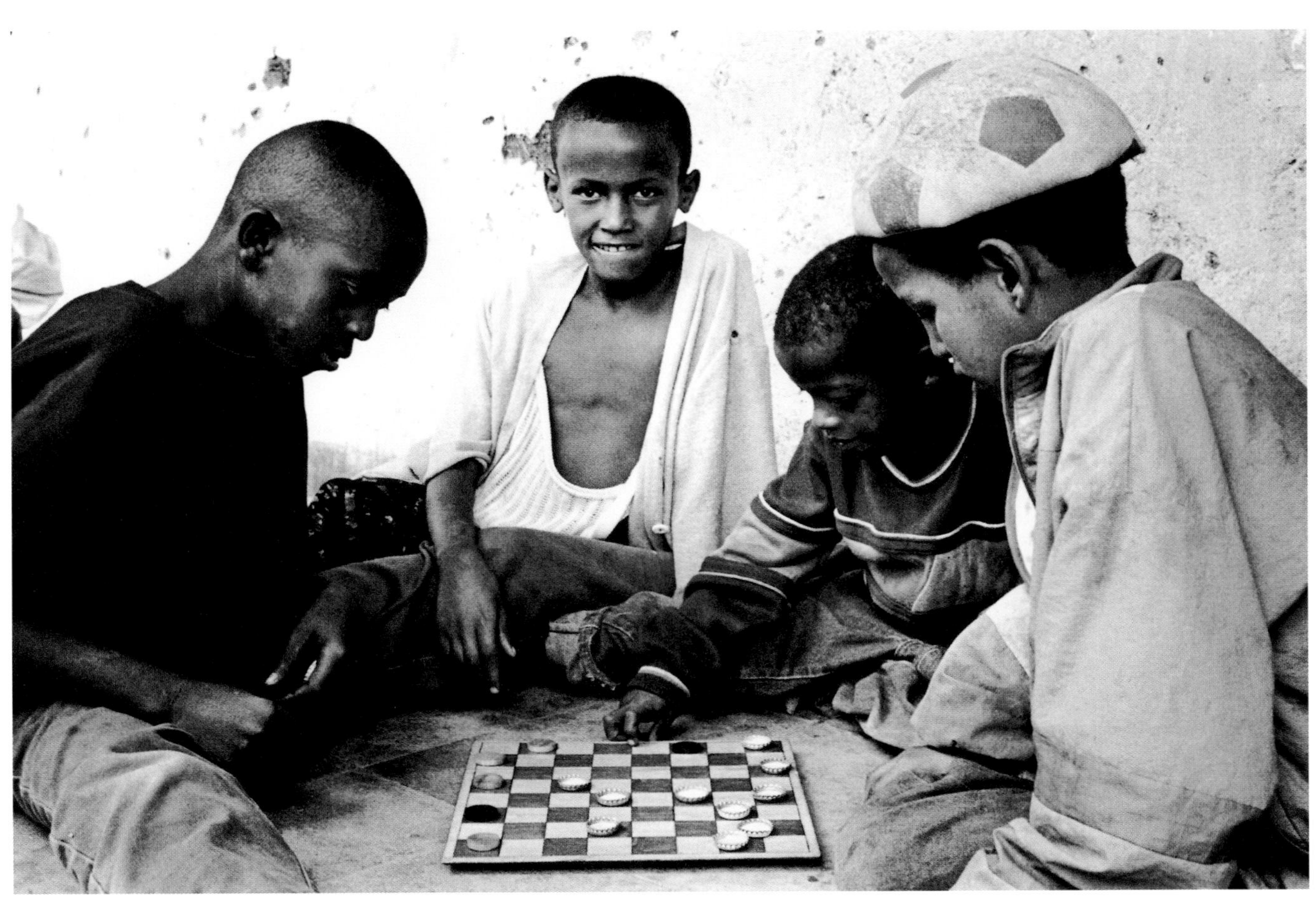

93 **DEMISSE, YEWO, MIHIRET & HABTAMU**

GOAL STREET CHILDRENS PROJECT, WOREDA 15, KEBELE 35, ADDIS ABABA, ETHIOPIA

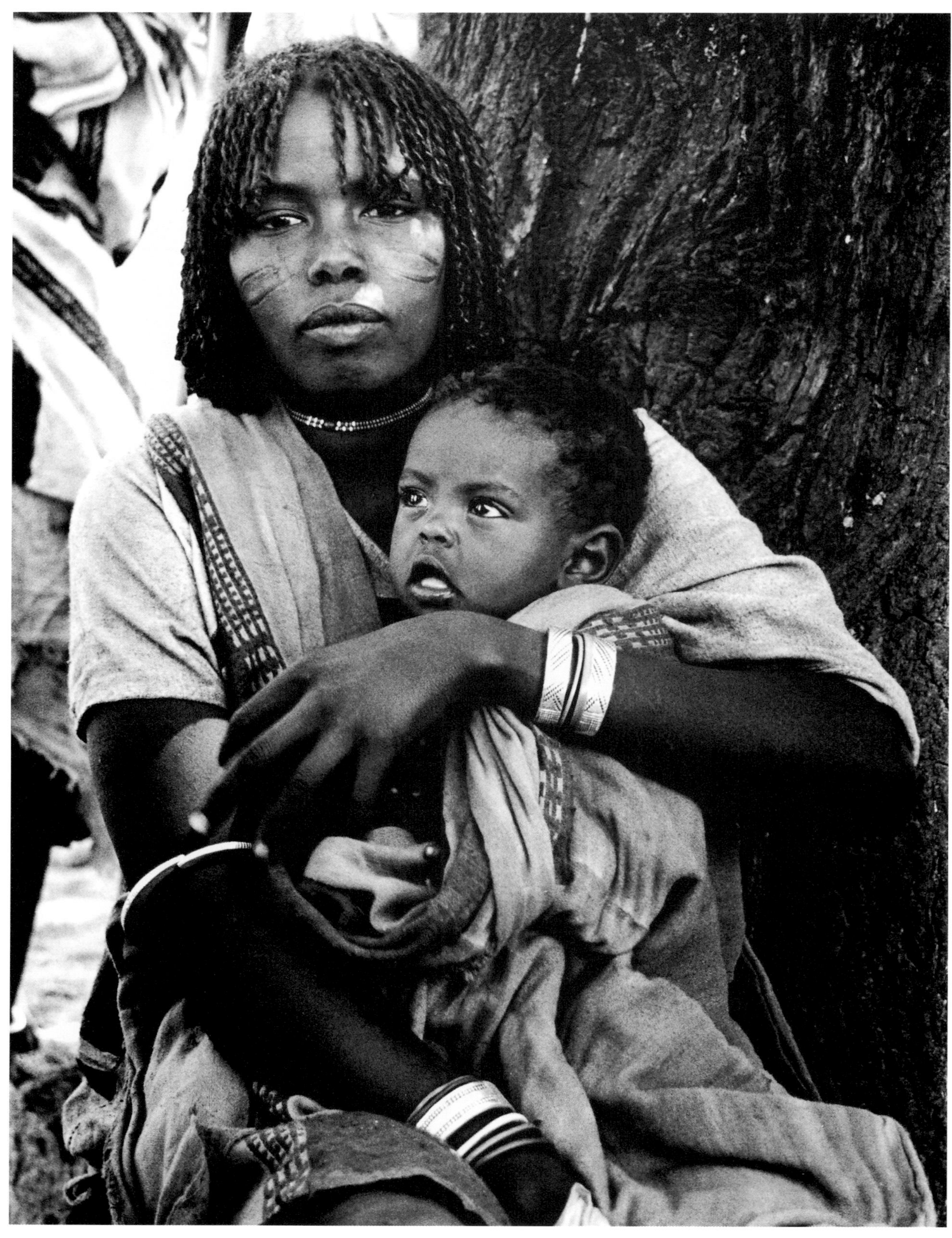

94 **LIMU GELO & SORSE TAYE**

KEREYOU TRIBE, DHEBITY, METAHARA, EAST-SHOWA, ETHIOPIA

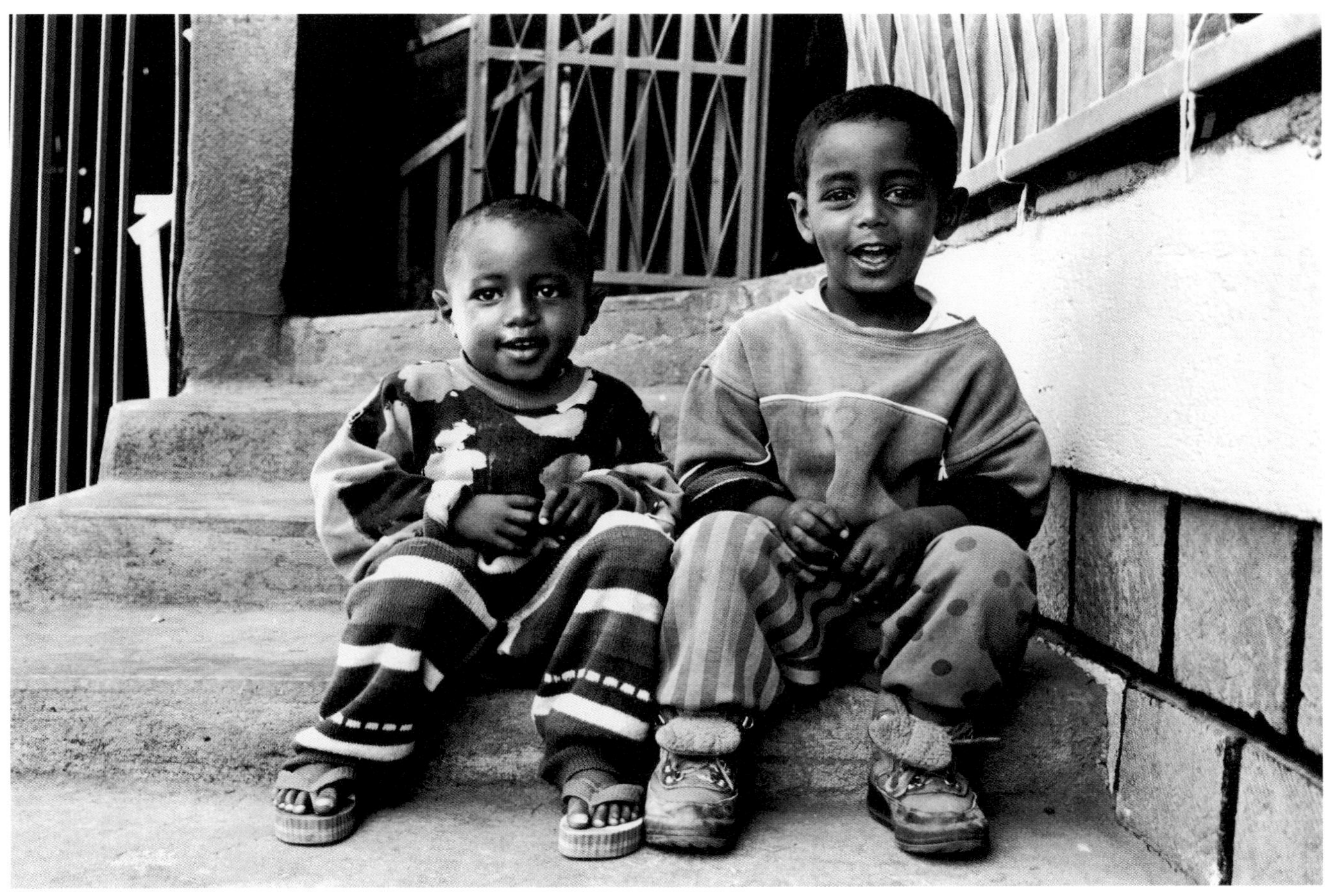

95 **HAILEMARIAM FOLENA & EYOB SENTAYEHU**

ABEBECH GOBENA ORPHANAGE & SCHOOL, ADDIS ABABA,

ETHIOPIA

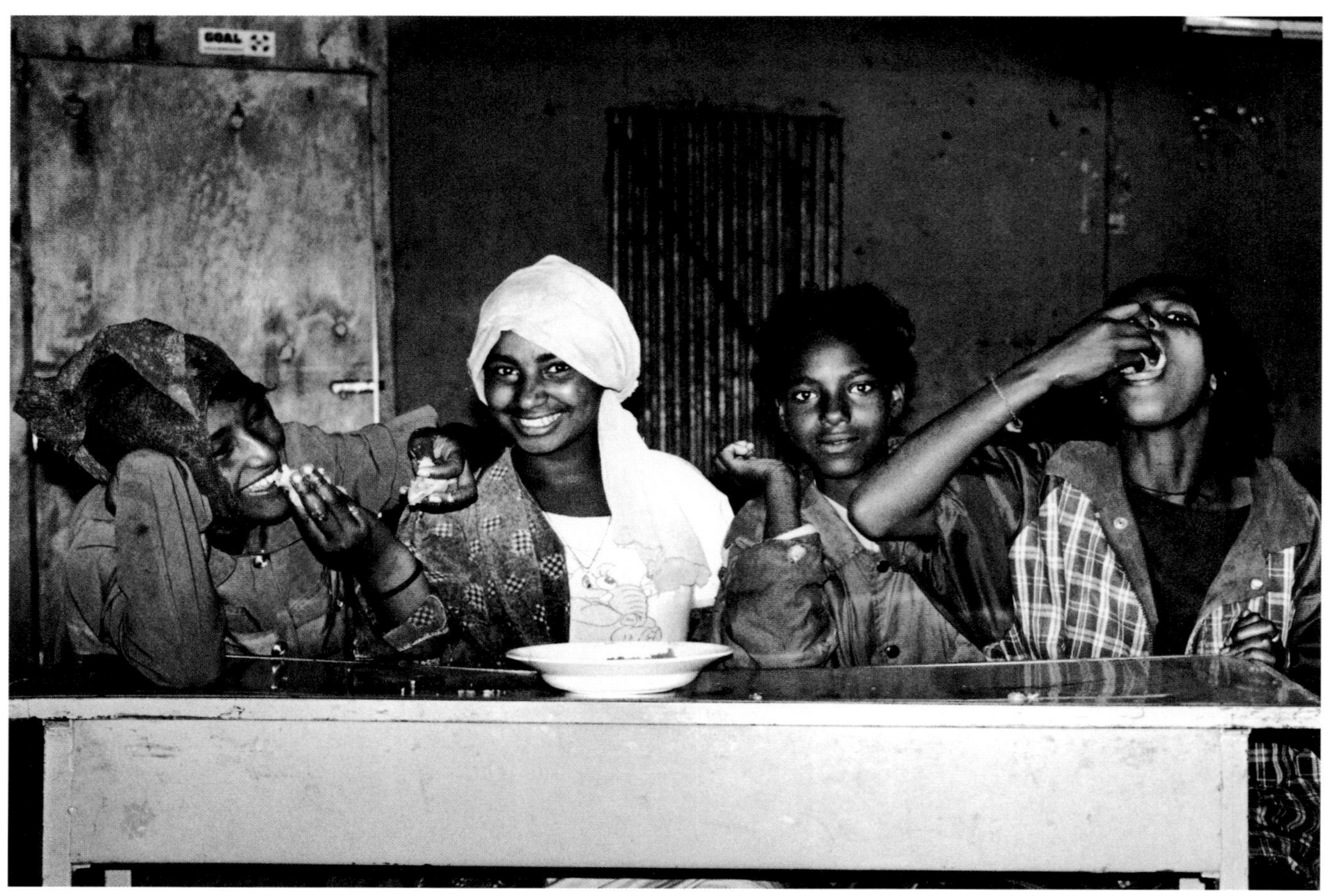

96 **MELAT, HIWOT, AYNALETN & NSRIEOT**

GOAL STREET CHILDRENS PROJECT, WOREDA 15, KEBELE 35, ADDIS ABABA, ETHIOPIA

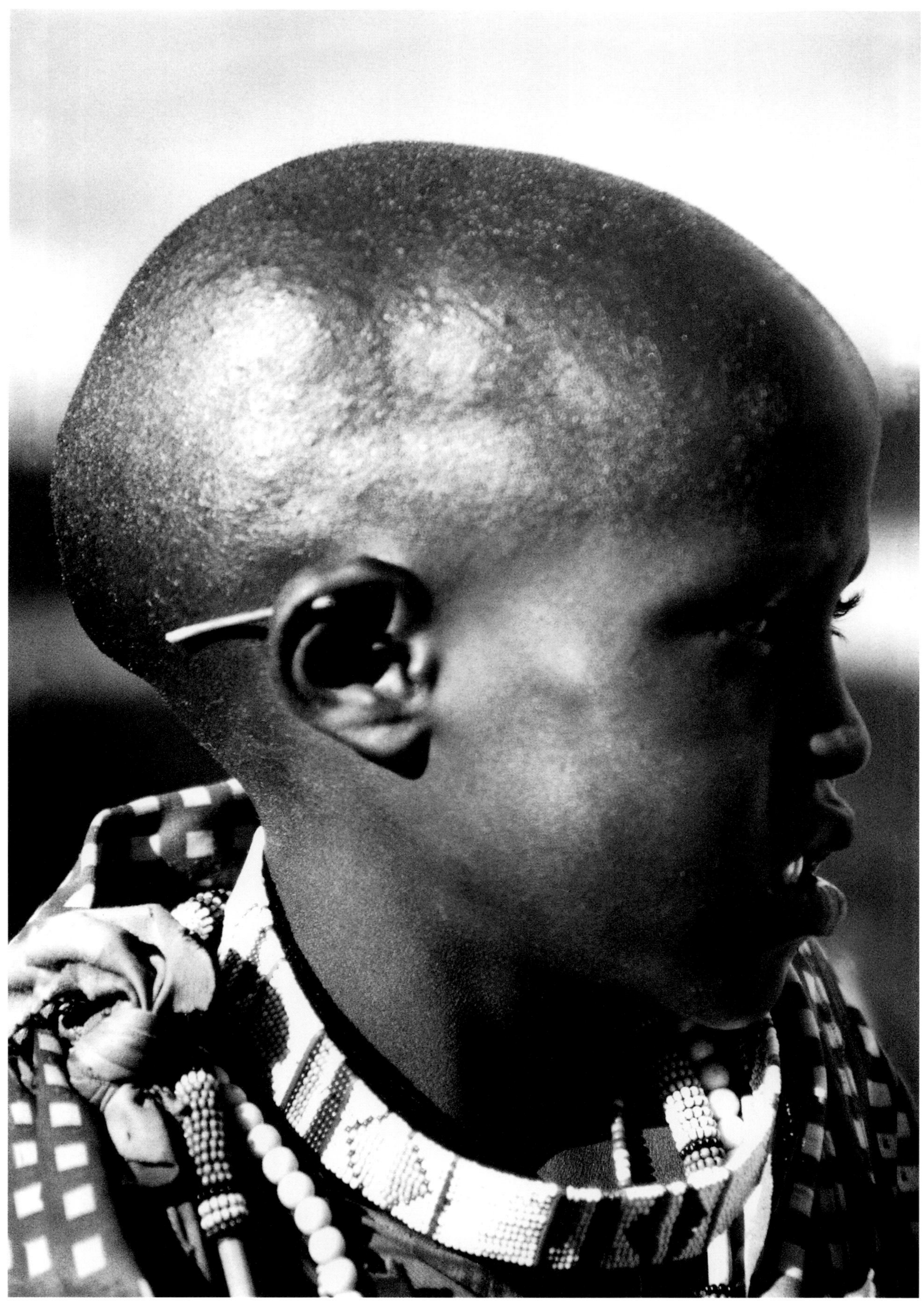

97 **ESELENKEI**

MAASAI WEDDING, LOITA HILLS, MORIJO,

KENYA

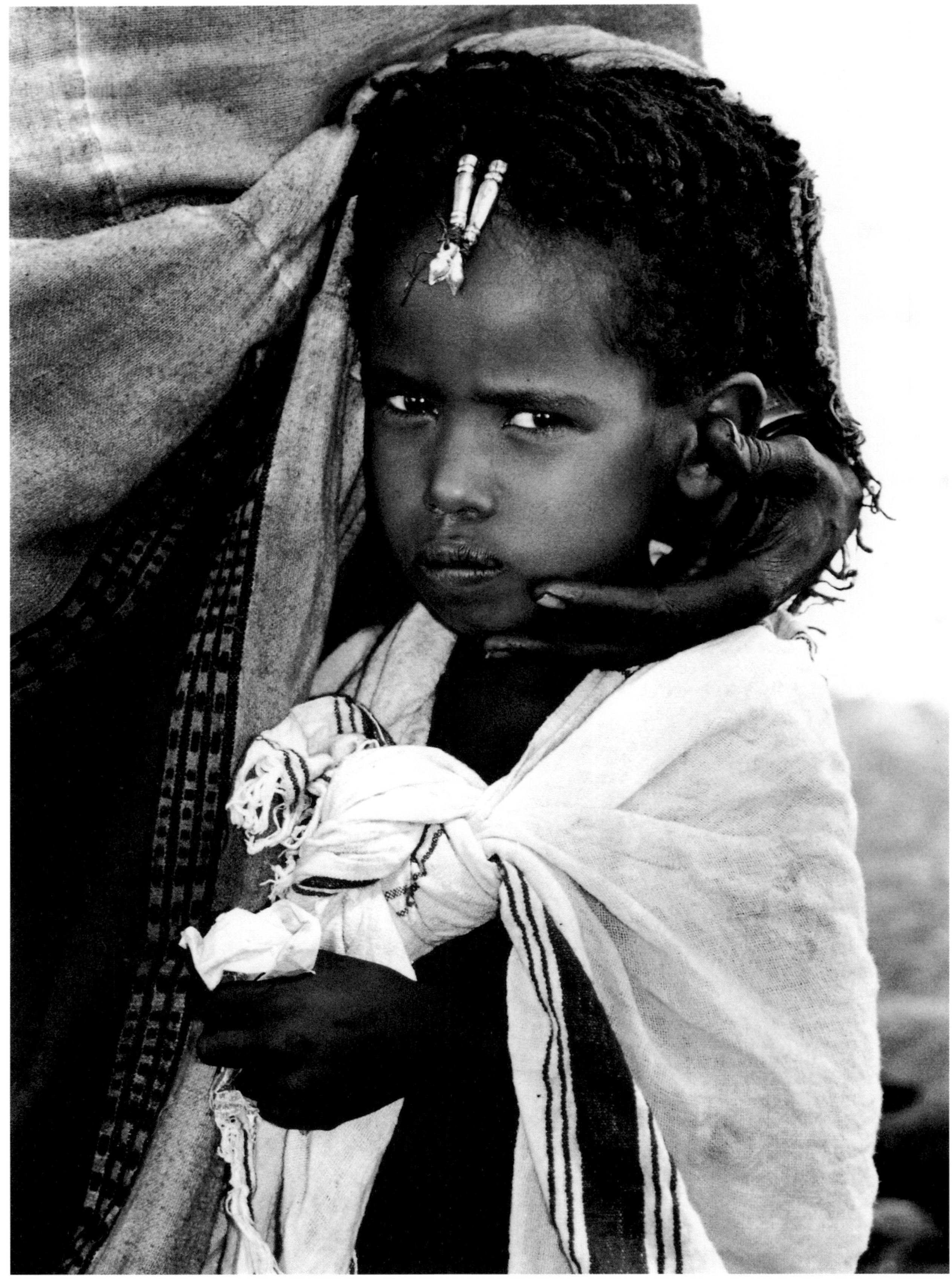

98 **AYE BORU**

KEREYOU TRIBE, DHEBITY, METAHARA, EAST-SHOWA,

ETHIOPIA

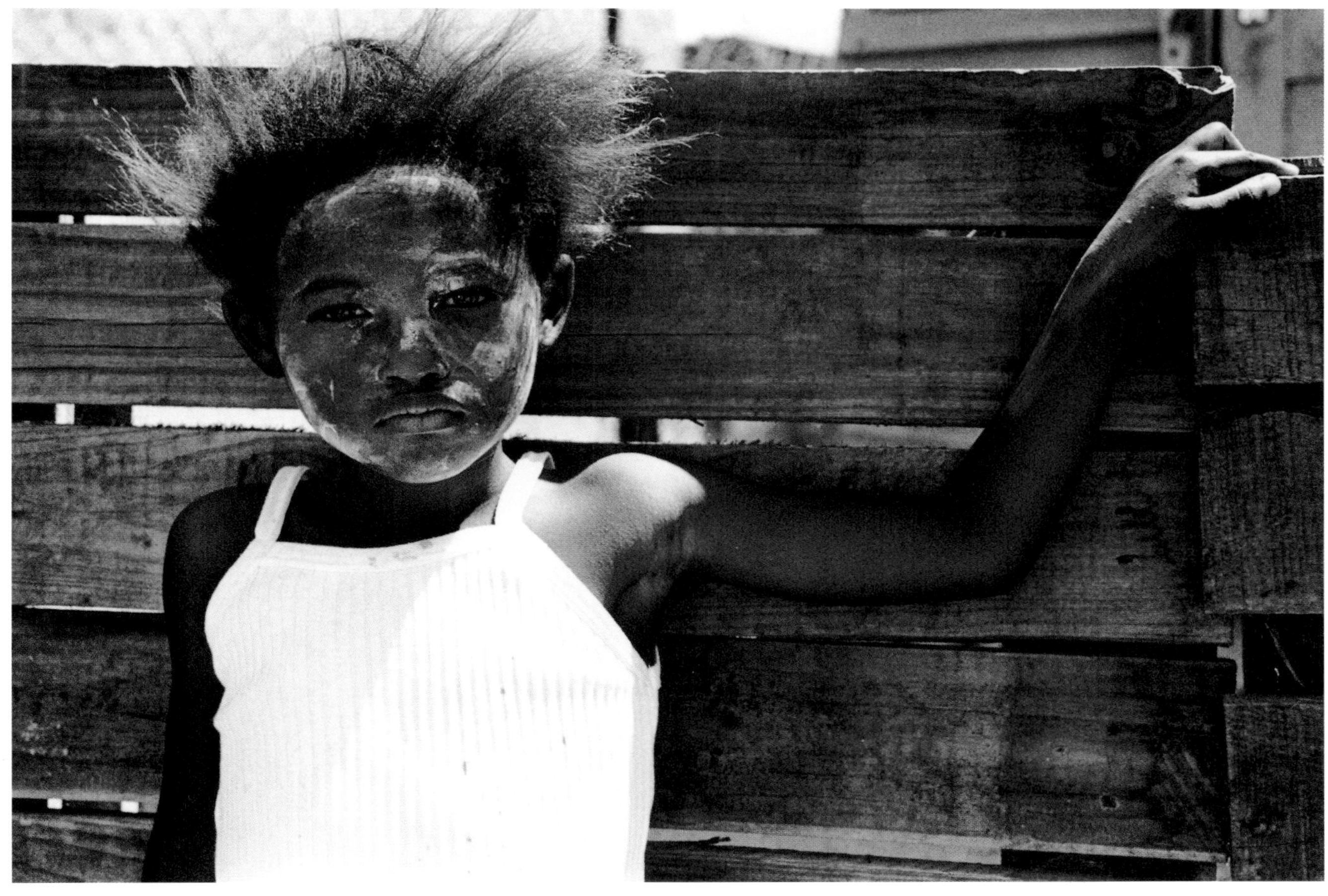

99 **NTOMBI**

LANGA TOWNSHIP, CAPE FLATS, WESTERN CAPE PROVINCE,

SOUTH AFRICA

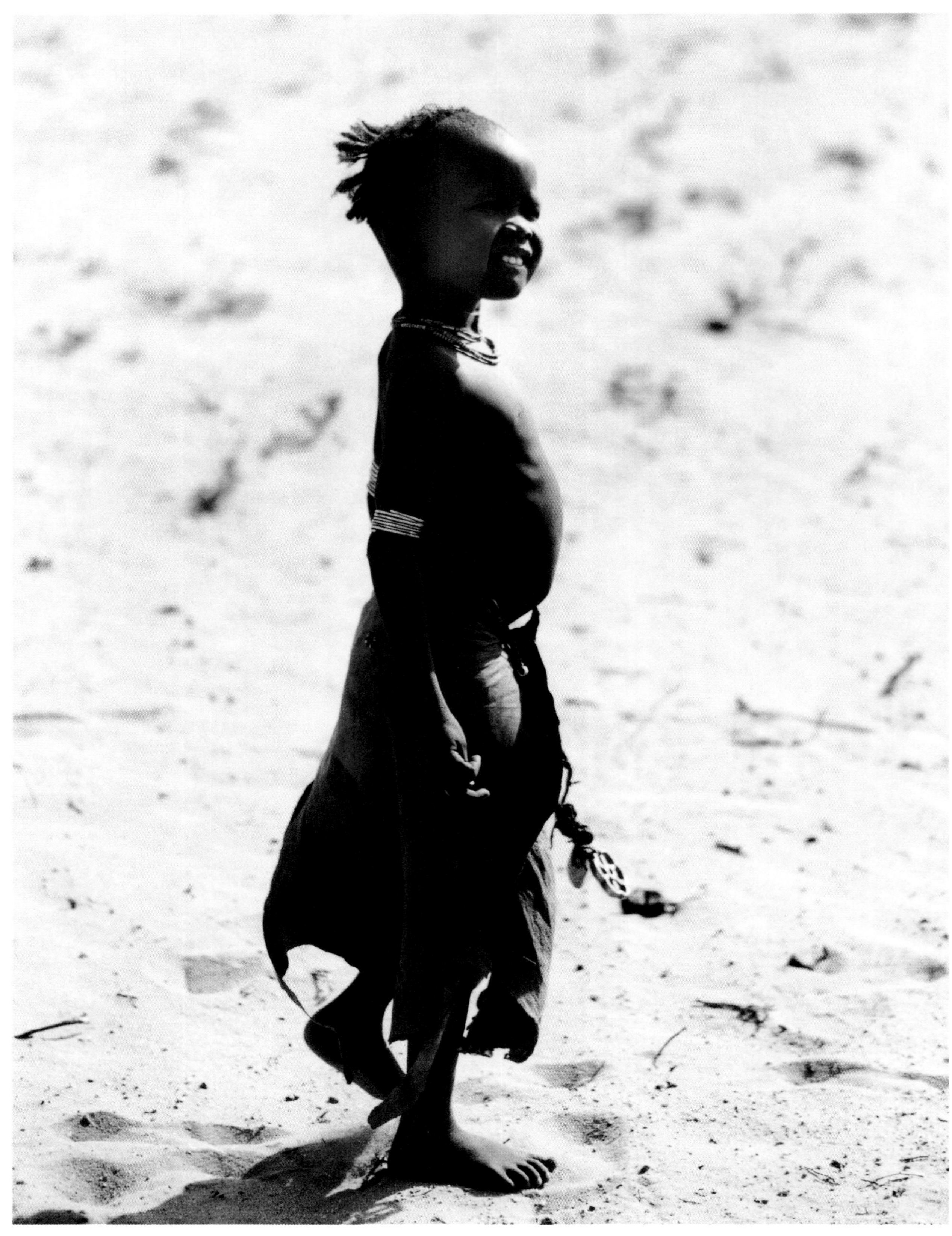

100 **NASSIA**

DAASANACH TRIBE, GAMO – GOFA,

ETHIOPIA

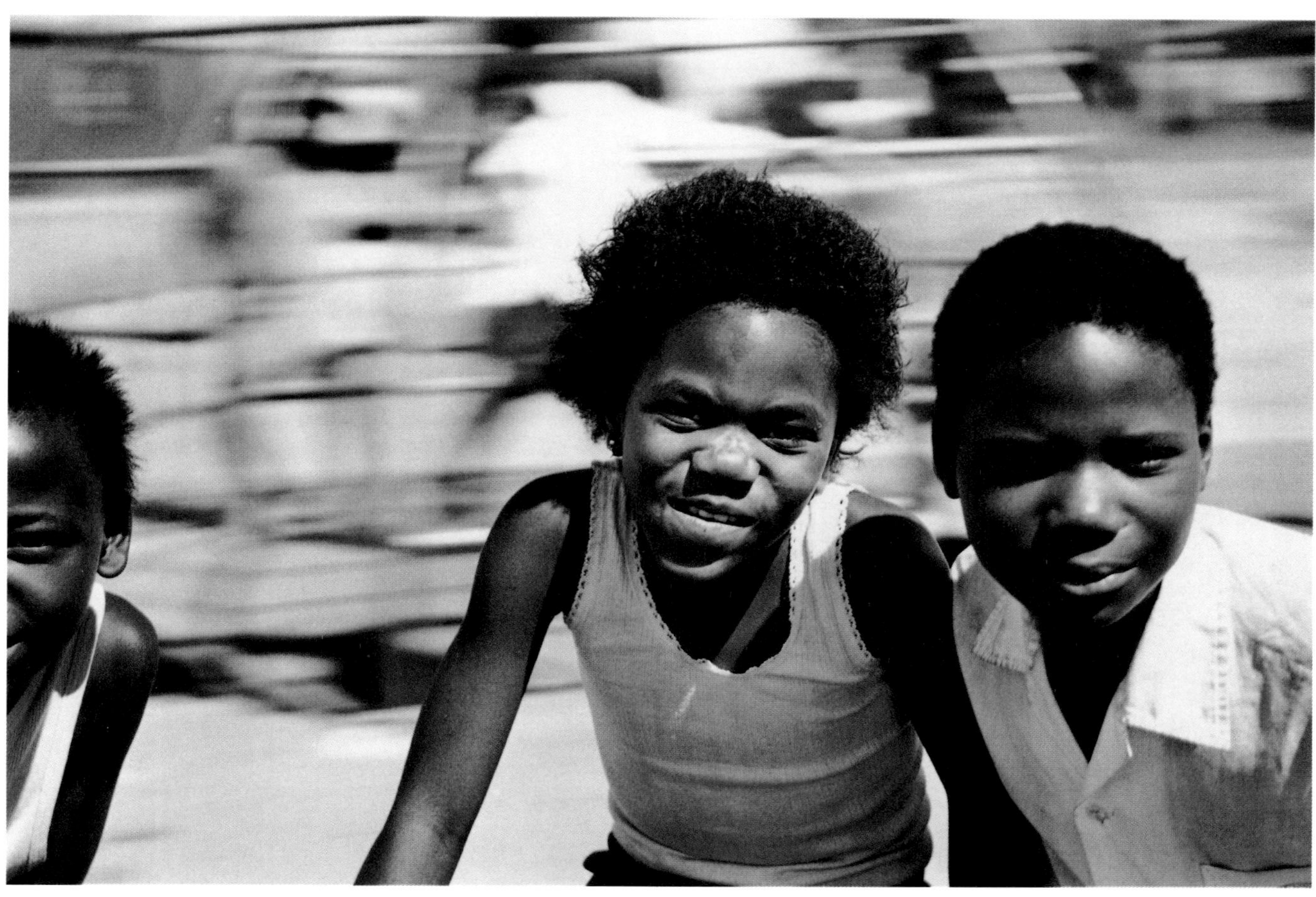

101 **KHUHULWA, ANALISA & CECEKA**

LANGA TOWNSHIP, CAPE FLATS, WESTERN CAPE PROVINCE, SOUTH AFRICA

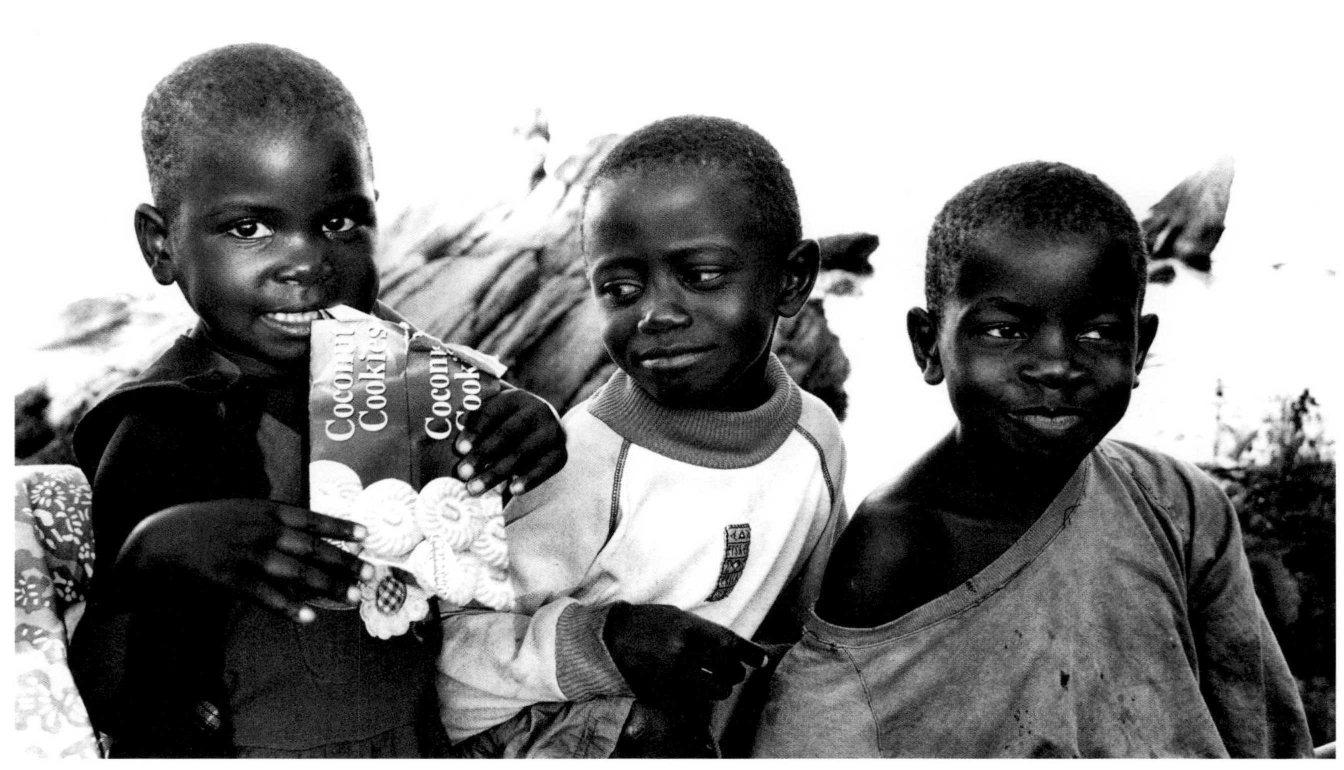

102 **FLORA, TEMWA & MALUMBO**

NKATHA BAY, NORTHERN PROVINCE,

MALAWI

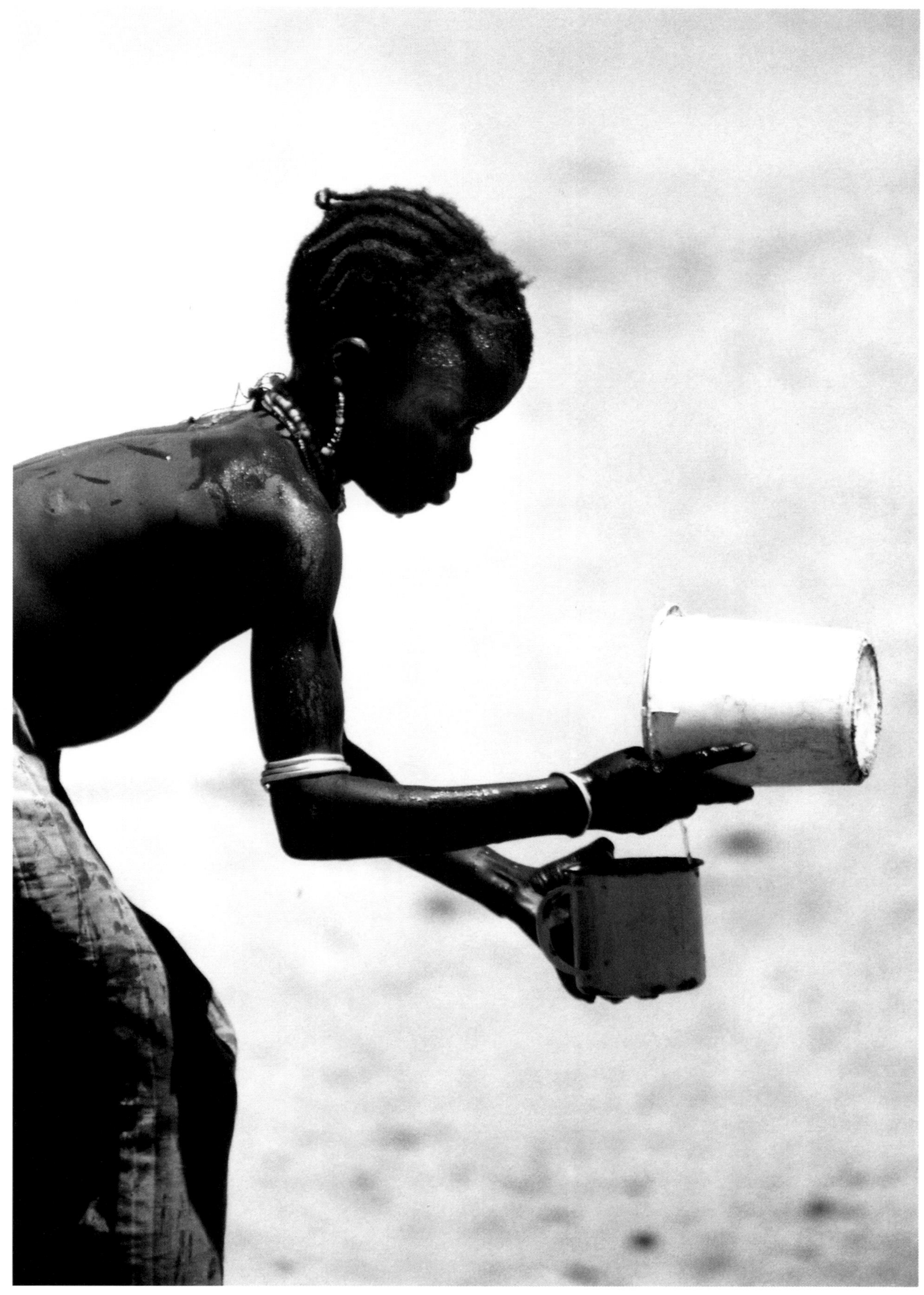

103 **NARAMA**

DAASANACH TRIBE, GAMO – GOFA,

ETHIOPIA

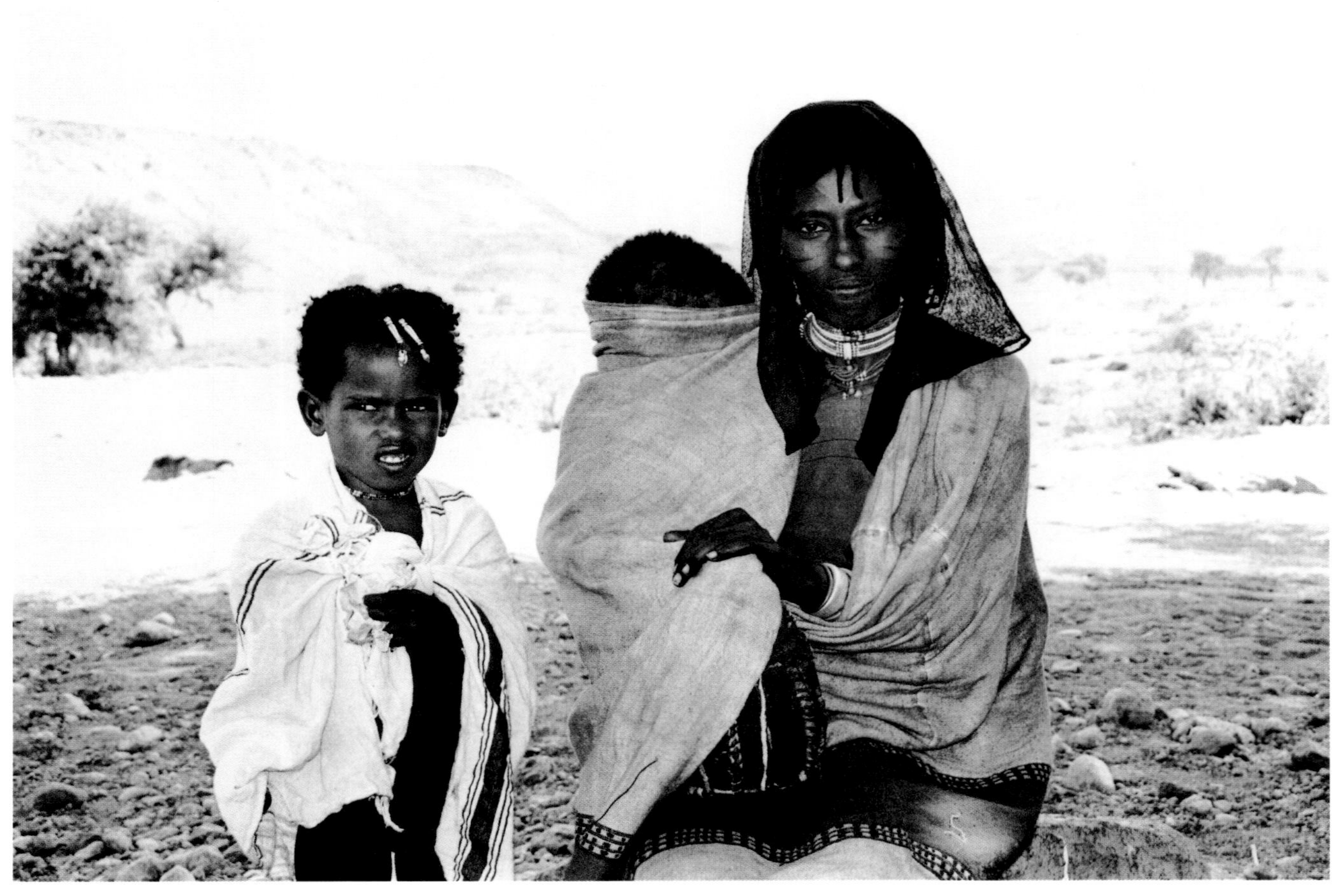

104 **GUYE ELEMO, ROBE BORU & AYE BORU**

KEREYOU TRIBE, DHEBITY, METAHARA, EAST-SHOWA, ETHIOPIA

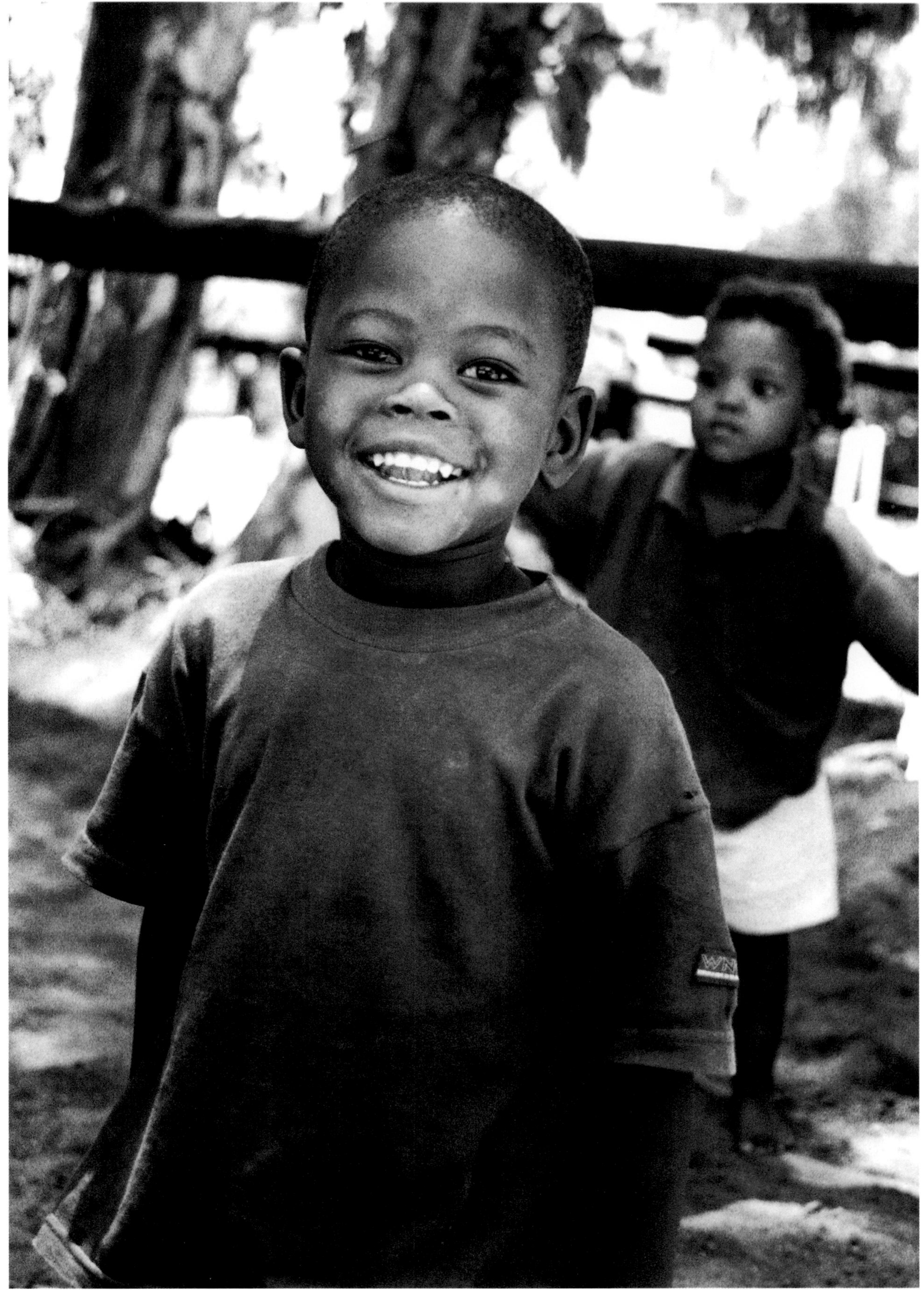

105 **SIPHO**

FOURWAYS CROSSING, JOHANNESBURG, GAUTENG,

SOUTH AFRICA

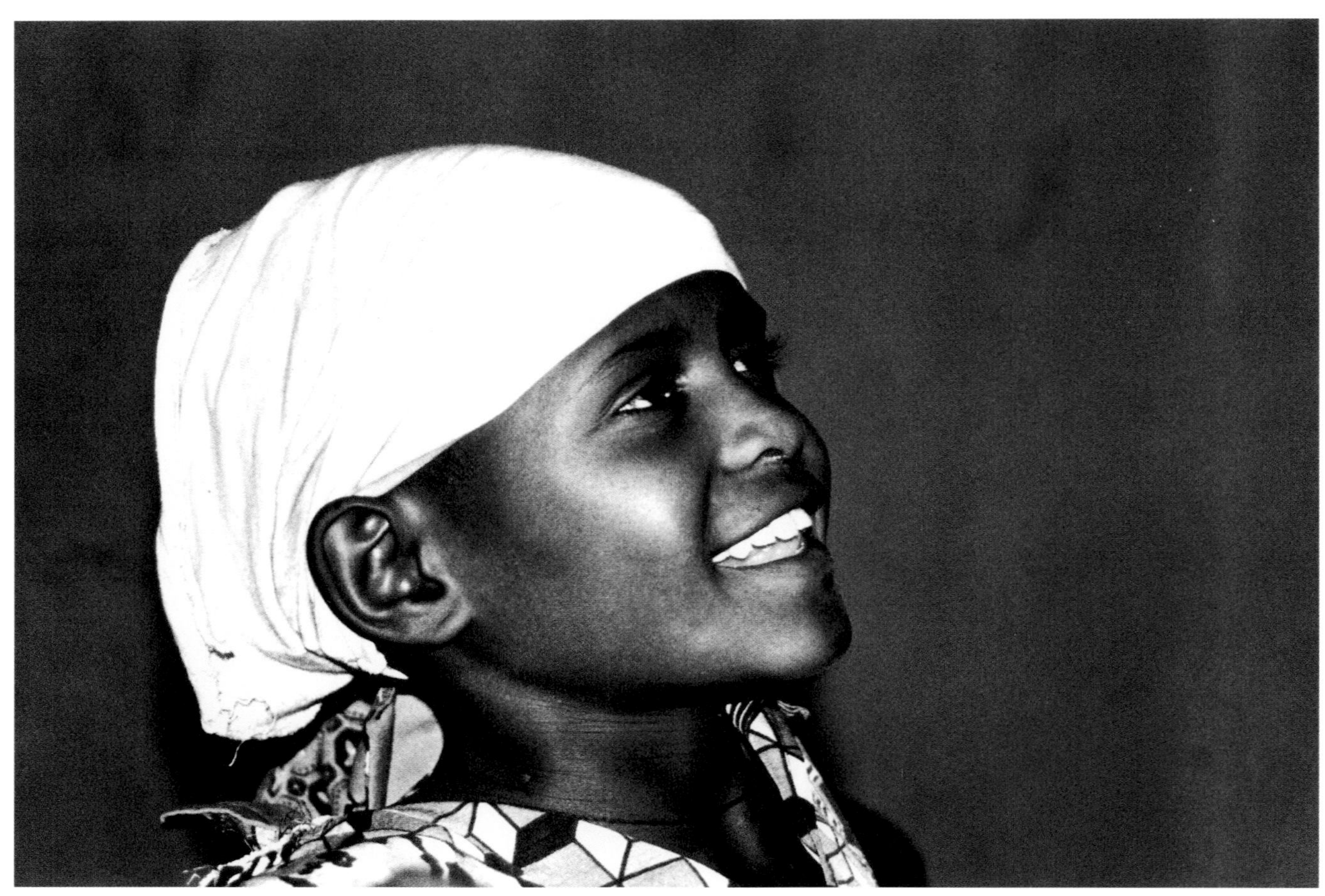

106 **MEKDES NEGUSE**

GOAL STREET CHILDRENS NIGHT SHELTER, WOREDA 21, KEBELE 13, ADDIS ABABA, ETHIOPIA

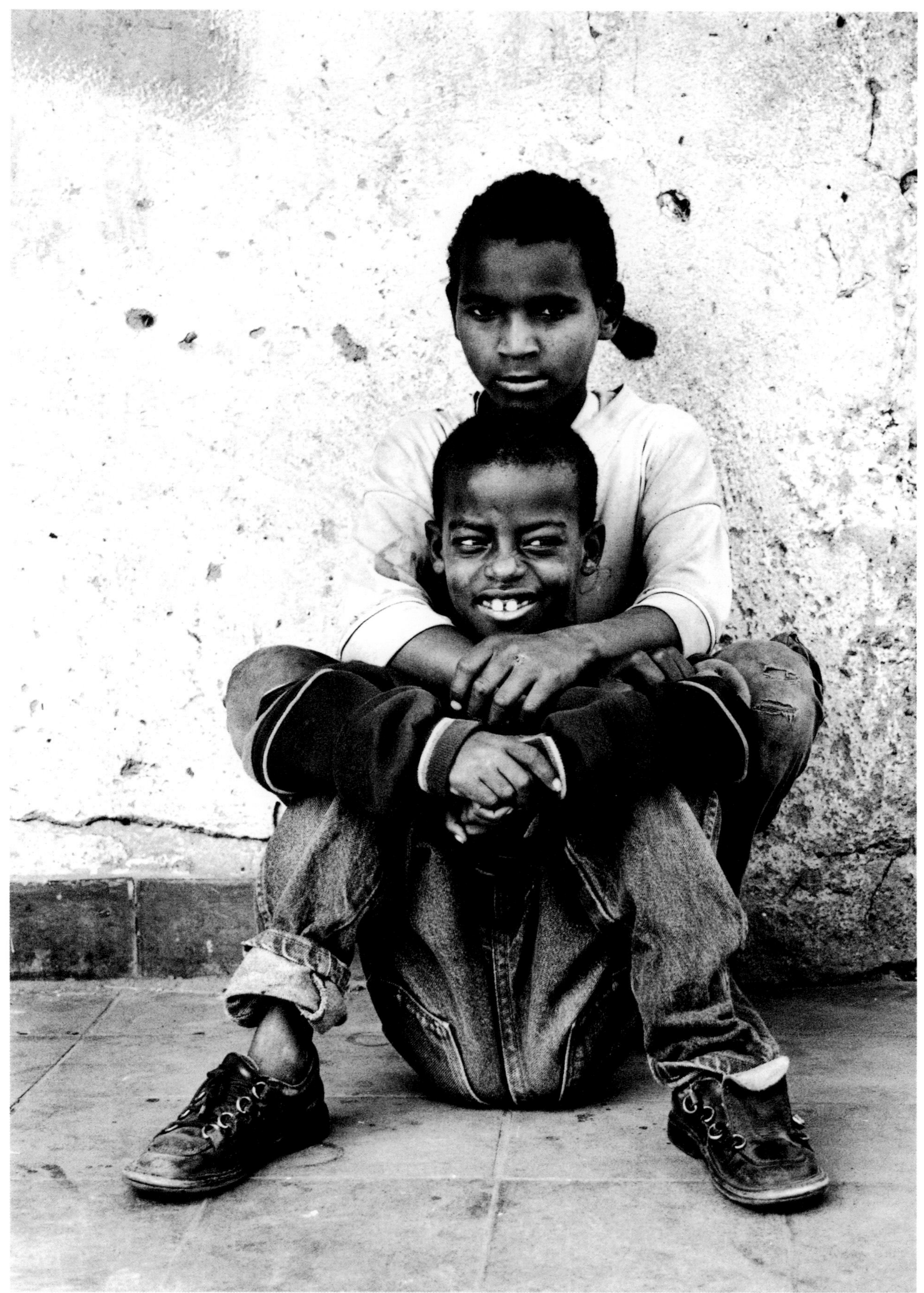

107 **MIRET & ABDURAJAK GURAGE**

GOAL STREET CHILDRENS PROJECT, WOREDA 15, KEBELE 35, ADDIS ABABA, ETHIOPIA

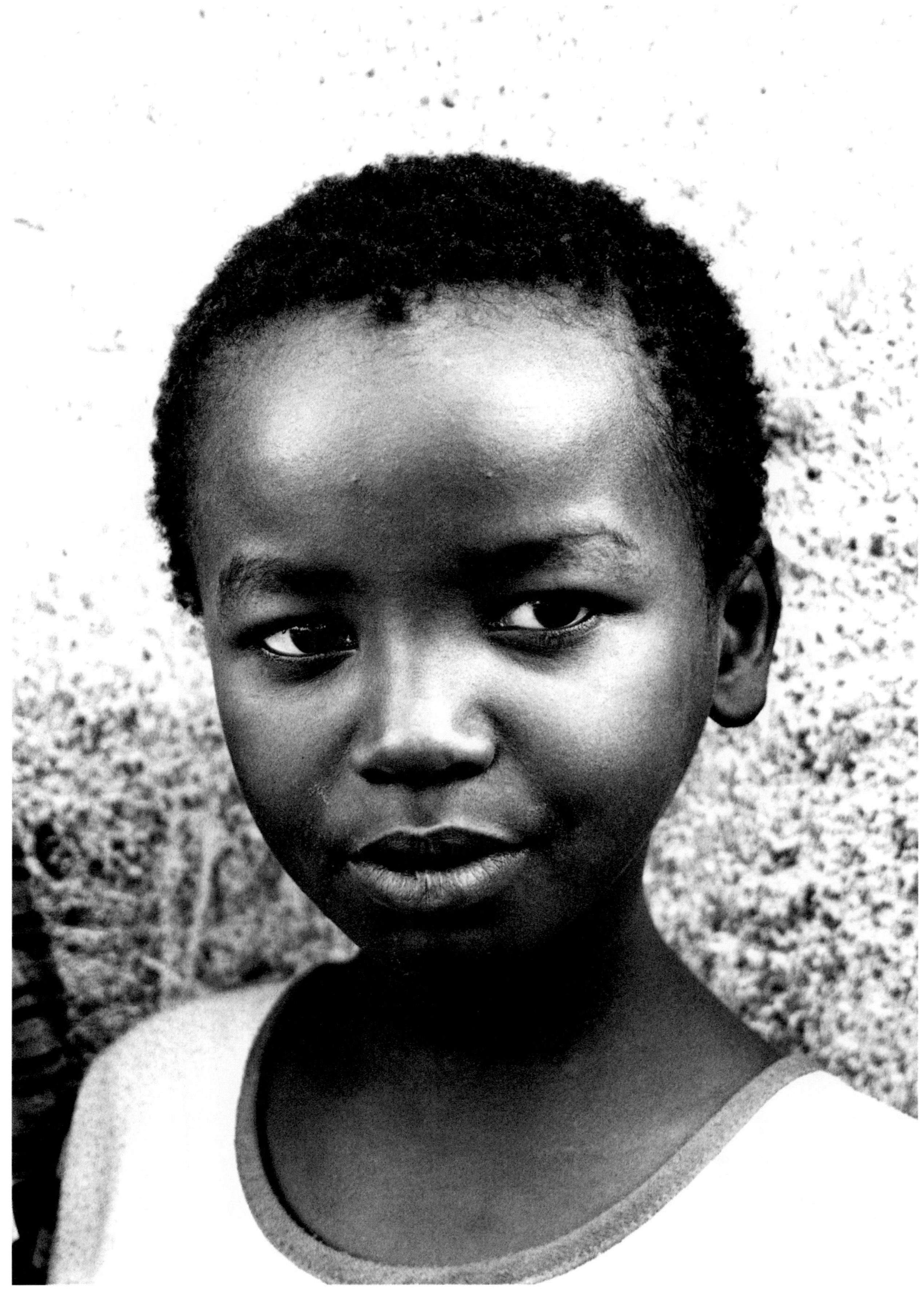

108 **MWANGI MACHARIA**

DAGORETTI CORNER STREET CHILDRENS PROJECT, NAIROBI,

KENYA

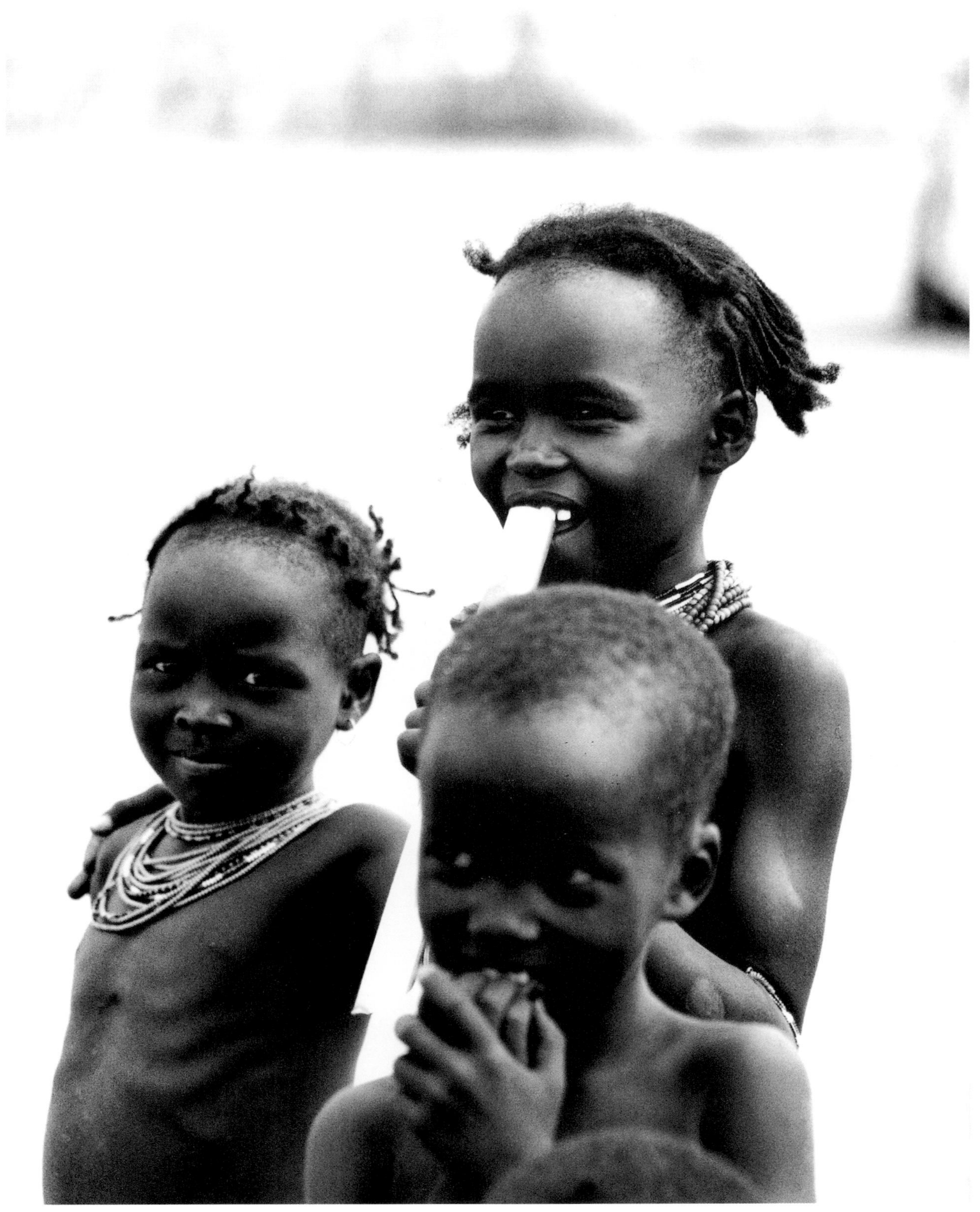

109 **AYUNI**

DAASANACH TRIBE, GAMO – GOFA,

ETHIOPIA

THE CHILDREN'S STORIES

Front Cover & 30 FATIMA
LAMU TOWN, LAMU ISLAND, KENYA
Fatima radiated great vitality, dignity and spirit. As soon as I saw her I knew that she would be perfect for the front cover – the embodiment of what I wanted to highlight in the book.

7 HANA ASEFA CHERENET
GOAL STREET CHILDRENS PROJECT, WOREDA 21, KEBELE 13, ADDIS ABABA, ETHIOPIA
Hana is one of those special kids that, if given the opportunity, would have the confidence and the ability to achieve great things. As I arrived at the street children's project, she was holding court representing her fellow street kids to the centre's staff. At 14 years of age she gave a five minute speech on why the kids on the programme who don't end up going into formal or vocational education should be supported as they end up distracting the rest of the children and unable to support themselves in the future. In addition, she highlighted that there were plenty of other children on the street who would give everything for the opportunity of a place on the programme and the chance of an education. At 9 years of age her mother died and her father kicked her out – she made her own way from Dira Dawa in the east of the country to Addis and a life on the streets. She has been with the GOAL programme on and off for about four years.

9 HAMUZA KINTU, ALEX BISO & SHARIYA BISO
BUJUGALI FALLS, NILE RIVER, JINJA, UGANDA
I met with their uncle at a fire on the banks of the Nile the night before and asked him about photographing the kids the next day for the book. I asked him to make sure that they came in their normal attire and not to make any special effort. Sure enough when they arrived the next morning they had been polished from head to toe and dressed immaculately.

10 GELLE BOSSET
KEREYOU TRIBE, DHEBITY, METAHARA, EAST-SHOWA, ETHIOPIA
Gelle is a Kereyou pastoralist nomad. Her tribe ply the arid lands around the Awash River down in the rift valley for pasture for their cattle, goats and camels. Their range area is particularly affected by drought and famine. Inter-tribal raids for cattle and women are another feature that have been part of their culture for thousands of years – only nowadays the spears and clubs have been replaced by the ubiquitous AK47.

11 ZUKO, MALIBONGWE, ATTIE, LOZO & DAKI
LANGA TOWNSHIP, CAPE FLATS, WESTERN CAPE PROVINCE, SOUTH AFRICA
These kids had managed to turn a couple of old mattresses into a playground. Zuko was the local king of spin and was trying to perfect his flip – he would like to represent South Africa in the Olympics someday.

13 TRISTAN SHAXSON
MOUNT SELINDA, MANICALAND, ZIMBABWE
Tristan's photo usually receives great surprise from viewers in the first world yet in many senses he is as African as every other child in this book. His preferred language is Shona and he is very much a part of the country's landscape. In keeping with a lot of the other kids along my route his future is unpredictable at best.

15 MAASAI INKERA
KANJIRO SENETO MAASAI BOMA, NGORONGORO, TANZANIA
These Maasai kids live a very traditional life looking after their family's herds. Their lifestyle has been largely unchanged for thousands of years. Basic education is starting to feature for some of the boys but the girls are largely expected to stay within the Boma or homestead to work. In Africa, like other pastoralists, the Maasai are highly susceptible to ravages of drought and famine.

16 ZERIHUN MENGESTE
GOAL STREET CHILDRENS PROJECT, WOREDA 21, KEBELE 13, ADDIS ABABA, ETHIOPIA
Zerihun's parents both died in 1996. He was on the streets for a while and joined the GOAL street kids programme for about a year – he eventually dropped out because of peer pressure. He occasionally attends the drop in centre. He's now 13-years-old.

19 EDAPAL EKWAKOL
TURKANA TRIBE, LOKALALEI, WEST TURKANA, RIFT VALLEY PROVINCE, KENYA
Edapal and his family live in one of the worst drought affected areas of the continent. Living by the Lomekwi laga, a dry riverbed on the west side of Lake Turkana, his family have lost much of their livestock to the drought and rely heavily on food programme handouts. Their government has largely forgot them and Edapal considers Kenya to be some far off place near Nairobi.

20 BEHAILU GEBESA, YETAYU LEYEKUN, BELELEGNE ABESA & HUSEN JEMALE
STREET KIDS, BOLE ROAD, ADDIS ABABA, ETHIOPIA
During the days its not so bad, but in the rainy season and at night time it can get very cold on the streets – Addis is the third highest city in the world at 2'500 metres asl. When it's cold you will normally find street kids huddled together for warmth and the safety of numbers.

21 PATIENCE, ORBIN, DIOS & ISAAC
LAKE BUNYONYI ROAD, KEBELE, UGANDA
As tough as it may seem, in the context of some of the other children in this book, these kids have a reasonable life labouring on the roads around their village. The main problem is that they miss quite a bit of school and end up with low levels of literacy. Isaac's mangled toe is also a painful reminder of the perils of his job.

23 FAITH
CHINOTIMBA TOWNSHIP, MATABELELAND NORTH, ZIMBABWE
Faith was found at three months of age in a plastic bag in the township dump. She was in very bad shape when she was brought to the hospital. The nurses and staff christened her Faith on account of her circumstances. Normally she lies listlessly in her cot waiting for someone to pick her up and give her some affection. On doing so the change in her is incredible, she becomes instantly animated. Full of smiles and life... until it's time to go and the tears begin.

24 NAKWAR AND FRIEND
DAASANACH REFUGEES, GAMO – GOFA, ETHIOPIA
For the desert pastoralists of Africa, water is the primary focus of everyday life. It's liquid gold. Like most work in Africa, the collection and management of this valuable resource is left in the hands of the females – you can see the care that Nakwar is exercising in its collection. The Daasanach from Southern Ethiopia and Northern Kenya have always suffered greatly from the droughts and resultant famines that plague their corner of the world.

25 LUNGISA IBHAYISIKILI
KHAYELITSHA TOWNSHIP, CAPE FLATS, WESTERN CAPE PROVINCE, SOUTH AFRICA
The kids of South Africa's townships have a very different set of problems to contend with. As you can see with the bikes and the shoes, they have greater access to resources than most of their contemporaries further north. However, they have to contend with the social problems manifest in communities suffering from chronic levels of crime, high unemployment and a HIV/Aids epidemic of monstrous proportions. These problems are hugely exacerbated by weapons saturation unseen in any other country not at war on the continent.

26 ATHMAN
LAMU TOWN, LAMU ISLAND, KENYA
Athman was a real character. As soon as he heard that a Mzungu was in town taking photos of kids he made it his business to become part of the circus. At one stage, I couldn't reach for my camera without him trying to muscle into centre frame. This is the only shot I have of him unaware – it's a little soft but I like it. I nicknamed him Hollywood – by the end of the day all the kids were calling him by that name. He was a born showman.

27 ROBERT ZEWIS
GLUE SNIFFING STREET KID, NAIROBI, KENYA
Robert is one of the thousands of street kids that deal with life on the streets of Nairobi by sniffing glue. It just about makes a life of random violence, rape & sexual abuse, petty crime and begging tolerable. Without family to fall back on they are treated as pariahs by most people – they have a few friends within the local and the international community. However the reality is it's hard to get off the street. It is estimated that there are between 20'000 and 30'000 street kids in Nairobi.

28 GENOCIDE ORPHAN

KIGALI, RWANDA

This poor guys name became a smudge in a soggy notebook. His African name was too difficult to remember, unlike his story. He like tens of thousands of others lost his parents in the genocide. He managed to survive by playing dead under the weight of his dead family's corpses until nightfall before making off in the dark. He survives on the streets of Kigali like all the other kids – another victim of Rwandan violence and the great first world's apathy.

29 NELOITA

MAASAI WEDDING, LOITA HILLS, MORIJO, KENYA

13-year-old Neloita is just about to be married. In keeping with Maasai cultural tradition, she has been circumcised to ensure her virginity and chastity for her 49 year old husband who has taken her as a second wife. His daughter from his first wife is older. Female circumcision or Female Genital Mutilation (FGM) is without doubt the single biggest crime (from a long list) committed against women in Africa.

31 STEVEN KARIKO

MIDDLE OF THE DESERT, DAMARALAND, NAMIBIA

Steven is a 4-year-old from Darmaraland in Namibia. He wants to be a teacher when he grows up. If you ask a kid in Africa what they'd like to do when they grow up chances are it will be a career that allows them to give something back to their community. His leg scar healed up eventually without any stitches.

33 LONGUTT

KANJIRO SENETO MAASAI BOMA, NGORONGORO, TANZANIA

As you can see by the weathering on 3-year-old Longutt's hand the Serengeti receives all of the elements in the extreme. Throughout each year, as he tends the family animals, he must endure the blistering heat, shattering cold, phenomenal floods and then drought conditions – not to mention predators such as lion, leopard, cheetah and hyena to name a few.

34 MUSA ASEFA

STREET KID, FOOTBALL STADIUM, ADDIS ABABA, ETHIOPIA

Like most of the estimated 40'000 street kids in Addis Ababa, Musa isn't in a street kid's programme. He spends all of his time on the street pitting his wits against everything just to survive. For the majority of kids in his situation that means a life of begging, petty crime and prostitution – whatever it takes to survive.

36 JOHN MWANGI

GLUE SNIFFING STREET KID, NAIROBI, KENYA

When we were photographing John he was barely lucid but he kept insisting on having his picture taken. His friends were in slightly better shape and could talk coherently in Kiswahili. He had been on the street a long time and couldn't deal with life on the street without sniffing glue.

39 YONAS GIZAW

GOAL STREET CHILDRENS PROJECT, WOREDA 21, KEBELE 13, ADDIS ABABA, ETHIOPIA

Both of his parents died when he was about 6 years of age. He had a grandmother but she was too old to work so he hit the streets to try and support her. He joined the GOAL street kids project in 1998 and is doing well in school. He has a sister somewhere but has no way of finding her. He wants to finish his education and go into business for himself.

41 JOSEPH

TURKANA TRIBE, LOKALALEI, WEST TURKANA, RIFT VALLEY PROVINCE, KENYA

We had to fly up and rescue an American geologist who's Landrover had broken down in the middle of nowhere north west of Lake Turkana. After a bush landing and a hike through the drought stricken desert we located the Landrover and Bob Campbell, it's proud owner, began to play doctor on it. After half an hour Joseph appeared from nowhere – a herder without a herd. He hung around for a while amused at the goings on and then just took off and vanished back into the desert.

45 ABERASH LEGESSE

GOAL STREET CHILDRENS PROJECT, WOREDA 21, KEBELE 13, ADDIS ABABA, ETHIOPIA

Aberash was one of the real characters at the street kids programme. She joined it in 1998 at the age of 12. When her father died Aberash and her mother left Wellega province and came to Addis to find her brother. They survived by begging on the street and eventually found the brother after two years. She is attending formal school and doing very well.

49 KORINYANG

DAASANACH TRIBE, GAMO – GOFA, ETHIOPIA

Korinyang is a Daasanach pastoralist from the Ethiopian / Kenyan border area. Her family traditionally range their animals back and forth across the border depending on available forage. It was one of the worst hit regions in the drought that afflicted a large part of the horn of Africa last year. She is suffering from kwashikor or malnutrition but is receiving foodaid at a feeding station in Ileret. She and many other Daasanach children attend the school in Ileret. Part of the proceeds of this book will go to building a new school for these children. In January this year the rains finally came and the Daasanach returned to their range, secure in their existence – until the next drought.

52 NAKWAN

TURKANA TRIBE, ILERET, MARSABIT DISTRICT, EASTERN PROVINCE, KENYA

Nakwan, meaning pale child in Kiturkana, set about his business with an air of confidence and pride befitting someone at the top of their game. A brief acknowledgement and he was on his way. Completely unfazed by the presence of a camera.

54 NAHIDA, ALYA & SADIA

LAMU TOWN, LAMU ISLAND, KENYA

Nahida and Alya took turns in hiding behind Sadia as she constantly tried to stare me out. It would last for about a minute before we all gave in to fits of laughter. Sixty seconds later, recomposed, off she'd go again.

55 HACKO ROBA, GELE JICCO & GUYE ROBA

KEREYOU TRIBE, DHEBITY, METAHARA, EAST-SHOWA, ETHIOPIA

When I first met with the Kereyou they were attending a GOAL operated field clinic under a tree in the bush – some had walked twenty kilometres to attend. I approached the matriarch about the book and she was intrigued by the shots that I showed her of the kids along my route from South Africa. However she let me know in no uncertain terms that their children were off limits as far as photographs were concerned. Thinking that it was taboo, I of course accepted her wishes and left Ato Bekale to translate my apologies and thanks. After five minutes of frantic conversation between the two of them I discovered that her reasons were not cultural after all. In times past some other white visitor had taken their photos and promised to send them on a copy – they never materialised. Here was a group of people with absolutely nothing who'd allowed a foreigner to photograph them and, like most of the time, they had been let down by them. Once they realised I was with GOAL and they accepted my promise to send them a complete set of copies, the matriarch quickly set about turning the field clinic into an outdoor studio. She had decided that every Kereyou in running distance was going to have their photo taken that day. You can see by this shot the different reactions I got – I'm not sure if it was me or because the old woman was ordering the girls around and telling them what to do.

59 SCHOOL CHILDREN

SALAM BIRR ELEMENTARY SCHOOL, WOREDA 24, KEBELE 9, ADDIS ABABA, ETHIOPIA

Thanks to the Women and Childrens Development Organisation (WCDO), an indigenous NGO, these children get to attend formal school on a fully sponsored programme. Their families are not in a position to pay for their education but the programme provides each child with a years tuition, books, a school uniform, lunch every day and a school bag. There are over 100 children in this WCDO programme which costs approximately £4'000 a year to run.

60 LAURA MABHENA

CHINOTIMBA TOWNSHIP, MATABELELAND NORTH, ZIMBABWE

If you ask any kid in an urban environment in southern Africa what it is they would like to do when they finish school, chances are they will come up with going on to be a teacher or a nurse or a doctor or a policeman. Laura on the other hand was quite sure that she wanted to be a super model. It was Laura's mother Violet who brought me around the township.

61 AYANTU JICCO, BEUITE TEDECHO & BERITE KUBI

KEREYOU TRIBE, DHEBITY, METAHARA, EAST-SHOWA, ETHIOPIA

Ayantu and her grandchildren had to walk a twenty kilometre roundtrip through the mid morning heat of the desert to visit the GOAL field clinic. The clinic travels to thirty different outreach locations every month providing medical treatment and health education for the Kereyou people.

65 GUYE ROBA

KEREYOU TRIBE, DHEBITY, METAHARA, EAST-SHOWA, ETHIOPIA

When most Kereyou girls reach the age of thirteen or fourteen their families will organise an arranged marriage for them. Their potential suitor could range in age from his early twenties to his early sixties. Aside from the substantial age gap the girls often go into marriage without any advice or education as to what lies ahead. Guye is 13-years-old.

68 GINA & ANASTASIA

GLUE SNIFFING MOTHER & CHILD, NAIROBI, KENYA

Without doubt this is one of the saddest photos in the book. At 15 year's of age Gina is a glue sniffer and mother trying to get by on the streets of Nairobi. She became pregnant with Anastasia after being raped. It's people in her circumstances that really need help.

72 PRIORITY NDEBELE

CHINOTIMBA TOWNSHIP, MATABELELAND NORTH, ZIMBABWE

Priority was born with a club-foot. He was recently given an oversize pair of sneakers that he is very proud of – he has also discovered to the amusement of his friends that running in oversize shoes can be a calamitous affair.

74 MAJAHANA NGWENYA

CHINOTIMBA TOWNSHIP, MATABELELAND NORTH, ZIMBABWE

Majahana was born one hundred percent healthy. He had to go in for a simple hernia operation just after he was born and complications occurred. He is now paralysed and suffers from brain damage.

75 OLGOLMONI

MAASAI WEDDING, LOITA HILLS, MORIJO, KENYA

As a Maasai male, Olgolmoni will pass through a number of eight year age sets on his path to being an elder. He has recently been initiated into the Moran or warrior age set where he will undergo an established set of rituals on his route to manhood. Traditionally the morani leave their families between the age of 14 and 22 after their circumcision ceremony to spend the next eight years amongst other warriors in their own manyatta or village. It is only when they pass through this age set and become an elder that they are eligible for marriage.

83 VIOLET MOYO, MARGARET & FAMILY

CHINOTIMBA TOWNSHIP, MATABELELAND NORTH, ZIMBABWE

Violet works occasionally for a safari company and Margaret is a schoolteacher in the township's primary school. Both of them brought me around the township to help with the book. As a separate settlement to the town of nearby Victoria Falls, it is a legacy from the days of Rhodesia. Since independence it has flourished into a thriving town in its own right with far greater atmosphere and charm than it's neighbouring tourist trap and it's transient inhabitants. Chinotimba has been badly hit by the fall in tourism since Comrade Bob decided to maintain power at any price up to and including the collapse of the country. Violet is now out of work and Margaret is trying to teach on much depleted resources.

84 JOSEPH VAN SCHALKWYK

KIMBERLEY, NORTHERN CAPE PROVINCE, SOUTH AFRICA

Joseph was the first kid I photographed for the book. It was an amusing encounter. He was wild and full of spark. He's really short for his age but strong for his height – a potential jockey. He lives with his family on the horse yard where his father works. If he calms down a little as he grows up, he will have the opportunity to go and train to be a champion jockey.

85 ERRMI & NASSIA

DAASANACH TRIBE, GAMO – GOFA, ETHIOPIA

Along with their traditional clothing first world hand me downs have made their way to the pastoral lands of the Daasanach. This seemingly charitable practice is not quite what it seems. Aside from the cultural consequences that the flooding of these cast offs carry, they can often damage the local clothing industry on price.

86 SHEFERAW TESHOME & ABUBEKER MOHAMMED

GOAL STREET CHILDRENS PROJECT, WOREDA 21, KEBELE 13, ADDIS ABABA, ETHIOPIA

These guys are preparing to go to bed at one of the GOAL night shelters. Sheferaw came to Addis with his father when his mother died – they lost each other at the station and he ended up on the street. He has been in the programme since 1998. He is in school and generates some money by collecting cans and rubbish. Abubeker's father died and his mother doesn't make enough money as a day labourer to support him. He was on the streets at 7 years of age and has been in the GOAL programme for 3 years. He is also in school and makes some money shining shoes.

87 PIRIAS

MAASAI WEDDING, LOITA HILLS, MORIJO, KENYA

Contrary to the concerns of people who've seen this photograph, Pirias is not suffering from serious burns. She has been painted with Ochre for the wedding of Neloita and Julius.

93 DEMISSE, YEWO, MIHIRET & HABTAMU

GOAL STREET CHILDRENS PROJECT, WOREDA 15, KEBELE 35, ADDIS ABABA, ETHIOPIA

At the drop in centre the kids that aren't in formal education or come in to relax and play. Draughts is very popular with the guys and games can get pretty heated. It's all part of the informal educational programme that the centre operates.

95 HAILEMARIAM FOLENA & EYOB SENTAYEHU

ABEBECH GOBENA ORPHANAGE & SCHOOL, ADDIS ABABA, ETHIOPIA

Abebech Gobena was one of the most remarkable people I met while shooting this book. In the late 70's she went to visit a famine site in the south of the country. During her trip she came across a baby suckling on its mother's breast – but the mother was dead. She took the baby and another lost child back to Addis and set up an orphanage. Her family disowned her and her husband divorced her so she set about building up an orphanage and school. It is now one of the most impressive set ups that I've seen in the world. She has 400 children in fulltime care and education, she has an excellent clinic that caters for about 1'500 people in the community in addition to the kids and she manages a community wide feeding programme for the WFP. The class rooms are as well equipped as the best schools in Europe and her vocational training has spawned a number of micro industries that provide jobs for her school leavers and contribute to the running of the centre. Abebech succeeded against all odds without the benefit of an education herself. She continues to be the principal initiator of all new projects and fundraising drives both at home and abroad. Hailemariam pictured here is one of 10 children that contracted HIV from their mothers who have subsequently died. She wants them to have a good quality of life during their stay.

96 MELAT, HIWOT, AYNALETN & NSRIEOT

GOAL STREET CHILDRENS PROJECT, WOREDA 15, KEBELE 35, ADDIS ABABA, ETHIOPIA

The kids at the drop in centres get lunch every day. They have to pay a nominal few pence for their meal if they are not in formal education. This plays an important part in promoting a culture of self-help. The children attending formal education receive their meals for free as they attend school all day and don't have the time to generate any money.

99 NTOMBI

LANGA TOWNSHIP, CAPE FLATS, WESTERN CAPE PROVINCE, SOUTH AFRICA

Langa township on the Cape Flats is on of the hottest places in southern Africa. It can often get up to 45 degrees centigrade in the summer and unlike the wealthy neighbourhoods of nearby Capetown, the township doesn't benefit from the cool Atlantic breeze. Ntombi has a flour paste on her face to protect her from the sun's harmful rays.

101 KHUHULWA, ANALISA & CECEKA

LANGA TOWNSHIP, CAPE FLATS, WESTERN CAPE PROVINCE, SOUTH AFRICA

These girls are playing on a roundabout in a playground in the township. Since democracy finally arrived in South Africa in 1994 efforts have been made to improve the facilities in townships all over the country.

102 FLORA, TEMWA & MALUMBO

NKATHA BAY, NORTHERN PROVINCE, MALAWI

Gladys, their mother, befriended us as soon as we arrived in Nkatha Bay. Like most mothers in Africa she had a natural head for business and a drive created by her desire to provide the best life possible for her children. She'd run errands or do laundry – a regular monument to job creation. Flora, Temwa and Malumbo would come and help when not in school. They even stared in a demo commercial that we shot with a director friend who'd joined us during our stay in Malawi for his holidays.

106 MEKDES NEGUSE

GOAL STREET CHILDRENS NIGHT SHELTER, WOREDA 21, KEBELE 13, ADDIS ABABA, ETHIOPIA

Mekdes had only been with GOAL for about four months when I took this. Her mother and father are dead and her two brothers and sister are also in the street kids programme. She's not in formal education at the moment but hopes to go into it next year if she is still with GOAL. She was singing a song for me when I took this photo.